Debating Late Antiquity in Britain AD300–700

Edited by

Rob Collins
James Gerrard

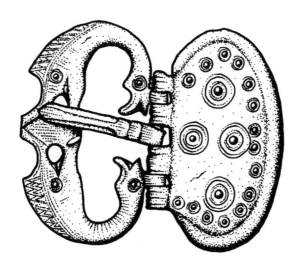

BAR British Series 365
2004

This title published by

Archaeopress
Publishers of British Archaeological Reports
Gordon House
276 Banbury Road
Oxford OX2 7ED
England
bar@archaeopress.com
www.archaeopress.com

BAR 365

Debating Late Antiquity in Britain AD300–700

ISBN 1 84171 585 9

Printed in England by The Synergie Group

Cover illustration: Late Roman belt buckle decorated with dolphins. Drawn by Sven Schroeder after Nick Griffiths, Anne Jenner and Christine Wilson *Drawing Archaeological Finds* (1991: fig 12c).

All BAR titles are available from:

Hadrian Books Ltd
122 Banbury Road
Oxford
OX2 7BP
England
bar@hadrianbooks.co.uk

The current BAR catalogue with details of all titles in print, prices and means of payment is available free from Hadrian Books or may be downloaded from www.archaeopress.com

Contents

List of Tables

List of Figures

List of Contributors

Rob Collins: Archaeology Department, University of York; rc132@york.ac.uk

John Davey: Department of Archaeology, University of Bristol

Simon Draper: Archaeology Department, University of Durham; s.a.draper@durham.ac.uk

Dr. Neil Faulkner: Institute of Archaeology, University College London; neilfaulkner2000@yahoo.co.uk

Dr. Ralph Fyfe: School of Geography, Archaeology and Earth Resources, University of Exeter;
r.m.fyfe@exeter.ac.uk

James Gerrard: Archaeology Department, University of York; jfg101@york.ac.uk

Prof. Martin Henig: Institute of Archaeology, University of Oxford; martin.henig@archaeology.oxford.ac.uk

Daniel Hull: Archaeology Department, University of York; danielhull@yahoo.com

Dr. David Petts: Research Associate, Department of Archaeology, University of Durham;
d.a.petts@durham.ac.uk

Prof. Philip Rahtz: c/o Archaeology Department, University of York

Dr. Stephen Rippon: School of Geography, Archaeology and Earth Resources, University of Exeter;
s.j.rippon@exeter.ac.uk

Christopher Sparey-Green: Canterbury Archaeological Trust, Canterbury; christopher@sparey.evesham.net

Dr. Sam Turner: Archaeology Section, Devon County Council; SCTurner@devon.gov.uk

Dr. Howard Williams: Department of Archaeology, University of Exeter; H.M.R.Williams@exeter.ac.uk

The opinions expressed in this volume are those of the individual authors. The editors cannot be held responsible for any errors or misconceptions.

Foreword

Philip Rahtz

The June 2003 conference at York was especially welcome to me because I had been involved in its subject for over half a century. Over this period there have been both many new discoveries and a wide range of interpretations concerning the late Roman and post-Roman centuries in Britain.

In the conference there were three principal areas of interest. The first was the fate of what had been Roman Britain. Over the past fifty years I have been exposed to many different viewpoints about the extent of survival of the Roman way of life after the conventional date of AD410. These range from an argument that while the economy and the degree of central control changed radically, the way of life remained much the same (notably for the peasants), to Neil Faulkner's forceful demonstration at the conference of just how great the differences were in life in the fourth century and the fifth.

The second area of debate was about the extent to which Anglo-Saxon material, so well known in the cemeteries of eastern England reflected a ?violent immigration from the continent on a large scale; or alternatively the influence on the material culture by a few ?peace-loving farmers (or none in the extreme view!).

The third point of interest (very much related to the second) was about the fate of the 'British' population in the West, whether it was augmented by 'refugees' from Eastern Britain, and was still able to maintain autonomy for up to three centuries (depending on location) – the Arthur syndrome.

An especially intriguing aspect of this has been the interpretation of sherds of amphorae and table-ware from the Byzantine areas of the east Mediterranean and North Africa. These imported ceramics were first recognised in the 1930s (when I was a boy) by C. A. Ralegh Radford. He was one of my mentors when in the 1950s I became an archaeologist. Radford had found this material at Tintagel, a site that has maintained its archaeological importance down to the present day. Once Radford had defined the areas of origin for the imports, they were recognised on many sites. They have been found mainly in Cornwall, Devon, Somerset and Wales; and, in a few cases, in the north-west of Britain (notably Whithorn) and Ireland. The sites where they were found were 're-occupied' hillforts or hilltops, possibly early monasteries or chieftain strongholds; and, in contrast, costal beach-heads, seen as trading places. The latter may be the locations of points of entry, especially the recently excavated site at Bantham Bay, Devon. The debate about their significance ranged from the minimalist view that all the ceramics came from a single ship (blown off course from the west Mediterranean) to the view, when more sites were known, especially the putative ports-of-trade, that there was in the later fifth-sixth centuries regular trading between Western Britain and Byzantine areas, involving ships carrying not only the amphorae and table-ware, but valuable low-volume/high value goods (such as silks and spices), which were being traded in exchange for tin and anything saleable the British could offer.

The last argument has been recently extended to a higher level of trade, not only involving daring sea-captains, but the machinations of international diplomacy (Harris 2003) – with Byzantine emperors thereby gaining a foothold in Western Britain, or at least wanting to make friends and influence people.

A different and equally fascinating body of evidence has been recognized in the last half century, cemeteries that appear to be of indigenous British in the west, but not conventionally Roman or Anglo-Saxon. They are characterised by being sparse in grave-goods. The graves are orientated west-east, mainly in rows. The largest of these known, and also the type-site, is Cannington in Somerset (Rahtz et al. 2000), where about five hundred graves were excavated near an Iron Age and later hillfort; at least a further five hundred to one thousand graves had been destroyed by earlier quarrying. Finds in and around the graves included Late Roman coins and other artefacts, some of Anglo-Saxon derivation, and a few sherds of the Byzantine amphorae referred to above. A substantial number of skeletons provided radiocarbon determinations; these extended from the middle of the fourth century to the late seventh and eighth centuries AD.

The cemetery thus exhibited the mixed material culture of the burying community, who may have lived in or around the adjacent hillfort. Cemeteries of the Cannington type provide alternative data to consider in assessing the characteristics of the Western British in late antiquity and beyond.

Finally, I would make a plea that we seriously consider the implications of Baillie's case for a major environmental disaster in the late AD530s, caused by a cometary impact or something equally drastic (Baillie

1999). If he is right, we might suggest that this marks the end of the '?Golden Age' witnessed by the imports from the Byzantine area; and the resumption of pressure from Germanic expansion.

The department at York and the 'Dark Ages'

I have been fortunate enough to be involved since 1950 in a series of sites which have provided fuel for the debate of the 2003 conference. This began with an eighth-century glass jar in the fill of the well of the Late Roman temple at Pagan's Hill in North Somerset. Perhaps the temple was still in use? Excavation at Pagan's Hill was followed by the Cannington site, mentioned above. This was followed by Byzantine amphora sherds in the numinous context of the summit of Glastonbury Tor, possibly an early monastery. Then, in the 1970s, a major hill-fort settlement at Cadbury Congresbury. This had various structures and numerous imported sherds and metal finds. This may be a site of mixed functions – secular and religious.

Not surprisingly, my late and post-Roman experience was influential in shaping the new department at York in 1978, with an early mediaeval bias. My first member of staff, Tania Dickinson, was highly involved in Anglo-Saxon studies. The Late Antiquity bias at York was also continued after my retirement by my successor, Martin Carver, with his brilliant campaign at Sutton Hoo and his greater expansion into Europe – the new emphasis in these studies is certainly an attempt to understand a much wider horizon.

It is therefore appropriate that York, on the 25th anniversary of its founding, was host to the 2003 conference, resulting in this volume, where the principal archaeological problems dealt with in this foreword are seen in a wider interdisciplinary context.

Bibliography

Baillie, M. 1999. *Exodus to Arthur*. Batsford: London

Harris, A. 2003. *Byzantium, Britain and the West*. Stroud: Tempus.

Rahtz, P. Hirst, S. and Wright, S. 2000. *Cannington Cemetery*. Britannia Monograph 17, London

1: Preliminary Perspectives

Rob Collins and James Gerrard

Leading up to the debate...

This volume is the proceedings of a conference hosted by the Department of Archaeology at the University of York in June 2003. The idea of the conference first came into being during our MA programmes in 2001. We were both dissatisfied with the current state of Dark Age/Early Medieval archaeology. Respectively, we were interested in the North and the South West of Britain in the years after AD 400. These interests disenfranchised us from the dominant academic spheres of post-Roman studies. We were neither Anglo-Saxonists nor Britto-Celticists, with their respective theoretical agendas. Instead, we sought to examine the post-Roman centuries in an integrated fashion that gave equal weighting to all cultures and societies. This is not to say that we believed we could be objective; we simply wanted to draw together and address some of the issues that have governed the study of the 5th to 8th centuries.

The situation is clearer on the continent, where an integrative discourse is found in the concept of Late Antiquity (e.g. Brown 1971; Cameron 1993). Ken Dark (e.g. 1994; 2000) has been the most prolific advocate of a Late Antique categorization of the late and post-Roman centuries in Britain. More recently, Esmonde Cleary (2001) has utilised this concept in his discussion of integrative frameworks for the Roman to medieval transition. It was only natural that our choice of title for the conference would be 'Debating Late Antiquity in Britain, AD 300-700'. This title, we hoped, would not only stimulate Romanists and post-Romanists, but also highlight the inconsistent use and understanding of the concept of Late Antiquity. Therefore, our primary aims were 1) to critically consider and debate the validity and relevance of the Late Antique label, as applied to Britain, and 2) to explore how this period could be accessed archaeologically by drawing together individual approaches.

Whether we were successful or not in our primary aims is a matter for debate in itself. We, like Dark and Esmonde Cleary, saw Late Antiquity as an integrative term. Yet in some ways, the contributors demonstrated that this was clearly not the case. For example, Howard Williams was the only representative of the Anglo-Saxon research community that presented a paper (although several eminent Anglo-Saxonists attended). In contrast, our session on the South West of Britain attracted several papers, forcing us to be highly selective so as to maintain some semblance of regional balance. Representation of Wales and the North was limited to three papers, which does not reflect the relevance of this debate to those regions. In addition to the regional and periodic under-representation evident at the conference, there was also a lack of artefactual and ecofactual studies. Late Antiquity may not have succeeded as an integrative term. However, it did enable several important themes to be drawn out during the conference. These are summarised below, before we draw out the implications for the whole debate on Late Antiquity in a concluding section.

As a further note, the papers in this volume were not the only ones delivered at this conference. For a variety of reasons, a number of participants were unable to contribute to these proceedings. These include Christopher Bowles (Post-Colonial Identity in Late Antique Britain), Kurt Hunter-Mann (Gildas and a Fifth Century Transition), Dominic Perring (Ideology, Power, and Regionality in Late Roman Britain), Colin Wallace (Romans, Saxons, *Brittunculi* and Their Pottery), and Tony Wilmott (The End of the Roman Frontier in North Britain). This group of papers complemented those published in this volume and provided much food for thought.

The main positions summarised

Central to the conference was a critique of Late Antiquity juxtaposed with an exemplary articulation of the Late Antique concept. Those who attended the two papers by Neil Faulkner (*con*) and Martin Henig (*pro*) will remember these pithy and humourous, yet accurate addresses. Faulkner forcibly argued that the concept of Late Antiquity is not only theoretically bankrupt, but also that the material record of post-Roman Britain does not uphold such an interpretation. Henig, on the other hand, demonstrated the continued Romano-Christian influence seen in portable art, particularly jewelry, and argued that the shadow of Rome was long indeed.

The four papers on southwest Britain all approached the period with a landscape perspective, but built their arguments on different forms of evidence. Sam Turner suggested that in the well-studied landscapes of Devon and Cornwall, little change can be seen around the year 400. Arguing from a palynological perspective, Ralph Fyfe and Stephen Rippon concurred with this view, noting that agricultural change does not occur in Exmoor until the 8th-10th centuries. John Davey's research with the South Cadbury Environs Project similarly argued for landscape stability between the 3rd and 7th centuries. Simon Draper critically reexamined the conclusions of Desmond Bonney's theory regarding the antiquity of parish boundaries and demonstrates that in Wiltshire, parish boundaries are a late Saxon phenomenon. Therefore, all four papers argued that the post-Roman landscape of the South West was a landscape that was developed in the Roman period and continued to be important after the political fragmentation of the early 5th century. Archaeological changes in the landscape only become visible in the 7th-10th centuries.

One of the few artefact based approaches highlighted how constrained the current state of knowledge is in reference to typologically dating the 5th and 6th centuries. James Gerrard challenged the temporal division of material culture in Somerset and Dorset around the year 400. This study of Black-Burnished ware demonstrated that 'the End' of Roman Britain was not as clear, in ceramic terms, as is generally believed. Studies such as this remain rare but are fundamental to refining our understanding of the 5th century.

Another theme that generated considerable interest was the session on death and burial. David Petts' wide-ranging survey of burial traditions of the former Western Empire strongly suggested that western Britain was in the mainstream of Late Antique mortuary traditions. These rites were focused on unaccompanied inhumations aligned west-east within a Christian ideological tradition. Set against this was Howard Williams' thought-provoking paper focused on the ideology and significance of the Anglo-Saxon cremation rite and associated funerary objects. These accompanied cremations were divergent from the mainstream of Late Antique funerary practice and are best seen within a northern European and Germanic context. Christopher Sparey-Green successfully bridged the gap between burial and settlement, arguing that the site of Poundbury, Dorset was not only a cemetery but also a focus for Roman and post-Roman religious activity, perhaps related to monastic practice. Daniel Hull also focused on the critical role of Early Christian monasticism at this time, drawing out the similarities and differences between Britain and Syria and, in the process, reminded us of the huge geographical and conceptual coverage of the label 'Late Antiquity'.

Finally, Rob Collins took us literally to the end of the empire with his discussion of the Late Antique frontier zone of Hadrian's Wall. Instead of simply arguing for regional continuity or discontinuity from a site-based approach, he employed an integrated landscape methodology. This attempted to put late and post-Roman evidence in the specific context of the supply and control of a frontier zone.

The debate

As is the case with most meetings tackling 'big subjects', the primary aims of the conference were only partially fulfilled. However, a number of themes can be drawn out from the papers in this volume. At a higher level is the tension between continuity and discontinuity either side of AD 410 seen in Faulkner's and Henig's respective approaches. Ultimately, this tension rests upon the difficulty inherent in dating sites, deposits, and artefacts of the early-mid 5th century. More specific themes, such

as agricultural/landscape activity, settlement, production, and ideological activity, can be resolved at the regional level.

Dark Age and Late Antique: different views of the same problems

Faulkner's Dark Age 'manifesto' is persuasive but problematic. He argues that, "Without some archaeological definition of 'Roman', discussion of 'Roman' continuity in the archaeological record has no basis." Yet his list of nine 'Roman' indicators reads like the definition of a 'Childean' culture. Indeed, his assertion that:

> The correct archaeological procedure is to start with basics like settlements, cemeteries, and distribution patterns, and to use these to build up a picture of economic life and social structure. These are the things archaeology is good at, and they provide the essential framework for more difficult problems like reconstructing political organization, cultural identities and belief systems.

is reminiscent of a Hawkesian ladder of inference. The problem is not the assertion, but the implication that we cannot achieve higher order understanding of the post-Roman centuries due to a lack of empirical evidence. Yet the evidence we do have is elite material culture, material from which we can interpret elite ideologies, as Henig does.

Henig unashamedly establishes his viewpoint with an elite and Romano-centric focus. The fashions visible in late Roman art and jewelry can be seen to continue as modified and transformed objects, objects that were nevertheless active pieces of material culture. These conferred *romanitas* to the bearers and observers because Rome was a dominant ideology in the West, as it continues to be today. Unfortately, the portable art only demonstrates the continued influence of Roman style through aspirations of political legitimation and imperial emulation. Can Late Antiquity really be demonstrated to be valid as anything more than an Art Historical concept once the imperial political framework is removed? Is there, in fact, a Late Antique 'stage' upon which the elite acted out their invented traditions rather than a Late Antique 'world' that connected successor states to the empire?

Dating: the crux of the problem

At our behest, Faulkner and Henig have taken polarised positions with their arguments to demonstrate the problems inherent in both extremes. Faulker's proposed scheme (this volume) is typical in that it relies upon accepted artefact chronologies. For example, the 'Age of Chiefdoms, AD 450/475-550/575' reflects the currency of imported Mediterranean ceramics. Yet in the absence of coinage, as Gerrard shows, our artefact chronologies are not stable and may be foreshortened. This problem with dating the 5th and 6th centuries has dogged our study of the period (Esmonde Cleary 1989: 141). Nor have we been willing to accept the possibility of 'late Roman' material culture dating to the 5th century, perhaps owing to the perceived rather than proven collapse of an integrated market economy in Roman Britain (e.g. Fulford 1979).

This poses the question: how do we transcend the models that are highly derivative of 'short chronology' dating? Clearly, new research needs to be carried out. Focused study on late Roman material culture and assemblage composition may challenge the notion of the complete demise of early 5th century specialist production (Cool 2000). In turn, this may allow us to identify 5th century deposits in otherwise 'Roman' sequences. Essentially, we need to completely reassess the dating evidence for 'the end' of Roman Britain and all that this notion implies from an archaeological perspective, rather than a pseudo-historical one.

Regional themes

Despite the difficulties of dating, the South West continues to be one of the most studied regions in Britain in reference to the 5th and 6th centuries. This is due to a combination of factors, principally that this region has benefited from long-term research, and therefore, recent studies have the advantage of decades of 'modern' scholarship and data to draw upon. This has enabled distinct methodologies to be applied to the region. The results of those studies found in this volume touch upon different themes, but are all interrelated and highly significant.

Agricultural production is a critical issue. The agricultural landscape, as investigated palynologically and geophysically, crucially demonstrates no major disruption from 'late Roman' practice until the 7th century at the earliest. Similarly, the settlement evidence from Cornwall suggests much the same thing, except that agricultural landscape change occurs between the 8th and 10th centuries. On a site level, Poundbury shows a continuous sequence from late Roman cemetery and settlement to post-Roman settlement that ends in the 6th or 7th century. This generalization can apply to the whole region, but it does not define the social and economic relationships between different settlements and their inhabitants. What is desperately needed is site-specific faunal and palaeobotanical data that would enable us to relate settlements and their inhabitants to the greater landscape. This will allow us to answer questions such as 'how long did the extraction of agricultural surplus continue after the demise of central Roman authority?'

A second regional issue is that of specialist production. The Roman period is characterised by mass-produced

goods, but at what point did this change? Is it the result of an economic catastrophe brought about by the collapse of a coin-using free market in the early 5th century (Evans 1990)? Alternatively, is the process far more drawn out but disguised by our difficulties in dating the period. Gerrard suggests that the latter view may be one that has not received enough attention.

Ideological and ritual activity is also an important topic of interest. The mortuary data clearly demonstrates that Britain can be divided into two halves: a Christian west and a 'pagan' east. What is more ambiguous, however, is evidence for ritual centres in the west. Sparey-Green's bold interpretation of Poundbury as a monastic site highlights the archaeological ambiguity of monasticism in Britain. This is particularly striking when compared to clearer archaeological imprints in other Late Antique provinces, for example Syria.

Finally, these themes have been explored to a greater or lesser extent in southwestern England. Does the evidence exist to explore them in other parts of the country? If so, will it resolve the relationship between Britain and Late Antiquity?

Afterthoughts

The relevance of the Late Antique paradigm to all of Britain remains a matter for debate that can be summed up in four simple questions. First, how does the concept of Late Antiquity relate to the disintegration of centralized state authority? Second, can Late Antiquity be used to integrate the archaeology of Britain on an intra-regional basis as well as with the continent? Third, is the limited application of Late Antiquity to Britain related to the archaeological invisibility of most of the population of the 5th and 6th centuries? Is Late Antiquity really a fashionable synonym for the non-Germanic zones? The answers to these questions will not be found in this volume, but we hope these proceedings have gone some way toward stimulating thoughts and theories on these issues.

Acknowledgements

We would like to thank many people for the support and advice that they freely gave us: Philip Rahtz kindly contributed to the atmosphere of the conference as well as this volume, for which the editors are indebted. Steve Roskams, Dom Perring, the secretaries of the Archaeology Department and the staff of King's Manor all provided help and assistance. Our thanks are extended to Jane Grenville, Head of the Archaeology Department, who had the vision and confidence to agree to our organising the conference and proceedings. Thanks must also be given to the research students of G65 and our respective partners who did so much to ensure the smooth running of the conference. Finally, a conference is only successful if it is attended by an interested and vocal audience to respond to the stimulating papers that our speakers graciously provided. We were fortunate enough to have both of these elements. Thank you to all.

Bibliography

Brown, P. 1971. *The World of Late Antiquity*, London: Thames and Hudson.

Cameron, A. 1993. *The Mediterranean World in Late Antiquity.* London: Routledge.

Cool, H. 2000. The parts left over: material culture into the fifth century, in T. Wilmott and P. Wilson (eds.), *The Late Roman Transition in the North*: 47-65. Oxford: British Archaeological Reports British Series 299.

Dark, K. 1994. *Civitas to Kingdom: British Political Continuity 300-800.* Leicester: Leicester University Press.

Dark, K. 2000. *Britain and the End of the Roman Empire.* Stroud: Tempus.

Esmonde-Cleary, S. 1989. *The Ending of Roman Britain.* London: Routledge.

Esmonde Cleary, S. 2001. The Roman to medieval transition, in S. James and M. Millett (eds.), *Britons and Romans: advancing an archaeological agenda*: 90-97. York: Council for British Archaeology.

Evan, J. 1990. From the end of Roman Britain to the Celtic West. *Oxford Journal of Archaeology* 9:91-93.

Fulford, M. 1979. Pottery production and the end of Roman Britain: the case against continuity, in P. Casey (ed.), *The End of Roman* Britain: 120-132. Oxford: British Archaeological Reports British Series 71.

2: The Case for the Dark Ages

Neil Faulkner

What constitutes a 'period' in archaeology? We all know that dividing the past into discrete periods is arbitrary but necessary. The past is an unbroken sequence of processes, but to study it we must cut it into manageable lengths of time. Knowing where to cut is always a problem, however. Usually we choose a time of transition, either a major change in material culture (an archaeological distinction) or in political authority (an historical one). Ideally, the two coincide, as, in the case of Britain in the first century AD, when the Roman Conquest is associated with clear and substantial (though not necessarily immediate) changes in archaeological evidence. Decisions about when a period starts and ends therefore reflect our interpretations of important transitions; they are partly a matter of academic convenience, but also statements about the significance we attach to perceived change in the past. Whatever their utilitarian purpose, in other words, archaeological periods are inescapably theory-laden.

To advocate a new period – a new way of dividing up past time – is to open up a debate. Have we misunderstood one of the great epochs of the past? Have we placed emphasis on superficial changes and ignored events of deeper significance? Do we achieve better understanding if we place the dividing lines in different places? If the answers are 'yes', and we adopt a new period, we have a paradigm shift: a change in the theoretical framework for understanding a specific chunk of past time. This is where I begin my discussion of the concept 'Late Antiquity'. Many scholars accept the usefulness of a time period extending from c.AD 250/300 to 600/800 (various start and end dates have been suggested). It brings together specialists who have traditionally approached one of history's great transitions – the decline and fall of the Western Roman Empire – from different starting-points. But there is more to the concept 'Late Antiquity' than a breaking down of sub-disciplinary barriers to facilitate scholarly debate; it implies an interpretation of the past which, to use the ugly jargon of currently fashionable theory, 'deconstructs' the process of decline and fall – an interpretation, that is, that denies the reality of the transition.

'Rather than emphasising the divisions and the breaks,' explains leading ancient historian Averil Cameron (1993a: 192), 'both the eastern and western empires can be seen as belonging to the longer history of Europe and the Mediterranean. This kind of approach has the advantage of taking our minds away for a while from the over-debated question of the end of classical antiquity and enabling us instead to look at issues like settlement, climate, exchange and political organisation over a much longer period.' Continuity and evolution are the dominant themes of Cameron's two syntheses on 'Late Antiquity', *The Later Roman Empire, AD 284-430* (1993a), and *The*

Mediterranean World in Late Antiquity, AD 395-600 (1993b). The view of the past she presents is an updated version of the old Whig interpretation of history, which sees the past as a seamless process of gradual change (if not actually of something called 'progress'), largely or wholly devoid of decisive clashes and revolutionary breaks.

Several archaeologists have applied this paradigm to British evidence, notably Ken Dark in two related studies, *Civitas to Kingdom: British political continuity, 300-800* (1994), and *Britain and the End of the Roman Empire* (2000). Dark (2000: 230) believes that Britain was a veritable model of Late Antique *Romanitas*:

> Rather than being the area of the former Roman West in which Late Roman culture was most entirely swept away in the fifth century, and in which exceptional curiously archaic local cultures flourished, quite the opposite would seem to be true. It was within the mainstream, but was the only part of the West in which the descendants of Roman citizens lived under their own rule, with their own Romano-Christian culture and in recognisably Late Roman political units, into the sixth century.

Dark's interpretation has been influential, spawning a second generation of scholarship in the same vein. Anthea Harris (2003), for instance, has recently argued that fifth and sixth-century Britain was subsumed within a Byzantine global supremacy, that it was part of a 'Late Antique' Byzantine commonwealth, and that contemporaries thought in terms of a Byzantine *oikoumene*, a Romano-Christian zone of 'civilised' peoples centred on Constantinople. This, she feels, was decisive in determining cultural identities in the West, where 'a continued sense of *Romanitas* amongst sub-Roman populations' meant that people still regarded themselves as inhabitants of the Roman Empire.

Claims like these must, I believe, be rejected. The 'Late Antiquity' paradigm (LAP) seems to me to be theoretically weak, methodologically suspect, and inadequately supported by either archaeological or historical evidence; so much so, in fact, that I suspect it of being an ideologically-driven interpretation whose well-springs lie far outside Early Dark Age studies. My aim in this paper is therefore as follows: a) to analyse the LAP's theoretical and methodological weaknesses; b) to summarise the evidence for fifth and sixth-century Britain; and c) to present an alternative hypothesis which both accommodates the evidence and provides a plausible explanatory framework for the period. (For clarity, throughout the paper, I use inverted commas or the abbreviation LAP when referring to the 'Late Antiquity' paradigm.)

What is wrong with the 'Late Antiquity' paradigm?

My critique of the LAP can be divided into four main areas of disagreement.

1. A theoretical vacuum

In the LAP view, the Western Roman Empire evolved rather than collapsed, and changes in political authority in the fifth century (from the rule of Roman administrators to Germanic kings) should be seen as secondary phenomena liable to obscure important underlying continuities. This argument is an impressionistic one in which terms are not defined and evidence is treated selectively. The LAP offers no definition of the Roman Empire as a social formation. Richard Reece and I have argued elsewhere that without such a definition, anything we choose – like Merovingian Gaul – can be called 'Roman' (Faulkner and Reece 2002). Indeed, in the extract quoted above, when Averil Cameron explains that the LAP allows us 'to look at issues like settlement, climate, exchange and political organisation over a much longer period', she reveals the theoretical vacuum at the heart of the enterprise. Instead of analysing a *specific* social formation, she offers us data collection for its own sake – an empiricism unconstrained by chronological limits or any research agenda. Because the LAP provides no analysis of the Roman Empire's social dynamic, it has no proper definition, chronological or otherwise, of its own subject of study.

2. Selective use of evidence

Equally important to any research programme is a definition of the range of evidence considered relevant to the matter in hand. In this case, if as archaeologists we are claiming things to be 'Roman', we need to define the Roman Empire's archaeological imprint. This, too, is a matter dealt with in detail elsewhere (Faulkner and Reece 2002), so here I shall merely summarise. The key point is the LAP's failure to provide any answer to the question, What counts as Roman? Instead, the paradigm seizes upon random bits and pieces – such as modest quantities of late-fifth-century Mediterranean pottery on a handful of western British sites – tears them from their wider archaeological context, declares them to be 'Roman', and proclaims this as evidence for a 'Late Antique' *oikoumene*. And, in the absence of any prior definition of what constitutes a Roman archaeological imprint, who are we to argue? Let us pursue points 1 and 2 further with an illustrative case-study.

A case-study in theory and method: Roman towns

As soon as we attempt to define our terms, and, on the basis of them, construct empirical tests for hypotheses using quantified evidence, 'Late Antiquity' turns out to be a world of emperors without clothes. Take the example of Roman towns.

Towns were essential features of Roman imperial civilisation for two reasons. First, they were local centres of political authority where tax collection and law enforcement were organised. They were the bolts which fixed the imperial superstructure of administrators and soldiers to its foundation blocks in the land and labour of rural producers dispersed across a hundred thousand villages. Without the towns to hold the two together, the flow of tribute would have dried up and the imperial system shrivelled. Secondly, the towns – with their orderly grids, standardised public-buildings, and grand houses decorated with mosaics, frescoes and classical statuary – were centres of 'Romanisation', uniting the many local elites who governed the empire into a single ruling class with shared cultural identity and uniform social aspirations. Politically and culturally, then, towns were vital to the integrity of empire. They cannot be compared in importance with the more superficial phenomena – such as the use of Latin or a taste for Mediterranean wine – sometimes cited by 'Late Antiquity' theorists as evidence of continuity. Celtic and Anglo-Saxon also became written languages. Some prestige goods were later imported from Scandinavia. Such developments did not turn the world upside down. The decline of the towns, by contrast, represents the passing of an entire political order that depended on them. Therefore, towns must be part of any definition both of what the Roman Empire was and of how we recognise it in archaeological sequences, and, in view of that, we must enquire, How do these essential features of the Roman archaeological imprint fare in the fifth and sixth centuries?

I will answer with reference to two studies, one a general overview, the other my own analysis of British evidence. Here is ancient historian Wolfgang Liebeschuetz (2003: 5) in his newly published study of towns from *c.*AD 400 to 650:

> The change can be summed up as a process of simplification. In many regions the appearance of cities had changed beyond recognition. The built-up areas had shrunk, secular monumental buildings were abandoned or neglected. Churches had replaced temples. Populations in the built-up core were much reduced. In the West probably only a very small number of cities retained a fully urban population profile, that is a propertied class together with a sizeable population of shopkeeper-traders, and a 'proletariat' of unskilled labourers, seasonal workers, and beggars.

The title of the book – a quite deliberate choice, I assume – says it all: *The Decline and Fall of the Roman City*. My work on the British towns involved a trawl through excavation data to produce detailed statistical analyses charting the urban histories of 17 major sites. The results have been published and discussed elsewhere (e.g. Faulkner 1996 and 2000a), and I shall do no more here than to restate this simple conclusion: there were no towns in Britain after *c.*AD 375, because on no site can a level of activity be demonstrated – whether measured by buildings under construction or buildings still occupied – sufficient to justify the description 'urban'. It is completely irrelevant to this conclusion that some sites show continuity of activity beyond c.AD 375. To repeat (because in many quarters the message has still not sunk in): there are no sites where a level of activity has been recorded for the late fourth century *sufficient to justify the use of the term 'town' to describe them.*

Britain is an extreme case, but Liebeschuetz's study (and many others; e.g. Rich 1992) has confirmed that sharp urban decline was the Late Roman norm. Nowhere, as far as I am aware, have 'Late Antiquity' theorists engaged seriously with this evidence. Some are simply in denial: random examples of late activity on former urban sites are cited as if they constituted effective counter-evidence to set against *the general trend established by quantitative analysis* (e.g. White 2002). Others appear oblivious to the whole issue, as if the decline of the towns were neither here nor there, 'Late Antique' civilisation apparently manifesting itself in other, more subtle ways than, say, the construction of urban bath-houses. But if towns, of all things, do not define the Roman Empire – if they are not an essential feature of the Roman archaeological imprint – then what is? There is no clear answer to this question so the LAP constitutes a hypothesis that cannot be tested. With neither a definition of the 'Late Antique' social formation, nor a set of archaeological attributes against which we can measure the 'Late-Antique-ness' of any specific instance, we are left with nothing but simple assertion.

[handwritten annotation: → cannot be proved w/out the presence of society / urbanism]

3. Failures in the analysis and interpretation of evidence

Left floating in this theoretical vacuum, unconstrained by any rules of method, it can be no surprise that evidence is abused. The correct archaeological procedure is to start with basics like settlements, cemeteries and distribution patterns, and to use these to build up a picture of economic life and social structure. These are things archaeology is good at, and they provide the essential framework for more difficult problems like reconstructing political organisation, cultural identities and belief systems. Only then, when archaeology has had the chance to tell its own story, is it legitimate to compare material evidence with that of written sources. Historical context comes towards the end of the process. The LAP fails in every respect. Material is not analysed in context; rather, some evidence is selected and separated. Even this is not analysed in its own terms – as an assemblage – but in relation to an *a priori* model of inherited or imported *Romanitas*. What matters is the degree to which the material corresponds to presumed 'Roman' types and reveals links with the 'Roman' world – which is why it was selected in the first place. Then, a simplistic equation is made between material culture, social identity and political organisation. Because there are late-fifth-century Mediterranean pots at Tintagel, the local chieftain was a Romanised client of the Byzantine Empire. Form and

content are simply conflated. A style of pottery, a taste for wine, even a conscious aping of 'Roman' manners are equated with *actual* social and political structures. There is no critical discussion of how material culture is manipulated to suit changed conditions, how old symbols get recycled, and how 'traditions' are constantly invented and re-invented (*vide* Hobsbawm and Ranger 1984). But the LAP view of the past is, anyway, essentially static. The Roman Empire is not viewed as an historical process with a beginning, middle and end; there is no sense of it as something contradictory, dynamic and changeable. Nor, therefore, is *Romanitas* ('Roman-ness') seen, as it should be, as a process – as a form of symbolic communication, a negotiation between social actors, and a repertoire of material culture that can be put to varied uses. Roman imperial rule and Roman provincial culture become rigid categories devoid of social content.

4. Bombs and books

I have argued that the LAP is theoretically vacuous, methodologically sloppy, and unsupported by evidence. My final criticism is directed at its ideological implications. As an archaeological perspective, the LAP is an extreme form of diffusionism, the idea that culture spreads outwards from a single advanced centre, bringing enlightenment and improvement to more backward regions, such that a standard of 'civilisation' is established against which each society or polity can be measured (Trigger 1989: 150-155 and *passim*). The implicit diffusionism of the LAP has two aspects. First, because of the inherent superiority of classical civilisation (or so the implication seems to be), the political and military collapse of the Western Roman Empire was not followed by an equivalent cultural collapse. The Church, in particular, played a key role as continuator of *Romanitas* in the former imperial territories; not least, perhaps, in western Britain. Secondly, Byzantium inherited and sustained the classical tradition in the eastern Mediterranean, and from here elevating cultural influences continued to be transmitted to western Europe during the fifth and sixth centuries. Thus, the Dark Ages were not dark at all, for they were illuminated by the brilliance of Byzantium.

Underlying this view is a thoroughly elitist conception of culture. Martin Henig, at least, is refreshingly honest about this. Believing that 'Roman civilisation was in general a 'good thing' and that it neither declined nor fell, only changed', he is equally clear that it was something for 'the educated, more or less well-to-do and above all Romanised section of society' (2002: 19, 153). This boils 'Late Antique' diffusionism down to its essence: a preoccupation with the Christianised 'high culture' of the Graeco-Roman elite. Roman imperialism, as the bearer of this tradition, becomes an act of benevolence and enlightenment. Instead of a ruthless system of violence to enrich the few, we have a bizarre cross between the United Nations and the National Trust. We have an empire to admire – and emulate.

Diffusionist theories were popular in the early twentieth century – that is, in the heyday of European imperialism. They are popular again now, in the age of Bush and Blair, in a world where economic progress and political justice are seen as gifts of the US army and Texaco, where Christian fundamentalism fuels the self-righteousness of empire-builders, and where the BBC inverts the meaning of language to call war 'peace-keeping', conquest 'liberation', and resistance 'terrorism'. The new imperialism has produced a new imperialist history to match. Niall Ferguson leads a group of prominent right-wing historians who are rewriting imperial pasts. In *Empire*, his successful TV series and book, he makes an explicit link between imperialism old and new, and, for him, an essentially beneficent British Empire provides a model for today's American Empire (2003). Whether they know it or not, advocates of the 'Late Antiquity' paradigm are peddling an equally sinister interpretation of the past.

In summary

I would encapsulate the case against the LAP by arguing that it fails these two key tests:

1. When the evidence is viewed *as a whole*, is there a distinctive 'Late Antique' archaeological imprint? If not, there is no coherent archaeological culture, and therefore no meaningful archaeological period.

2. Is there a convincing model of the dynamics of the hypothetical 'Late Antique' social formation? Can we explain the social action and processes of change indicated by the evidence in terms of a single model embracing the whole of the former Roman Empire? If not, the concept of 'Late Antiquity' is meaningless.

A new archaeological imprint

In the second part of this paper, I want to offer my own response to these two tests. My purpose here is two-fold: a) to demonstrate by counter-example the theoretical and methodological hollowness of the LAP; and b) to reject its claims about the character of fifth and sixth-century Britain by presenting an alternative perspective grounded in a more comprehensive analysis of evidence.

Let us begin by comparing two different archaeological imprints, that of Roman Britain, and that of what I shall persist in calling 'Early Dark Age Britain' (in the absence of any other term for the fifth and sixth centuries that is not equally loaded with ideological baggage). I present first a list of what I consider to be diagnostically 'Roman' material evidence. (It has been published elsewhere (Faulkner and Reece 2002), but I reproduce it here for convenience.) I stress that the list is no more than a suggestion. The crucial point is that without some such archaeological definition of 'Roman', discussion of

'Roman' continuity in the archaeological record has no basis.

1. A cultural assemblage that is broadly uniform from Britain to Syria between the first and fourth centuries AD – for example, Roman army buildings and equipment, the design of forum-basilica complexes and other monumental urban buildings, and similar representations of a well-defined pantheon of deities.

2. Evidence for a long-distance communications network defined by ports, canals, roads, bridges, *mansiones*, and *mutationes*.

3. Numerous high-status settlements present – administrative towns, small towns, forts, and villas.

4. Evidence for centralised authority, planning and regulation in the layout and ordering of settlements – for example, regular street-grids not encroached upon by private buildings, water-supply by aqueduct, and drainage and rubbish-disposal systems.

5. Many public buildings with much monumental architecture and artistic embellishment – such as forum-basilica complexes, baths, amphitheatres, theatres, temples, *mansiones*, and arches.

6. Much use of mortared masonry – notably, in public buildings, town-houses, barracks, villas, and walls around forts and towns.

7. Evidence for mass production and long-distance distribution of a wide range of artefacts – such as Roman imperial coinage, fast-wheel-thrown and high-fired pottery, and oil and wine transported in amphorae.

8. Evidence for a range of luxury crafts reflecting Graeco-Roman Mediterranean taste – fresco painting, floor mosaics, and naturalistic statuary in bronze and stone.

9. A repertoire of art and architecture rooted in Graeco-Roman Mediterranean culture – for instance, naturalistic representation of form, the use of straight lines and right angles in settlement layout and building design, and the use of standard decorative motifs like Corinthian capitals on sculpture, floral swags on fresco, and guilloche borders on mosaic.

Now compare this imprint with what follows in the Early Dark Ages. Here is a new list summarising the archaeological evidence for western Britain in the fifth and sixth centuries – amounting, in my view, to a diagnostically 'Early Dark Age' imprint for this region.

1. Fortified secular elite sites – e.g. hilltop enclosures, including reused hillforts, coastal promontory forts, and reused Roman walled settlements.

2. Ecclesiastical sites – cemeteries, churches, monasteries – mostly new foundations, but some continuing or reusing Roman sites.

3. Small coastal trading sites – promontory forts with harbours or beaches, and 'sand-dune' sites.

4. Small farms, often enclosed, sometimes reusing high-status Roman sites, sometimes continuing low-status Roman sites, sometimes new foundations.

5. Vernacular architecture includes small round-houses (in stone), small rectangular halls (in stone or timber), and some larger rectangular halls with aisles and partitions (in timber).

6. Small and impoverished local assemblages include domestic pottery, brooches, knives, bracelets, combs, and pins. Some residual Roman material still in use – e.g. fineware pots repaired with lead rivets. High-status artefacts include penannular brooches with decorated terminals and hanging-bowls with decorated escutcheons.

7. Imports of luxury goods from the Byzantine East and Frankish Gaul at some sites.

8. High-status inscribed memorial stones.

The contrast between the two imprints is one of the sharpest in the British archaeological sequence. Moreover, there is no basis for regarding this as anything other than reliable evidence for an equally sharp contrast between two past worlds of social experience. It is to this that we must now turn.

A new world order

How is the Roman Empire to be defined as a social formation? What was its structure and dynamic? What sort of world system is represented by a 'Roman' archaeological imprint? My definition (also published elsewhere and repeated here for convenience; 2002) comprises three main elements:

1. Rome was an ancient military imperialism, a system of robbery with violence, in which inflows of wealth through successful war enriched and empowered the Roman state and those who controlled it. This struggle for plunder was driven forwards by military competition – that is, by the need to accumulate military resources to wage war a) against rival states on Rome's borders, b) within the highly fractious Roman elite, and c) against attempted revolts from below among the subject classes of the empire.

2. The Roman Empire constituted a 'military supply' economy, in which state tax collection and arms expenditure, oiled by state supply of coin (the 'tax-pay cycle'), pump-primed the entire economy. This created a powerful two-tier economy. A primary economy of local subsistence production continued, but it was overlain by a secondary economy of production, exchange and distribution through regional, provincial and imperial marketing networks.

3. Rome was at root a traditional agricultural society, and its two heaviest foundation-blocks were land and labour. Maintaining the infrastructures of empire and civilization – soldiers, forts, towns, villas, 'the world of taste' – depended upon effective elite control over the countryside, exploitation of peasant labour, and accumulation of agricultural surpluses.

This system was highly unstable. For half a millennium it was aggressive, predatory and expansionist. In this period it seized control of virtually all the developed agricultural land in the Mediterranean and Europe. But it then came up against two insuperable barriers. In central Europe and in the far north and west of the continent, most land was unploughed and remained a relative wilderness. The population was sparse and impoverished, and its exploitation did not yield the surpluses necessary to support an infrastructure of forts, towns and villas. Empire and 'civilisation' was restricted to the plough-lands. Secondly, in the East, the Romans faced a rival imperialism powerful enough to block eastward expansion. The wealth of Mesopotamia's ancient cities combined with the first-class military recruiting grounds of the Iranian steppes gave successive Persian empires the strength to throw back repeated Roman assaults down the centuries. After the great conquests of the first century BC, therefore, the Roman Empire, hemmed in by *barbaricum*, gained little further territory. By the time of the Roman invasion of Britain in AD 43, such military adventurism was exceptional.

The inflows of plunder which had fed imperial expansion had now largely dried up. The soldiers, the frontier defences, the imperial aristocracy, the monumental building, the largesse of 'bread and circuses', the whole system, in short, by which Rome defended its territory and maintained internal peace, came to depend on resources raised from *within* the imperial territories. Taxes went up. Labour services increased. Forced requisitioning was widespread. As the proportion of surplus siphoned away by the state increased, provincial life decayed. Resistance – usually passive, occasionally active – prompted governments to centralise administration and deploy military force. The Late Roman state therefore developed as a bureaucratic, paramilitary, totalitarian authority. And then, under the weight of this oppressive infrastructure, the system gradually collapsed. Over-taxation ruined the towns, the villa-owning gentry, and the agricultural basis of the entire social formation. Marginal land went out of use. Some villages were abandoned. Sections of the peasantry gave up and became bandits, revolutionaries, or fifth-columnists for the 'barbarians'. As the tax base thus shrank, the imperial system was caught in a classic 'scissors crisis': increases in state surplus extraction to make up shortfalls and maintain military expenditures simply increased the resistance and decay that were destroying the empire's resource base.

This is the thesis I have advanced at much greater length in *The Decline and Fall of Roman Britain* (2000b). It has not, of course, found universal favour – or, indeed, much favour at all. It does, however, enable us to explain the salient changes in the evidence for Roman Britain between the late first and late fourth centuries. To summarise, in the Early Roman period (*c*.AD 50-225/50), a Romanised settlement pattern had developed rapidly. It comprised a network of forts and roads in the upland areas of north and west, and about 20 major towns, 100 small towns and 1000 villas in the lowland areas of south and east, in all cases associated with large assemblages of Romanised artefacts. By contrast, in the Late Roman period (*c*.AD 225/50-375/425), the towns declined from an early third century peak, the villas from an early fourth century peak, and overall the Romanised settlement pattern and associated material culture had collapsed to almost nothing by the late fourth and early fifth centuries.

This much has been argued before, notably, in the first instance, by Richard Reece (1980 and 1988). But I think this account of decline-and-fall can take us further – into the fifth and sixth centuries, when the evidence points, not to the immediate replacement of one form of 'complex society' by another, but to a profound hiatus, in which for a time 'complexity' ceased altogether, to be replaced by 'simplicity', and was only gradually restored in the generations that followed. The term 'complex society' is an academic obfuscation: all 'complex societies' are in fact class societies driven by competition between and within classes for control over surpluses. And what the evidence for the immediate post-Roman period indicates – a period of between 50 and 100 years after *c*.AD 375 – is an almost complete collapse not only of Romano-British class society, but of any sort of class society at all. There is a clear material culture gap separating the final collapse of Romanised settlements and assemblages in *c*.AD 375/425, and the emergence of distinctive Early Dark Age ones from *c*.AD 450/75 onwards. This gap has been much discussed (e.g. Brooks 1986 and 1988), but usually as if it were a lacuna in the evidence recovered due to a problem of archaeological 'invisibility'. I want to argue here that the evidence could be taken at face value. Why should it not reflect the collapse of the Romano-British ruling class and a shift of power and wealth in favour, not of an alternative ruling class, but of the British peasantry?

Is this possibility really so difficult to accept? Not only is it what the archaeological evidence implies; it also finds good support when various fragments of historical evidence are pieced together. This is not the place to review these in detail. I shall merely list the fragments to show that my archaeologically generated hypothesis does not have to stand alone: it can be supported by a number of pieces of written evidence which may imply (I put it no more strongly than that) revolutionary change, popular revolt and radical politics in the period *c*.AD 375-475. Missionaries and monks built a popular Christian movement in the former western provinces of the Roman Empire in this period, and I suspect that the radicalism of their message has often been underestimated. The western monk Pelagius argued that people had free will, that they could choose to act righteously, and that this was the only route to salvation. In contrast to those like St Augustine, who believed that 'sin' was inevitable and that God's 'grace' could be earned by 'faith' and 'obedience' alone, Pelagius believed that people were responsible for their own actions and that it was deeds not words that counted (Chadwick 1990: 225-235); this was a much harder road for the rich to follow, since it required them not merely to profess to be Christian, but to act in a positively Christian manner. The contrast between orthodox grandees and the ascetics of popular Christianity is evident in the life and work of St Patrick. He describes himself as uneducated (*Letter*, 1), expresses scorn for 'priestly intellectuals' (*Confession*, 13), and tells us with bitterness that some elements in the hierarchy had attempted to prevent his mission (*Confession*, 26ff). The Church we glimpse in Patrick's writing was, then, deeply divided by class. It is in this context, perhaps, that we should read the references in Orosius to Constantine III, who, we are told, rose from the ranks, had a son who was a monk, and chose to promote militant monks to Gallic bishoprics (Dark 1994: 57). And what role, we are bound to wonder, did the most radical of the Christian preachers play in the revolts of *bagaudae*, the bandits and peasant rebels of the Late Roman countryside that are attested for Gaul, Spain and perhaps Britain by fleeting references in the classical sources (Thompson 1952 and 1977)?

It seems possible that the later 'conservatism' of the Celtic Church was rooted in a tradition of popular asceticism and radicalism that had endured in the British Isles because of the near-complete collapse of elite culture in the years after *c*.AD 375. The supreme representative of this tradition is the early-sixth-century monk and pamphleteer Gildas. Compared with the ghastly, power-worshipping panegyrics of the fourth century, *The Ruin of Britain* is a delight to read, for Gildas was a dyed-in-the-wool 'red' who hated the rulers of his age. Not only does he condemn the 'tyrants' for corruption, injustice and oppressing the poor, but he has withering contempt for the clerical toadies who attached themselves to royal courts, the spin-doctors of the Early Dark Ages, who, he says, 'do not look to the good of the people but to the filling of their own bellies'. It is perhaps worth adding that Gildas stands very much in the tradition of Judaeo-Christian apocalyptic literature – a tradition which runs from the Jewish prophets of the Old Testament to the Fifth Monarchists of the English Revolution, where religion, instead of being a stale litany of dogmas, becomes a living language for voicing the anger of the oppressed. Why, we must ask, was Gildas so radical and so angry? Perhaps because he represented a popular tradition which, as a new elite emerged in the early sixth century, was being destroyed by new forms of class exploitation. This is a good point to return to the archaeological evidence to see whether we can pick up a story there of a new class society in the making.

We have noted already how profoundly different is the archaeological imprint of the period after *c.*AD 450 or 475 from that of Roman Britain. Whatever measure we take – settlement hierarchies, site characterisation, artefact assemblages, distribution patterns – provided we assess matters statistically, not selectively, we are witness to a transformation. The process of change, moreover, was continuous. Between the late fifth and the early seventh century, we see two major developments. First, in broad terms, a large number of small elite sites in western Britain was replaced by a smaller number of larger sites; in other words, a fairly flat settlement hierarchy evolved into a more extended, differentiated one. Secondly, we see an increase in the density and a spreading westwards of distinctively 'Anglo-Saxon' material, which at the outset had been confined to a limited number of sites in eastern Britain. I hardly need add that our historical sources imply that the entire period was characterised by conflict and change, including two major phases of warfare between 'Britons' and 'Anglo-Saxons', the first in *c.*AD 450-500, the second in *c.*AD 550-600. What explanatory framework might be offered to account for this epoch of apparent storm and strife?

I am not an Early Dark Age specialist, but a Romanist who enjoys flying kites. The evidence summarised here has been culled from secondary sources; it is the evidence used, amongst others, by 'Late Antiquity' theorists. My argument is that this evidence does not support the claims frequently made for it, and that instead, if archaeology is allowed to tell its own story, and if that story is then compared with the fragmentary historical references available to us, much more convincing models for Britain between the late fourth and the early seventh century AD can be constructed. I conclude, therefore, by offering one such model.

The Anarchy, *c.*AD 375/425-450/75

Break up of the Roman army due to the cessation of army pay and partial troop withdrawals, and consequent collapse of the Roman imperial state in Britain.

Popular ('bagaudic') resistance to tax-collectors and landlords, supported by Christian radicals, challenges ruling class control over land, labour and the social surplus.

Land becomes controlled by primary producers. Elite surplus appropriation is ended. The Romano-British ruling class disintegrates. Residual local state activity ceases. Britain becomes a region of largely self-sufficient,

independent peasant farms, with only localised networks, and balanced exchanges of goods and services.

The Age of Chiefdoms, *c.*AD 450/75-550/75

Military insecurity and threats to property gives rise to war-chiefs and war-bands offering protection in return for tribute.

Military competition between war-bands for control of territory, tribute and manpower compels war-chiefs to increase exploitation and accumulate larger surpluses.

Political instability gives way to growing consolidation of war-bands and their territories, and increasingly effective surplus accumulation by the emergent ruling class.

Increasingly sophisticated legitimation strategies include the 'invention of tradition', fake geneaologies, the use of Roman titles, and patronage of the Church.

The Emergence of Kingdoms, *c.*AD 550/75 onwards

Military competition between war-chiefs gives rise to unstable and contested centralisation of power under kings.

The consolidation of royal power leads to larger territories, more stable authority, the establishment of state infrastructures, elaborate ideologies of political legitimation, a more secure and powerful ruling class, and more efficient, bureaucratically-controlled surplus appropriation.

Military competition continues mainly as conflict between tributary royal states.

Acknowledgements

I am grateful to Richard Reece for reading this paper in draft and offering critical comments.

Bibliography

Brooks, D. A. 1986. A review of the evidence for continuity in British towns in the fifth and sixth centuries. *Oxford Journal of Archaeology* 5(1): 77-102.

Brooks, D. A. 1988. The case for continuity in fifth-century Canterbury re-examined. *Oxford Journal of Archaeology* 7(1): 99-114.

Cameron, A. 1993a. *The Later Roman Empire*. London: Fontana.

Cameron, A. 1993b. *The Mediterranean World in Late Antiquity*. London: Routledge.

Chadwick, H. 1990. *The Early Church*. Harmondsworth: Penguin.

Dark, K. 1994. *Civitas to Kingdom: British political continuity, 300-800*. London: Leicester University Press.

Dark, K. 2000. *Britain and the End of the Roman Empire*. Stroud: Tempus.

Faulkner, N. 1996. Verulamium: interpreting decline. *The Archaeological Journal* 153: 79-103.

Faulkner, N. 2000a. Change and decline in late Romano-British towns, in T. R. Slater (ed.), *Towns in Decline, AD 100-1600*. Ashgate: Aldershot.

Faulkner, N. 2000b. *The Decline and Fall of Roman Britain*. Stroud: Tempus.

Faulkner, N. and Reece, R. 2002. The Debate about the End: a review of evidence and methods. *The Archaeological Journal* 159: 59-76.

Ferguson, N. 2003. *Empire*. London: BBC Books.

Harris, A. 2003. *Byzantium, Britain and the West: the archaeology of cultural identity, AD 400-650*. Stroud: Tempus.

Henig, M. 2002. *The Heirs of King Verica: culture and politics in Roman Britain*. Stroud: Tempus.

Hobsbawm, E. and Ranger, T. 1984. *The Invention of Tradition*. Cambridge: Cambridge University Press.

Liebeschuetz, J. H. W. G. 2003. *The Decline and Fall of the Roman City*. Oxford: Oxford University Press.

Reece, R. 1980. Town and country: the end of Roman Britain. *World Archaeology* 12: 77-92.

Reece, R. 1988. *My Roman Britain*. Cirencester: Cotswold Studies.

Rich, J. 1992. *The City in Late Antiquity*. London: Routledge.

Thompson, E. A. 1952. Peasant revolts in Late Roman Gaul and Spain. *Past and Present* 2: 11-23.

Thompson, E. A. 1977. Britain, AD 406-410. *Britannia* 8: 303-18.

Trigger, B. G. 1989. *A History of Archaeological Thought*. Cambridge: Cambridge University Press.

White, R. 2002. Reviews. *Britannia* 33: 387-88.

3: Remaining Roman in Britain AD 300-700:
The evidence of portable art

Martin Henig

The subject matter of this paper is inevitably diffuse and it is easier to define what it is not about than to give an easy resumé of its aims. Firstly, it is not really concerned with the detail of typologies, a field which numerous students of Migration period archaeology have made very much their own. Secondly, it does not attempt to paraphrase the quite brilliant study by Ellen Swift (2000), which looks at the distributions of various Late Antique jewellery types in the West and their later variants and 'Germanic' successors, even though inevitably it will cover some of the same ground. It does not attempt to argue for 'continuity' in a narrow sense, because the period between AD 400 and 700 is so full of changes that we have to be prepared for the possibility, indeed the strong likelihood, that grandparents were wearing totally different dress/jewellery from their grandchildren and probably talking a different language and embracing a different religion. Incidentally, all of these statements happen to be personally true of the author of this paper, living in the early twenty first century, which bids fair to be at least as tumultuous as the fifth century. He began the text of chapter 7 of his survey, *The Heirs of King Verica* (2002: 127), with the following statement: 'Their favourite stories were all of metamorphosis, of men and women changing into other men and women, or into animals and plants'. Such imaginative adventures concerning transformations in culture can be equally applied to the way people dressed because, apart from the language people spoke, clothing and its accessories were the surest way to express identity.

The continuity of western culture

This paper is an inevitably hasty and superficial attempt to survey some of the evidence from afar, rather like an overview of a landscape observed from the air. With luck it gives the main lines of a topography. Hopefully, the enquiry allows one to go on to 'ask' the people of Britain during these so-called 'Dark Age' centuries whether they were 'Roman' in their aspirations. This same question can be posed whatever the ethnicity of the subjects, which I believe in any case to have been very mixed in most instances. Embraced within this question are far larger ones connected with the development of European culture as a whole. Is there, indeed, a sense in which we ourselves, living in the twenty-first century might describe ourselves as still Roman despite the even more momentous changes from the eighth century onwards? That this is by no means a ridiculous question is demonstrated if one only looks at late Roman coins, then the coins of Charlemagne, issues of later Medieval kings throughout Europe and finally at current British or

European coins; or at the clothes and regalia of Medieval monarchs and at their castles and feasting-halls. The centres of power of the Medieval Monarchy (castles and palaces) and of the Church (cathedrals and abbeys) are ultimately derivative from the palaces and basilicas of the late Roman Empire. Similarly the vestments, liturgical vessels and liturgy of the Orthodox and Catholic traditions of the Church are still Roman. It is on such broad continuities of Western culture that one can muse when reading, for example, John Steane's splendid book *The Archaeology of the Medieval English Monarchy* (1993).

All too often archaeologists adopt dry, evolutionary approaches which strive to place specific labels on people and their material culture and this is all very well in its way. However, in a diverse symposium such as this one it is worth taking a broad-brush approach to Western culture. It is said that if you are on a ship and encounter the Gorgon you may be asked the question: 'How is it with Alexander?' To which the only safe reply, should you wish to avoid shipwreck, is 'Alexander lives and reigns' The Gorgon is Alexander's sister, still searching for her brother, and if she is told that Alexander has died, she will sink the vessel (Yalouris 1980: 20). Alexander is, of course, a central figure in our culture today and he was also seen as a king of magical power in the Romances beloved in the Middle Ages, flying into the air on a throne raised by four griffins (Yalouris 1980: 16, figs 3 and 4) as well as plumbing the depths of the sea (Yalouris 1980: 17, fig.5). Similarly, let us also not forget Arthur, a probable Dark Age chieftain and most plausibly a name used of Ambrosius Aurelianus. Gildas (25.30) wrote of Ambrosius that 'his parents had worn the purple', a victor of many battles including *Mons Badonicus* (26.1) which was afterwards ever associated with Arthur. Arthur, like Alexander, was important as the epitome of medieval kingship and of continuing *Romanitas*. They both remain key figures today in modern culture, but it is not very useful to take on the one hand the two ends of the Alexander story in fourth century Greece and in his medieval metamorphosis, or on the other the Ambrosius of Gildas and the Arthur of Malory (or T.H. White), and to look for specific continuities. But the use and reuse of these figures by different societies over the past two millennia shows that there are broad themes and continuities running through Western civilization. Thus it is the contention of the writer of this paper that the 'decline and fall' of Rome, as some have painted it, has been much exaggerated, and that the concept was in large measure a Renaissance construct invented for the purposes of contemporary politics!

Figure 3.1: Tombstone of M.Favonius Facilis. 1ˢᵗ cent AD (Institute of Archaeology, Oxford)

There were of course major changes to the form which Romanness took and indeed a transformation over time: The titles of the admirable book and exhibition catalogue edited by Leslie Webster and Michelle Brown (1997), *The Transformation of the Roman World AD400-900* and with a narrower geographical scope - rather too narrow because it does not take account of the so-called 'Anglo-

Saxon' areas of Britain is Ken Dark's *Civitas to Kingdom: British Political Continuity 300-800* (1994) provides exciting new approaches. Nevertheless, for many early Romanists, Medievalists and the vast majority of the general public, rigid stereotyping persists. The Romans can so easily be defined by a series of cliches: militarism as represented by marching legions, the rulers wandering around in impractical togas and talking Ciceronian Latin, gladiators in the amphitheatre, brash and mechanical buildings and a sort of coarsened Hellenism in art which need not be taken too seriously. This image might be summed up by the Prima Porta statue of Augustus or, in Britain, by the tombstone of M. Favonius Facilis from Colchester (Fig. 3.1). To a degree this caricature has a little truth in the first century, but tends to lose credence later. As John Onians (1999: 162-289), that most perceptive of ancient historians in our generation, has proposed what chiefly distinguishes Rome is its use of symbol and its openness to the imagination. The aesthetic and intellectual journey from, say, the column of Trajan (Onians 1999: 186 fig. 149) to the apse mosaic of San Apollinare in Classe (Onians 1999: 278, fig. 224) is a very long one but it is not one of decline in any respect and I would argue that, if anything, the opposite is the case.

In writing about imperial Rome we should never forget the strong persistence of local culture which affected all aspects of life including language, jewellery and dress. Visitors to Gaul or Britain outside the provincial capitals and the *Coloniae* which initially housed legionary veterans would certainly have known immediately that they were not in Rome. Everyone would have been wearing brooches to fasten native-style garments while the spoken language would either have been Latin with the admixture of Celtic terms or Celtic, and the cults would have been Romano-Celtic too. The enormously varied output of artists in Roman Britain alone as shown in an earlier book (Henig 1995) demonstrates the difficulties in adopting too prescriptive a definition of Roman art. Presumably even in the first century the same person could well have owned and have worn both a 'Celtic', Aesica-type brooch (Henig and Booth 2000: 134-135, fig. 5.19) and a 'Roman' intaglio-set signet ring (Henig and Booth 2000: 138, fig. 5.21).

Local culture and the continuing Roman tradition

In the third century even what we might have characterised as truly Roman was beginning to change very markedly indeed. In a real sense it was becoming just as different from the early Roman world as that of the early Middle Ages was from it. For example, jewellery became much showier with considerable use of large plain stones and open-work cut gold employed for flashy keeled rings, bracelets and neck-chains (Henig 1981). This was an age too when institutions such as the army and the administration were transformed out of recognition and by the end of the fourth century there

Figure 3.2: Wallpainting from house-church at Lullingstone, Kent. End of 4ᵗʰ century AD
(Institute of Archaeology, Oxford)

were no longer any legions who could possibly 'go home', as one has to remind people again and again, any more than a cook can reconstitute the original ingredients of a ragout or a curry. Certainly the Roman upper classes, especially the emperors and their families, wore wonderful jewelled diadems and brooches and gorgeous clothes, as can be seen for example in the figures of the *orantes* from the Lullingstone house-church (Meates 1987: 33-34, pl. xii) (Fig. 3.2). Even ordinary people of some rank were clad in lovely bright clothes – clothes which, on inspection, remain strangely familiar, as the chasubles and copes of our priests to this day. Christianity had arrived even in remote Britain and, as certain examples of portable art show us from fifth, sixth and seventh century contexts, as well as textual evidence, was here to stay. Nevertheless, the ancient classics, especially Vergil and Ovid, continued to be read alongside Biblical texts. There is no way in which the culture need be regarded as any less Roman than what had come before (unless one defines culture in terms of the economy and drains which I certainly do not!). Indeed, it would seem that it is only in Late Roman times that the great tradition of insular Latinity really gets going. In terms of material culture treasures like those associated with the cult of the god Faunus from Thetford, Norfolk (Johns and Potter 1983) and the secular - Christian Hoxne Treasure from Suffolk exemplify the fourth/early fifth-century style at its apogee (Henig 1995, chapter 7) and it is from such jewellery and accompanying dress and other items that we should approach Late Antiquity, Peter Brown's term for our period being a far more satisfactory term than the Dark

Ages as these years were very far from being dark (see now Brown 2003)!

Continental Romanitas

Before considering evidence for continuing *Romanitas* from Britain itself, it is well to glance at the Continent. During the fifth century the political hold of emperors ruling in Western Europe loosened and although the emperor reigning in Constantinople retained at least nominal hegemony power passed to successor states under rulers, often of 'barbarian' origin but frequently with a Roman background and education who would often endeavour to look like Romans as would their followers. Striking ornament and fiery jewels may not look very Roman to people whose views of what an emperor looks like are resolutely Augustan, but such 'Byzantine' styles were certainly anticipated in the regalia of late Roman rulers. In the fourth century, as shown on the famous *Missorium of Theodosius* (Volbach 1961: 322, pl. 53), emperors wore diadems on their heads and circular jewelled brooches on their shoulders while lesser aristocrats wore splendid crossbow brooches (of which a very few have, indeed, been found in Britain). The tomb of Childeric I (*d.* AD 482) included a wonderful cross-bow brooch but also a signet-ring engraved with his portrait in the style of contemporary late Roman/early Byzantine imperial signets and his title 'CHILDERICVS REX' (MacGregor 1999) (Fig. 3.3).

As for people at levels a little below emperors or kings, take the well-known ivory diptych of the late fourth/early

Figure 3.3: Impression of intaglio ring, and objects from the tomb of Childeric, Tournai. Late 5th century AD (Institute of Archaeology, Oxford)

kingdoms on the verge of the Christianisation. Of the Anglo-Saxon ruling families, continuity of aspiration is to be seen whether we are looking at the Britons or the assumed Germanic settlers. For both we can begin with very late Roman material, with cross-bow brooches from Richborough, the belt-buckle and other jewellery from the Thetford Treasure (Johns and Potter 1983: 2-29) and the rich assemblage including much female jewellery from Hoxne. For the Britons of the fifth and sixth centuries the main sources are textual and theological, but used intelligently, we can see both continuities with Roman Britain and exciting new ideas coming in from elsewhere (see Sharpe 2002). It is easy enough, however, to extrapolate sufficiently to show that Western Britain, and at least British enclaves further east together with the Ireland of Patrick, were reasonably ordered while the corruption which Gildas finds in contemporary rulers and clergy, while centred on lust and violence were at least suggest a world where material comfort and personal status mattered. There were certainly connexions with the Continent. As Sharpe (2002: 154) concludes in his important survey, which should be read by every archaeologist concerned with this subject: 'The world of late antiquity did not end on the Channel coast'.

fifth century *magister militum*, Stilicho, and his wife Serena, now in Monza (Volbach 1961: 324, pls. 62 and 63) (Fig. 3.4). He wears a richly embroidered tunic held in place by a splendid belt and the equally rich fabric of his cloak is fastened at his right shoulder by a cross-bow brooch. He has elegant shoes and perhaps leggings. Stilicho's weapons are a spear, which he holds in his right hand, and a sword, whose scabbard hangs from a baldric. He steadies a large shield with his left hand. Similar dress and weapons are to be seen worn by those who accompany Justinian on the famous mosaic in San Vitale (Volbach 1961: 343, pl. 164). Here the use of coloured tesserae brings out the startling richness and sophistication of the dress, including the shoes at court, are truly dazzling by any of the standards of the early empire. The guards carry spears and a single shield with a chi-rho emblazoned on it serves for all of them. Belts and swords are not visible but the only positive absence lies in cross-bow brooches. On this mosaic these are reserved for high civilian officials (Volbach 1961: pls. 166 and see 167). Instead the guards have striking pendants suspended from their necks. Serena (Volbach 1961: pl. 62) is also richly clothed, with her long tunic held in place by a somewhat narrower, more highly decorated belt. Around her neck she has a necklace of gems, perhaps amethysts, and she has prominent ear-rings. These features are, once again, matched at San Vitale, this time by the ladies of Theodora's court (Volbach 1961: pls. 165, 167).

Roman fashion in late- and post-Roman Britain

Turning to Britain, kingly jewellery is not really to be found before the late sixth century with the Anglo-Saxon

Unfortunately we do not, on the whole, get descriptions of physical appearance, dress and jewellery. The nearest we come is Constantius' description of the 'Pelagian' *curiales*, presumably of *Verulamium*, who encountered St Germanus in AD 429 (Constantius, *Vita S. Germani* 14). They were *conspicui divites veste fulgentes* probably alluding to their ostentatious pride as much as to the very strong likelihood that they would have resembled the Lullingstone Orantes (Fig. 3.2), in their gorgeous apparel. Material evidence has often seemed hard to find, or at least to date but it is slowly accumulating and the evidence is now most conveniently available in David Petts's excellent survey (Petts 2003). There are now recognisable Christian cemeteries such as Queenford Mill, Dorchester, Oxfordshire, and Cannington and Shepton Mallet, Somerset. These are indicators are borne out by the recognition of Christian structures, including the recently discovered seating for a large font, certainly designed for adult baptism, constructed on top of a mosaic floor in a villa at Bradford-upon-Avon (Corney 2003: 16-20). Until recently I was somewhat sceptical at various claims of baptisteries and churches elsewhere in the countryside but taken together the argument is

Figure 3.4: Cast of diptych of Stilicho and Serena c. AD 400(Institute of Archaeology, Oxford)

Figure 3.5: Enamelled penannular brooch from Bath. 4ᵗʰ or 5ᵗʰ century AD (Institute of Archaeology, Oxford)

persuasive. In addition there is the rich tradition of early Christian memorial stones from the west (Thomas 1998) displaying remarkable textual sophistication. Two conclusions seem inescapable from a reading of the evidence: congregations of Christians were actually growing in the fifth and sixth centuries, not declining, and to be Christian was coming to be seen as the same thing as being Roman, as, indeed, it was almost everywhere else in Europe. This means that it makes no sense to speak or write of Roman Britain being in terminal decline: only superficial features like the economy had shrunk out of recognition, though even here, which economy are we being asked to consider?

For some reason archaeologists of the Roman period are resistant to the truth that civilization (literature and spirituality) do not need stone-built edifices or an efficient system of plumbing to flourish. However, even the Reece-Faulkner school of archaeologists would be at pains to stress how very different the early Roman economy was from the late fourth-century economy. Unfortunately, for the archaeologist, the Christian dead were almost invariably buried in shrouds without associated grave goods, they and their surviving relatives taking to heart the strictures against wealth. Presumably grave goods were believed to impede access to Heaven.

Obviously those interred here wore clothes and an assortment of dress accessories in life (such as enamelled penannular brooches) (Fig. 3.5) but believed that the ideal Christian position was one of holy poverty. The wealth one would acquire in the afterlife was of a totally different kind. Possessions were systematically removed from the corpse before burial, whether this was for the benefit of the heirs or for the church cannot be known. This means that the archaeologist lacks the finds assemblages, which are such a feature of so called 'Germanic' inhumations and cremations.

Anglo-Saxon graves of the fifth, sixth and even seventh centuries provide evidence for a pagan (or mainly pagan) culture of considerable interest and sometimes wealth. But it needs to be recognised that apart from the religious difference, the culture represented was neither more nor less 'barbarous' than that of the unfurnished British Christian graves. In a way it is in these graves that we should look for the heirs of the pagans of Thetford. Indeed this suggestion is supported by the presence of objects which seem to me to be characteristic of 'British' manufacture in 'Germanic' graves, such as the so-called 'quoit-brooches' in the fifth century (see Henig 1995: 170-173) (Fig. 3.6), and even the hanging bowls in the sixth and seventh (Youngs 1989: 47-52). The latter,

Figure 3.6: Quoit brooch from Sarre, Kent (British Museum) 5th century AD (Institute of Archaeology, Oxford)

Figure 3.7: Christian beaker from Long Wittenham, Oxfordshire. 5th century AD (Institute of Archaeology, Oxford)

write about his taste with some assurance but hardly decide whether he was a Christian or not, perhaps a member of the congregation of a nearby British church, or whether he considered himself as a Roman or as a Teutonic barbarian. In any case his ethnicity and religion may have owed a great deal to personal choice.

Being Roman in the Conversion period

The late sixth-century Augustinian Mission and perhaps some immediately preceding influences from Francia invigorated the culture of the native British church with the splendours of Rome and the Byzantine East (Harris 2003). For Augustine the problem was that he could not proceed to convert 'barbarians' in isolation as though there was a *tabula rasa* but had to engage with a living church which had been here from early in the fourth century if not earlier. The benefit was of course interaction between the two traditions perhaps best epitomised in Northumbria (Hawkes and Mills 1999). We can see the pendants and jewellery of the Conversion period and later as having a close relationship to similar items from the Mediterranean world. In other words those who wore garnet jewellery were in a real sense Roman as has been recognised by William Filmer-Sankey (1996) and others (e.g. Wood 1997: 119). Characteristic items include gold and garnet cloisonne brooches (Webster and Backhouse 1991, nos. 31a, 32a) (Fig. 3.8) and pendants (Webster and Backhouse 1991, nos. 9 and 10) (Fig. 3.9). These included exotic garnets, and necklaces of amethyst beads emphasising the contemporary links with Rome and more properly the Roman East which we call the

indeed, may in the first instance have been designed for ecclesiastical use, possibly for baptism by *aspersion*, if they contained water. Their figural iconography including birds (doves) for escutcheons, doves, fish and dolphins and deer and the presence of these motifs on some crosses are suggestive. The problem is one for us (at least for the Anglo-Saxonists among us!), and not for them. It is, of course possible that some Britons, very possibly pagans, appear to us in Germanic guise through their grave goods. Who was the sixth or seventh-century man buried at Lowbury Hill (Harke 1994) with his shield and a spear enamelled in the British style? His grave also contained an enamelled British hanging bowl for good measure. Incidentally it is of some interest that a beaker carrying New Testament scenes was found not too far away at Long Wittenham (Henig and Booth 2000: 185-186, pl. 7.4) (Fig. 3.7). Whether Briton or 'Anglo-Saxon' the Lowbury Hill warrior surely looked rather like the Roman general Stilicho (Volbach 1961: pl. 65)! We can

Figure 3.8: Garnet cloisonné disk brooch from Milton, Oxfordshire. 6th-7th century AD (Institute of Archaeology, Oxford)

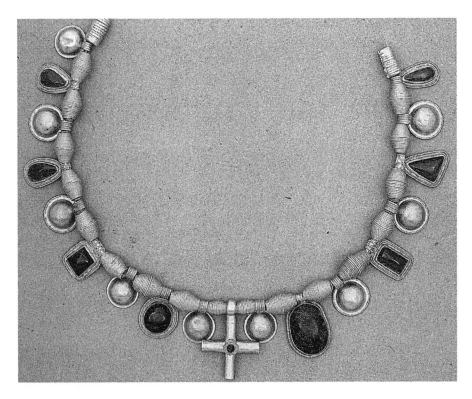

Figure 3.9: The Byzantine style: Desborough necklace, Northamptonshire 7th century AD (Photo: British Museum).

(1994), amongst others, has rightly said in no uncertain terms, most of Britain was British or at least non-Teutonic. Apart from the Irish and the Picts, Dumnonia, Wales and Cumbria were British as were the western counties of England, amongst them Gloucestershire, Somerset and Wiltshire. There were undoubtedly large groups of Britons elsewhere, for instance in the Chilterns, the Fen Country and the Middle Thames.

The most instructive story perhaps concerns Cumbria, which in the seventh century came under the hegemony of the Christian Northumbrian dynasty but seems to show unbroken Roman-Christian continuity with the past. When Cuthbert visited Carlisle and looked at its antiquities on on 20 May 685 he effectively stood in a surviving late Roman town, while the great High Cross at Bewcastle marked an ancient Romano-Celtic sanctuary Christianised (see Henig, *forthcoming*). The great culture of Northumbria's 'golden age', with its amazing manuscripts and impressive metalwork drew on the Anglo-Saxon, Roman, Byzantine, British and Irish traditions. But the very nature of the luxury of kingship would have made the Northumbrian kings think of themselves as deputising for the Emperor. Bewcastle and Ruthwell can be seen, I have surmised, as insular reflections of works such as Trajan's column (Fig. 3.10).

How the populace remained Roman

Below the high level of kings or chieftains like the man buried at Sutton Hoo it is impressive to see how many of the inhabitants of Britain, who could never have aspired to noble rank, wanted to be Roman, at least in appearance. In Roman times it is worth reminding ourselves that most of the very common cross-bow brooches from Britain are smaller than the massive examples depicted on consular diptychs, the Missorium of Theodosius and the like, and some of these brooches were surely worn by women as were many of the square-headed brooches, descended from cross-bow brooches, from later, Migration period graves. Circular brooches too are best known as very high status and Imperial insignia but archaeological finds from the later Roman Empire show that they were more widespread and there are considerable numbers of gilt-bronze examples from

Byzantine Empire (see Harris 2003). In the case of the pendants we can also see a link with possible late Romano-British base metal prototypes from Ickham, Kent and Alington Avenue, Dorchester, Dorset (Henig and Morris 2003) as well as from Disk Brooches and pendants from contemporary Byzantium like the well-known example from Benevento in the Ashmolean (Sena Chiesa 2002: 28 and 31, fig. 5). Seventh-century jewelled crosses too (e.g. Webster and Backhouse 1991, nos. 12, 13, 98) are clearly works which recall contemporary Byzantine jewellery, but their appeal within treasure-loving Anglo-Saxon culture was very great. Their appearance had a poetic dimension as evidenced by the 'Dream of the Rood' inscribed on the stone Ruthwell Cross. Frankish or Jutish kingship was always conscious of such Roman traditions. Further north in East Anglia burials at Snape and Sutton Hoo show kings surrounded not only with objects in Roman style but, especially at Sutton Hoo, with Roman objects. As Filmer Sankey has shown (1996) it is quite reasonable to see Raedwald or whoever was buried at Sutton Hoo as a typical Late Antique ruler, a king who perhaps saw himself as under the authority of the emperor in Constantinople, rather than as an emperor himself.

North and West

It is worth remembering that the Anglo-Saxon bias of post AD 400 archaeology on this island owes more to the plentiful grave goods of 'Anglo-Saxon' cemeteries and nineteenth-century prejudice than to reality. As Dark

Figure 3.10: The Bewcastle cross. 8th century AD and detail of carving (Institute of Archaeology, Oxford)

Roman Britain, some dating from as early as the third century; again, not items of the highest prestige. For Anglo-Saxonists circular saucer-brooches with geometric motifs including some with running spirals, suspiciously celticising though the classic type is to be found in the Saxon homeland near Hanover, though other varieties with rosettes and the like are surely of more local stylistic origin as is the use of the Late Roman technique of 'chip-carving'. These brooches are frequent in the Gewissean-Hwiccian lands of the Middle Thames with their mixed British and Germanic traditions (Dodd 1995). However, it is pertinent to ask whether the distinctions between 'Germanic' and 'Roman' would have been recognised by the wearers. Rather the wearers were surely doing their level best to 'look Roman'. What else would they have wanted to look like?

In late Roman times, buckles too were emblematic of *Romanitas*. Massive belts in precious metal, like the gold ones from the Tenes Treasure, Tunisia and from the Thetford Treasure or the fragmentary silver belt from Traprain Law are rare, but bronze buckles and buckle plates are an important part of Later Roman and early Anglo-Saxon assemblages. Some of the most characteristic and interesting of the late Roman belt-buckles are those of the so-called Hawkes type IB type. They are sometimes engraved with Christian ornament: peacocks, fish and trees of life (e.g. Brown and Henig

2002) (Fig. 3.11), but others are embellished in abstract chip-carved style, which has analogies with that to be seen on what may be slightly later quoit brooches (Henig 2000) which leads on to the ornament of belt buckles found in 'Anglo-Saxon' graves (Ager 1990: 157, pl. 2). Indeed, some type IB buckles are certainly found in such contexts. A belt was simply a proper part of a freeman's and free woman's dress and, on occasion, might be expressive of one having achieved a more elevated position in society.

It is probably always going to be difficult to give a totally coherent account of how the English people were composed. The most sensible statement to date is to be seen in Catherine Hills's book on the subject (Hills 2003). There may have been some small pockets of purely settler stock at least for a short period. Conversely, the western parts of Britain remained Celtic throughout our period but unfortunately, apart from a few penannular brooches and hand-pins, there is little that is diagnostic here in matters of dress. To the east the Hwicce and Gewissae, although partly – and in some parts of their regions mainly – British in origin, came to be largely absorbed into the Anglo-Saxon culture, art and linguistic ambit, while their ruling classes (whatever their actual ethnicity) regarded themselves as Saxons (Henig and Booth 2000: 178-201). The same holds true of Northumbria (Hawkes and Mills 1999). The use of old

Figure 3.11: Buckle-plate from East Challow (photo: Clive Brown)

Romano-British jewellery and other items will to a degree have further emphasised a desire to be Roman and this continued to manifest itself into the Conversion period (Geake 1997; White 1990). Under powerful influences from southern Europe, the people of Kent, the Thames Valley, the Midlands and East Anglia were not just continuing to look Roman in a general sense, but the availability of exotic items, chains incorporating amethysts or garnets (e.g. the Desborough necklace, Webster and Backhouse 1991: 28-29, no. 13) (Fig 3.9) and other rich items of jewellery, as well as silks and other textiles and metal vessels from the Eastern Roman Empire served to integrate them into the current East Roman Empire which we generally call Byzantine (Harris 2003). The pectoral cross from St Cuthbert's tomb (Webster and Backhouse 1991: 133-134, no. 98) and others like it can be compared with contemporary Byzantine jewelled crosses (Harris 2003: pl. 7). England was created with a subtle fusion of memory of Roman past with the Germanic inheritance of northwest Europe. The general resemblance of Anglo-Saxons of respectable family to the provincial Romans with whom they intermarried was especially apparent in the period of renewal in the late sixth and seventh centuries when we can see new Byzantine influences vying with old Romano-British *Romanitas*.

Art and propaganda

Propaganda has always played a part in establishing a 'new' Romano-Christian England, for us it is best represented by the brilliance of that great Northumbrian work of Late Antiquity, Bede's *Ecclesiastical History*. The result of the Augustinian mission through the seventh century and beyond was to allow the rulers of the separate, developing kingdoms to integrate themselves fully into the Catholic (rather than the British) church, and somehow to make themselves more Roman than the native kingdoms whose culture though partly derived from Roman Britain was also affected by eremitical traditions stemming from the Eastern Deserts. Such traditions which stressed the 'other', the opposite of the settled town or villa, rather the lonely headland or rock in the sea could seem a threat to those who desired an organised society, and might even be equated with

barbaricum! At any rate a British or Irish monastery could be seen as more distant in spirit from the world of Rome than was the court of an Anglo-Saxon king, replete with *royal* trappings. The word *apparently* needs to be stressed, because an explosion of creativity in the courts and monasteries of Ireland created an art (Youngs 1989) that was on occasion merged with the art of the East, especially in Northumbria where it is epitomised by the Lindisfarne Gospels of the 7th-8th centuries. In much of northern Europe Roman Christianity was returned by Irish and Anglo-Saxon missionaries, the products of a vibrant insular cultures whose beginnings can be traced back to the fourth century and whose end is still not in sight.

Bibliography

Ager, B. 1990. The Alternative Quoit Brooch: an update, in E. Southworth (ed.), *Anglo-Saxon Cemeteries. A Reappraisal*: 153-61. Stroud: Alan Sutton.

Boyle, A., Dodd. A., Miles, D., and Mudd , A. 1995. *Two Oxfordshire Anglo-Saxon Cemeteries: Berinsfield and Didcot*. Oxford: Thames Valley Landscapes Monograph 8.

Brown, C. and Henig, M. 2002. A Romano-British Buckle Plate from East Challow, near Wantage. *Oxoniensia* 67: 363-5.

Brown, P. 2003. *The Rise of Western Christendom*, second edition. Oxford: Blackwell.

Corney, M. 2003. *The Roman Villa at Bradford on Avon*. Bradford on Avon: Ex Libris

Cunliffe, B. and Poole, C. 2000. *Houghton Down, Stockbridge, Hants, 1994*. Oxford: English Heritage and Oxford University Committee for Archaeology.

Dark, K.R. 1994. *Civitas to Kingdom. British Political Continuity 300-800*. Leicester: Leicester University Press.

Dodd, A. 1995 . The brooches, in A. Boyle *et al., Two Oxfordshire Anglo-Saxon Cemeteries: Berinsfield and Didcot*: 75-80. Oxford: Thames Valley Landscapes Monograph 8.

Filmer-Sankey, W. 1996. The 'Roman Emperor' in the

Sutton Hoo Ship Burial. *Journal of the British Archaeological Association* 149: 1-9

Fulford, M.G. and Rippon, S.J. 1994. Lowbury Hill, Oxon: a re-assessment of the probable Romano-Celtic temple and the Anglo-Saxon barrow. *Archaeological Journal* 151: 158-211.

Geake, H. 1997. *The Use of Grave-Goods in Conversion-Period England* c.600-c.850. Oxford: British Archaeological Reports British Series 261.

Harke, H. 1994. A context for the Saxon barrow, in M. Fulford and S. Rippon. Lowbury Hill, Oxon: a re-assessment of the probable Romano-Celtic temple and the Anglo-Saxon barrow: 202-6. *Archaeological Journal* 151: 158-211.

Harris, A. 2003. *Byzantium, Britain and the West. The Archaeology of Cultural Identity AD 400-650.* Stroud: Tempus

Henig, M. 1981. Continuity and Change in the Design of Roman Jewellery, in A. King and M. Henig (ed.), *The Roman West in the Third Century. Contributions from Archaeology and History*: 127-143. Oxford: British Archaeological Reports International Series 109.

Henig, M. 1995. *The Art of Roman Britain.* London: Batsford.

Henig, M. 2000. A zoomorphic belt-buckle, in B. Cunliffe and C. Poole, *Houghton Down, Stockbridge, Hants, 1994*: 104-7. Oxford: English Heritage and Oxford University Committee for Archaeology.

Henig, M. 2002. *The Heirs of King Verica. Culture and Politics in Roman Britain.* Stroud: Tempus

Henig, M. forthcoming. *Murum civitatis, et fontem in ea a Romanis mire olim constructum:* The arts of Rome in Carlisle and the civitas of the Carvetii and their influence, in M. McCarthy and C. D. Weston (ed.), forthcoming conference transactions.

Henig, M. and Booth, P. 2000. *Roman Oxfordshire.* Stroud: Alan Sutton

Henig, M. and Morris, C. 2002. The copper alloy and lead alloy objects, in S. Davies, P. Bellamy, M. Heaton and P. Woodward (ed.), *Excavations at Alington Avenue, Fordington, Dorset, 1984-1987*: 180-81. Dorchester: Dorset Natural History and Archaeological Society and English Heritage.

Henig, M. and Plantzos, D. 1999. *Classicism to Neo-Classicism. Essays dedicated to Gertrud Seidmann.* Oxford: British Archaeological Reports International Series 793.

Hills, C. 2003. *Origins of the English.* London: Duckworth.

Johns, C. and Potter, T. 1983. *The Thetford Treasure. Roman Jewellery and Silver.* London: British Museum Publications.

King, A. and Henig, M. 1981. *The Roman West in the Third Century. Contributions from Archaeology and History.* Oxford: British Archaeological Reports International Series 109.

MacGregor, A. 1999. The Afterlife of Childeric's Ring, in M. Henig and D. Plantzos (ed.), *Classicism to Neo-Classicism. Essays dedicated to Gertrud Seidmann*: 149-62. Oxford: British Archaeological Reports International Series 793.

Meates, G.W. 1987. *The Roman Villa at Lullingstone, Kent II. The Wall Paintings and Finds.* Maidstone, Kent Archaeological Society.

Onians, J. 1999. *Classical Art and the Cultures of Greece and Rome.* New Haven and London: Yale University Press.

Petts, D. 2003. *Christianity in Roman Britain.* Stroud: Tempus.

Sena Chiesa, G. 2002. *Gemme dalla corte imperiale alla corte celeste.* Milan: Universita degli Studi di Milano.

Sharpe, R. 2002. Martyrs and Local Saints in Late Antique Britain, in A.T. Thacker and R. Sharpe (ed.), *Local Saints and Local Churches in the Early Medieval West*: 75-154. Oxford: Oxford University Press.

Southworth, E. 1990. *Anglo-Saxon Cemeteries. A Reappraisal.* Stroud: Alan Sutton

Steane, J. 1993. *The Archaeology of the Medieval English Monarchy.* London: Batsford.

Swift, E. 2000. *The End of the Western Roman Empire. An Archaeological Investigation.* Stroud: Tempus

Thacker, A.T. and Sharpe, R. 2002. *Local Saints and Local Churches in the Early Medieval West.* Oxford: Oxford University Press.

Thomas, C. 1998. *Christian Celts. Messages and Images.* Stroud: Tempus.

Volbach, W.F. 1961. *Early Christian Art.* London: Thames and Hudson.

Webster, L. and Backhouse, J. 1991. *The Making of England. Anglo-Saxon Art and Culture AD 600-900.* London: British Museum Publishing.

Webster, L. and Brown, M. 1997. *The Transformation of the Roman World AD, 400-900.* London: British Museum Press.

White, R. 1990. Scrap or substitute: Roman material in Anglo-Saxon graves, in E. Southworth (ed.), *Anglo-Saxon Cemeteries. A Reappraisal*: 125-52. Stroud: Sutton.

Wood, I. 1997. The transmission of ideas, Pp.111-127 in L. Webster and M. Brown (ed.), *The Transformation of the Roman World, AD 400-900*: 111-127. London: British Museum Press.

Yalouris, N. 1980. Alexander and His Heritage. *The search for Alexander*: 10-20. Washington D.C.: National Gallery of Art.

Youngs, S. 1989. *'The Work of Angels'. Masterpieces of Celtic Metalwork. 6th-9th centuries AD.* London: British Museum Press.

4: Coast and countryside in 'Late Antique' southwest England, *c*.AD 400-600

Sam Turner

Introduction

Southwest England is a region with a distinctive and individual history. Processes that were characteristic of other parts of southern Britain, like the nucleation of villages or the enclosure of open fields, either did not happen here or occurred at different times. As a result of its distinctive social, political and cultural history, the region has a strong local identity. For example, local agricultural and manorial customs have given the landscape of Devon and Cornwall a highly distinctive character that sets is apart from neighbouring parts of England. Whilst it is true that there are well-defined sub-regions where differences in geology, soil, climate and local custom have produced locally significant variations, the landscape of the South West peninsula is unified by certain common traits. Perhaps most prominent are the massive earth-built hedgebanks that so powerfully define the fields and tower over sunken lanes throughout the region; they make the experience of moving through the landscape here quite different to that in areas dominated by Parliamentary enclosure, with their flimsy, low-growing hedges.

The physical landscape of the South West has been only one of many elements contributing to a strong regional self-identity both now and in the past (Herring 1998: 77-82). Quinnell has argued that in the late Roman period, for example, material culture may have provided another mechanism through the manufacture and use of a distinctive group of stone artefacts (Quinnell 1993). In an area with a distinctive local identity and history, the period divisions that might be useful in other places will not necessarily apply. With southwest England in mind, it is clear that the term 'Late Antiquity' cannot be used to imply what it might in, say, northern Gaul or the eastern Mediterranean, but then neither can the term 'Roman'. Period labels of whatever sort always need to be understood within their local contexts; with these caveats in mind, 'Late Antique' might be a more accurate and specific term to describe this period than others like 'post-Roman' or the 'Dark Ages'. The history of the period between *c*.AD 400-600 in the far south-west of England is characterised by certain important processes that distinguish it from earlier and later centuries, including those typical of 'Late Antique' milieux elsewhere, for example the growing influence of the

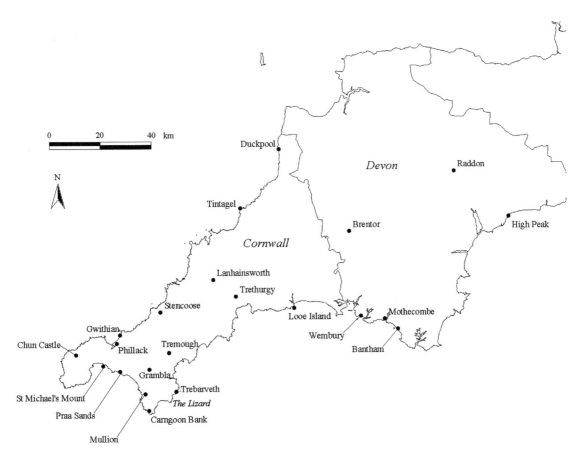

Figure 4.1: The location of sites mentioned in the text.

church and the continuing importance of 'Roman' material culture. The aim of this short paper is to highlight some of these with reference to some recent work that has been undertaken in the region (Figure 4.1).

Beachmarkets and Coastal Contacts

The best-known finds from the southwest of Britain dating to the fifth and sixth centuries are the ceramic imports from the Mediterranean. In contrast to much of Anglo-Saxon England to the east, little securely-dated locally-produced material has been identified in western Britain, so these imported objects have provided a useful key into the archaeology of a period that is relatively poor in surviving material culture.

Probably the best-known type of site to have produced this imported material, and certainly the ones with the highest profile in the public imagination, are the major fortified centres (for example Cadbury Congresbury and South Cadbury in Somerset: Rahtz *et al.* 1992; Alcock 1995, and Dinas Powys in south Wales: Alcock 1963). The greatest of all these, at least in terms of the volume of imported material dating to the late fifth and early sixth

centuries, is Tintagel in Cornwall (Morris and Harry 1997) (Figure 4.2). Thousands of sherds belonging to this period have been excavated here, an assemblage far in excess of that from any other contemporary site. These finds are associated with a large number of rectangular structures (Figure 4.3) that probably represent buildings used for a range of purposes including accommodation, storage and industrial activities (Thomas 1993; Morris and Harry 1997: 72-73; Morris *et al.* 1999: 210). When Tintagel has produced so much material it seems entirely reasonable to suggest it was a major centre for the rulers of Cornwall who emerged at this time (Morris and Harry 1997: 124). Nevertheless there are other sites that may have had a similar role. Recent work at St Michael's Mount in the west of Cornwall has identified a small assemblage of imported material from the island's summit. Peter Herring has suggested the site may have been an important power centre in the fifth and sixth centuries, as it became once again in the later middle ages (Herring 2000). Other examples may include places like High Peak in south-east Devon, a prehistoric cliff-top fortification where excavations produced a small assemblage of imported material (Pollard 1966), and potentially Looe Island off the south coast of Cornwall (Todd 1983).

Figure 4.2: The promontory site of Tintagel, general view.

Figure 4.3: Rectangular structures at Tintagel, occupation terrace Site C.

The second type of coastal site to have produced significant amounts of imported material are the sand-dune or beachmarket sites. Few of these have been methodically investigated and their significance and mode of use is far from clear. Most have only produced a few sherds of imported pottery from chance finds. However, at Bantham on the south coast of Devon, the recent construction of a modern building on the foreshore has allowed one of these sites to be excavated using modern methods for the first time in the South West. Exeter Archaeology's work on the site has produced some spectacular results, revealing phases of occupation including hearths and spreads of debris interspersed between layers of sand. Around 2400 pieces of bone were recovered, including some worked artefacts, and most importantly around 570 sherds of pottery, the vast majority of which was imported from the Mediterranean (Horner 2001; May and Weddell 2002). This massive haul is particularly striking considering that the relatively small excavation ($c.40m^2$) only affected a fragment of the site's total surface area, and a great deal more must lie unexcavated beneath the sand (see also Sylvester 1981; Griffith 1986).

Bantham lies at the mouth of the River Avon, and travelling north-west from here along the coast another probable beachmarket site has been identified at Mothecombe, adjacent to the estuary of the River Erme (Fox 1961). The site is subject to ongoing erosion from both the sea and people using the beach and coastal path, and several hundred square metres of desposits have been lost since the initial work on the site was reported by Fox in the early 1960s, potentially including a very large quantity of archaeological material. Preliminary work to assess the significance of the site has recently revealed a very rich palaeoenvironmental assemblage and continuing finds of imported Mediterranean ceramic material (Reed 2002). As at Bantham, there is a potentially extensive area of periodic occupation at the site with evidence for hearths and iron slag suggesting metal-working on site. Mothecombe is also important because it is one of a small but growing group of sites including Tintagel, Trethurgy, Gwithian, Bantham, and St Michael's Mount where imported Mediterranean pottery of the fifth and sixth centuries has been found stratified in the same levels as pottery produced in the South West (Thomas 1981; Quinnell 2000: 45). At Mothecombe this so far amounts to only two sherds in the Gabbroic fabric from Cornwall's Lizard peninsula, but at some other sites different forms and fabrics have also been found (e.g. Bantham: Allan 2001). This evidence supports Charles Thomas' contention that the use and production of pottery continued in Cornwall in the post-Roman period (Thomas 1968). Perhaps the main reason that Mothecombe is important, however, is its close proximity to Bantham. By comparing assemblages from the two sites, it may be possible in future to understand the relationships between the two sites, for example whether they were in use at the same time or not, whether they were used by the same kinds of people, and whether both saw activity on a similar scale.

Several theories have been put forward to explain the presence of the imported material from the Mediterranean region, and in particular the nature of the transactions that were taking place. Many scholars have suggested some kind of trading relationship between Britain and the eastern Mediterranean, and the famous mineral wealth of the South West, most importantly tin, is often cited as the likely motivation for this trade (e.g. Campbell 1996a: 88-89). It is virtually certain that tin production took place in Cornwall during the Roman period, and tin ingots have been found in several late-Roman contexts in the South West (Penhallurick 1986). These include Par Beach, on St Martin's in the Isles of Scilly, where an ingot was excavated within a late Roman building, and the settlement at Trethurgy, where an ingot was found in a fourth-century midden (Quinnell 1986). Work during the 1980s and early 1990s at the coastal site of Duckpool in north Cornwall demonstrated the presence of pewter-working in the late Roman period, which also required a supply of tin (Ratcliffe 1995). From this base it seems highly probable that the tin extraction industry would have been maintained in the post-Roman period and formed an important part of the local economy. Although no tin ingots have been dated securely to the post-Roman period, there are likely examples from Praa Sands in Cornwall (Penhallurick 1986) and from the estuary of the River Erme in Devon where around 40 ingots were discovered by divers in the early 1990s, just offshore of the possible beachmarket at Mothecombe (Fox 1995).

In a recent discussion, Harris has suggested that the major motivating factor behind these risky long-distance voyages from the Mediterranean was not tin, but rather the cultivation of political relationships between the Byzantine empire and the rulers of the South West (Harris 2003: 141-152). She has argued that the likely royal centre at Tintagel may even have contained a semi-permanent mercantile element from the eastern Mediterranean similar those attested in Gaul in documentary sources. Given the highly unusual nature of the site at Tintagel, these seem plausible theories. It is very likely that the elite at Tintagel were able to legitimate and bolster their power through their access to ideas and goods from the east Roman world. The form of Tintagel, for example, with its numerous buildings and dense occupation is quite unlike anything else so far known in contemporary south-west Britain, and it might be seen as reflecting urban models from the Mediterranean (see Dark 2000: 156; though Greeves 2003 has recently suggested that earthworks surveyed at Brentor, Devon may preserve the remains of a similar complex).

In seeking to emphasise the political or diplomatic relationships between Byzantium and west, however, Harris has marginalised the importance of the sand-dune sites. Harris suggests these were part of a different trade network to the major royal sites like Tintagel, and does not attempt to build them into her model of British-Byzantine political relationships (Harris 2003: 147-149). Her explanation does not seem convincing for sites like Bantham, where a very large quantity of imported material has been recovered without a known connection to a permanent secular centre. Whilst Harris' suggestion of a strong political motivation behind the movement of these goods is undoubtedly valid, it is not necessarily the case that the movement of imports was either completely controlled by the social elite or else was the result of a more random system of 'tramping' up and down the coast by speculative seafarers (see e.g. Thomas 1988; Wooding 1996; Campbell 1996b). We should perhaps be thinking in terms of a more complicated picture involving a mixture of primary and secondary trade and exchange across a range of sites. An increasing number of coastal sites are being identified showing that even the smallest of coastal inlets could be in active use during the fifth and sixth centuries (e.g. the most recent discovery at Wembury on the south coast of Devon (Reed 2003). These must be taken into account alongside sites like Bantham, and new models need to be built based on the detailed comparison of assemblages and site-formation

processes from a variety of different locations, both on the coast and elsewhere.

The Late Roman and 'Late Antique' Countryside

Imported Mediterranean pottery is not confined to coastal sites, but has also been identified at a number of settlements inland. By looking at rural settlements in addition to beachmarkets and royal centres, it may be possible in future to suggest how they functioned and how the overall landscape of settlement changed over time.

We know that structures of life in most of Devon and Cornwall were affected relatively little by 'Romanized' styles between the 1st and 4th centuries. In relation to material culture, for example, Henrietta Quinnell has noted that only small amounts of characteristically 'Roman' imported objects are found on many sites in Cornwall (Quinnell 1986). Whilst Roman forms may have influenced local manufacturers, around 95% of all pottery from Roman-period sites in the county was locally produced on the Lizard peninsula. This echoes the situation during the preceding Iron Age, when almost all the pottery in Cornwall derived from the Lizard, and suggests that distribution channels may have remained relatively undisrupted by any political changes.

The same kind of continuity is visible in the settlement patterns of Iron Age to Romano-British Cornwall. The most widely recognised type of late Iron Age settlements are known as 'rounds', and the sites of several hundred are known in Cornwall and west Devon. These were groups of buildings, commonly roundhouses, enclosed by a bank and ditch. As the name suggests they are often round, although rectangular, square and even triangular examples are also known (Johnson and Rose 1982). Sites like St Mawgan-in-Pydar (Threipland 1956), Castle Gotha (Saunders and Harris 1982), and Carvossa (Carlyon 1987) show that rounds date principally from the second century BC onwards, and that occupation continued into the first centuries of the Roman period with few changes. Only at one excavated round has abandonment been demonstrated before the beginning of the Roman period, Threemilestone near Truro (Schweiso 1976). While some went out of use in the second and third centuries AD, many new rounds were established at around the same time, including Grambla (Saunders 1972), Reawla (Appleton-Fox 1992), and Trethurgy (Miles and Miles 1973). By analogy with the rest of Roman Britain, Quinnell has argued that there is likely to have been an increase in the number of settlements in the second century AD to accommodate an expanding population (Quinnell 1986: 124).

If Cornwall seems to have been less 'Romanized' than other parts of Britain, it also appears to have been less severely affected than other areas by the 'ending' of

Roman Britain. In terms of settlements, this is shown by the rounds at Trethurgy and Grambla, which were both excavated in the 1970s and which have both produced imported Mediterranean pottery of the fifth and sixth centuries. Quinnell has argued that the distinctive material culture of these sites suggests a strong local sense of identity in the region during this period (Quinnell 1993).

Recent work by the Cornwall Archaeological Unit has identified several other sites of possible rounds that may have continued in occupation from the late Roman period into the fifth century. Disturbance in the churchyard at Mullion in west Cornwall was monitored by an archaeological watching brief that identified sherds of redeposited imported Mediterranean pottery along with Iron Age and Roman material. In his report on the site, Carl Thorpe suggests that the churchyard may have been established adjacent to a former round, and that the ceramic finds could relate to the clearance of domestic rubbish from its interior during the manuring of surrounding fields (Thorpe 2003: 27-28). Similar activity may also explain the presence of a few sherds of imported pottery close to the site of a Romano-British enclosure at Tremough (Lawson-Jones 2002: 22).

It seems likely that places like Trethurgy and perhaps Mullion would have been local power centres held by clients of the major royal centres like Tintagel. They probably represent the next step down the social scale in the fifth and sixth centuries. Both categories of sites were also occupied in the late Roman period, and places like Tintagel, St Michael's Mount (Herring 2000: 119-122) and Chun Castle in West Penwith (Preston-Jones and Rose 1986) seem to have received a similar range of goods in the fourth century as important rounds like Trethurgy and Reawla (Thorpe 1997: 82). This suggests that the major 'post'-Roman centres of Cornwall were in fact established as part of a late Roman settlement pattern (Dark 2000: 164-170). The changing ratios of imported ceramics and other goods probably reflect an increasing degree of social stratification and the establishment of increasingly sophisticated ruling class in the fifth and sixth centuries.

The increasingly common use of radiocarbon dating on sites without datable artefacts is leading to the recognition of a growing number of settlement from this period. In Devon, for example, the use of radiocarbon dating has recently allowed Exeter Archaeology to identify a phase of post-Roman activity at the enclosed hilltop site of Raddon not far from Crediton (Gent and Quinnell 1999). In addition, the recognition that local pottery production continued into this period raises the intriguing possibility that it may be possible to identify rounds that received locally produced wares, but not imported material. Quinnell's research has suggested that pottery production definitely continued in the Lizard into the fifth century (Quinnell 1995: 128), and the building evidence from sites like Gwithian, Tintagel, St Michael's

Mount, Bantham and Mothecombe suggests that it may be possible to identify fifth-century phases in future by re-examining the existing assemblages from the latest phases of sites currently assigned to the fourth century.

The exact location of the Lizard pottery kilns is uncertain, but other 'industrial' sites also appear to have continued from the Romano-British era into the fifth and sixth centuries. At Trebarveth in St Keverne a large quantity of late- and possibly post-Roman pottery was recovered from excavations in the early twentieth century close to the Roman saltworking site discovered later (Serocold et al. 1949; Peacock 1969; Johns and Herring 1996: 84). So-called 'grass-marked' pottery found nearby at Carngoon Bank, Landewednack suggests that this small production site may have continued in use into the sixth century or later (McAvoy 1980: 38).

The evidence from settlements and craftworking sites suggests that there were many continuities between the fourth and fifth centuries in the South West, and that the beginning of the fifth century did not mark a sharp break in social or political organisation. In broad terms, this also seems to be reflected in the palaeoenvironmental record for lowland areas (Fyfe and Rippon, this volume). Instead, it seems likely that there was an extended period of more gradual change. Nevertheless present archaeological evidence suggests that a significant proportion of sites with late Roman occupation were no longer used after the fourth century. Whilst there may have been some decline in population levels at this time, this probably also reflects an increasing degree of polarisation in social relationships during the fifth and sixth centuries. So whilst there was certainly a degree of continuity in patterns of settlement and production into Late Antiquity, there were also some important changes and it is these processes that give the period much of its distinct identity.

The end of occupation at an increasing number of rounds marks the beginning of an important change in the settlement pattern. Based on place-name evidence, Oliver Padel has suggested that at this time there was a shift from settlement in rounds to the unenclosed farmsteads that formed the basis of the medieval settlement pattern (Padel 1985). Whilst unenclosed settlements may have existed in Roman period Cornwall, very few have been identified outside west Penwith (Quinnell 1986: 120). Settlements whose place-names begin with distinctively early medieval elements like *tre-* and *bod-* probably represent the earliest stratum of a new settlement pattern (Padel 1985; Turner 2003). Some of the Cornwall Archaeological Unit's recent work has produced exciting results relating to these long-hypothesised but up to now archaeologically obscure settlements. At least three new sites have been identified in recent years, not through artefactual analysis but by radiocarbon dating sites excavated along pipelines. Two sites were located in the corridor of the Bear's Down to Ruthvoes pipeline in central Cornwall, including one at Lanhainsworth near St

Columb Major where features interpreted as possible gullies around roundhouses were radiocarbon dated to the fifth or sixth centuries (Lawson Jones 2001). A third site at Stencoose near St Agnes was also revealed during the construction of a pipeline. An excavated structure here produced no dateable finds but has been radiocarbon dated to around the beginning of the seventh century (CAU 1997: 29).

The field systems around settlements are also suggestive of landscape change during this time. There is an increasing number of examples where Romano-British field boundaries have been identified underlying medieval field patterns on different alignments (discovered through both aerial survey, e.g. Trenithan Bennett (Rose and Preston-Jones 1995) or Dewcombe, Lawhitton (English Heritage National Mapping Programme), and through geophysical survey and excavation, e.g. Trenowah (CAU 1998: 37-38) or Tremough (Lawson Jones 2002). This suggests a discontinuity between the agricultural systems of the two periods, a process of change in the landscape that probably began in Late Antiquity (Herring 1999a; 1999b).

Ewan Campbell has suggested that the social elite who controlled sites like Tintagel in Late Antiquity were no longer able to maintain their position without access to the trade in imported Mediterranean objects which seems to have ended in the late sixth or early seventh century (Campbell 1996a). With the possible exception of St Michael's Mount, all the major enclosed settlements in mainland Cornwall became disused in the late sixth and early seventh centuries, marking the end of the Iron Age and Roman settlement pattern.

There was, however, one aspect of Late Antique culture that continued to thrive and indeed lead the transition to the early middle ages. Christianity may have been introduced into Cornwall in the late Roman period, though the earliest evidence in the form of sculpted chi-rho monograms and inscribed stones probably date to the fifth century (Thomas 1994). Major ecclesiastical centres had almost certainly been established by the sixth century, though little evidence has been uncovered to date and no churches from this period have so far been excavated in the South West. The most likely sites include places like St Matheriana's on Glebe Cliff at Tintagel, and Phillack on the Hayle estuary, which have produced small amounts of imported Mediterranean pottery and possible evidence of Late Antique burial practices (Nowakowski and Thomas 1992; Thomas 1973; Thomas 1994). Unlike the secular elite fortress on Tintagel Island, however, early Christian centres seem to have survived the end of the Late Antique period. The possible establishment of an early religious community could help explain why a Late Antique centre like St Michael's Mount was still occupied in the ninth or tenth century and later became a significant monastic centre (Herring 2000: 122-125). Elsewhere, important early

medieval churches like St Kew, St Buryan, St Keverne and Tintagel became central places in the contemporary landscape and acted as foci for patterns of settlement and farming (Turner 2003).

Conclusion

The fifth and sixth centuries represent a highly distinctive period in the history of southwest Britain, and one that is broadly united by certain historical processes. These include long-distance coastal trade and exchange, increasing social stratification and the development of kingship, changes in the structure of the settlement pattern, and the introduction and consolidation of Christianity. The nature of these processes clearly resulted from a range of internal and external factors, and it is unlikely that exactly the same combination would be identified elsewhere. Bearing in mind these local variations, however, the term 'Late Antique' can usefully be applied to a period when elements of late Roman civilisation were incorporated and transformed to create a new type of society and landscape. It is clear that the fieldwork undertaken in the last decade is beginning to revolutionise our understanding of the period, both through research excavation at major sites like Tintagel and through the planning process at places like Bantham and Tremough. As the body of available data begins to grow we will increasingly be in a position to refine our models of the region's distinctive Late Antique history, and it is important that further research builds on this new foundation.

Bibliography

Alcock, L. 1963. *Dinas Powys, an Iron Age, Dark Age and Early Medieval Settlement in Glamorgan.* Cardiff: University of Wales Press.

Alcock, L. 1995. *Cadbury Castle, Somerset: the Early Medieval Archaeology.* Cardiff: University of Wales Press.

Allan, J. 2001. The pottery from Bantham Ham. Unpublished conference paper given at *Archaeology in Devon 2001*, University of Exeter, November 2001.

Appleton-Fox, N. 1992. Excavations at a Romano-British round; Reawla, Gwinnear, Cornwall. *Cornish Archaeology* 31: 69-123.

Campbell, E. 1996a. The archaeological evidence for external contacts: imports, trade and economy in Celtic Britain AD 400-800, in K. Dark (ed.), *External Contacts and the Economy of Late-Roman and Post-Roman Britain*: 83-96. Woodbridge: Boydell.

Campbell, E. 1996b. Trade in the Dark Age west: a peripheral activity?, in B. Crawford (ed.), *Scotland in Dark Age Britain*: 79-91. St Andrews: University of St. Andrews.

Carlyon, P. 1987. Finds from the earthwork at Carvossa, Probus. *Cornish Archaeology* 26: 103-144.

CAU. 1997. Excavations at Stencoose, St Agnes. *Archaeology Alive: a Review of Work by the Cornwall Archaeological Unit* 5: 28-29.

CAU. 1998. St Austell north east distributor road. *Archaeology Alive: a Review of Work by the Cornwall Archaeological Unit* 6: 37-38.

Dark, K. 2000. *Britain and the End of the Roman Empire.* Stroud: Tempus.

Fox, A. 1961. Archaeology and early history. *Transactions of the Devonshire Association* 93: 79-80.

Fox, A. 1995. Tin ingots from Bigbury bay, South Devon. *Devon Archaeological Society Proceedings* 53: 11-23.

Gent, T. and Quinnell, H. 1999. Excavations of a causewayed enclosure and hillfort on Raddon Hill, Stockleigh Pomeroy. *Devon Archaeological Society Proceedings* 57: 1-75.

Greeves, T. 2003. Was Brentor a Dark Age centre? *Dartmoor Magazine* 71: 8-10.

Griffith, F. 1986. Salvage observations at the Dark Age site at Bantham Ham in 1982. *Proceedings of the Devon Archaeological Society* 44: 39-57.

Harris, A. 2003. *Byzantium, Britain and the West: the Archaeology of Cultural Identity AD 400-650.* Stroud: Tempus.

Herring, P. 1998. *Cornwall's Historic Landscape: Presenting a Method of Historic Landscape Character Assessment.* Truro: Cornwall Archaeological Unit.

Herring, P. 1999a. Farming and transhumance at the turn of the second millennium (Part 1). *Cornwall Association of Local Historians Journal* Spring 1999: 19-25.

Herring, P. 1999b. Farming and transhumance at the turn of the second millennium (Part 2). *Cornwall Association of Local Historians Journal* Summer 1999: 3-8.

Herring, P. 2000. *St Michael's Mount, Cornwall. Reports on Archaeological Works, 1995-1998.* Truro: Cornwall County Council.

Horner, W. 2001. Secrets of the sands. *Devon Archaeological Society Newsletter* 79: 8-9.

Johns, C. and Herring, P. 1996. *St Keverne Historic Landscape Assessment.* Truro: Cornwall Archaeological Unit.

Johnson, N. and Rose, P. 1982. Defended settlement in Cornwall: an illustrated discussion, in D. Miles (ed.), *The Romano-British Countryside: Studies in Rural Settlement and Economy*: 151-208. Oxford: British Archaeological Reports British Series 103.i.

Lawson Jones, A. 2001. *Bear's Down to Ruthvoes, Cornwall. Archaeological Watching Brief.* Unpublished report, Cornwall Archaeological Unit No. 2001 R007. Truro: CAU.

Lawson Jones, A. 2002. *Tremough Campus, Penryn. Phase 1 Excavations and Landscaping Works.* Unpublished report, Cornwall Archaeological Unit No. 2002 R017. Truro: CAU.

May, J. and Weddell, P. 2002. Bantham: a Dark Age puzzle. *Current Archaeology* 178: 420-422.

McAvoy, F. 1980. The excavation of a multi-period site at Carngoon Bank, Lizard, Cornwall, 1979. *Cornish Archaeology* 19: 31-62.

Miles, H. and Miles, T. 1973. Excavations at Trethurgy, St Austell: interim report. *Cornish Archaeology* 12: 25-30.

Morris, C., Batey, B., Brady, K., Harry, R., Johnson, P. and Thomas, C. 1999. Recent work at Tintagel. *Medieval Archaeology* 43: 206-215.

Morris, C. and Harry, R. 1997. Excavations on the lower terrace, Site C, Tintagel Island 1990-1994. *Antiquaries Journal* 77: 1-144.

Nowakowski, J. and Thomas, C. 1992. *Grave News from Tintagel: an Account of a Second Season of Archaeological Investigation at Tintagel Churchyard.* Truro: Cornwall Archaeological Unit.

Padel, O. 1985. *Cornish Place-Name Elements.* Nottingham: English Place-Name Society Vols. 56-57.

Peacock, D. 1969. A Romano-British saltworking site at Trebarveth, St Keverne. *Cornish Archaeology* 8: 47-65.

Penhallurick, R. 1986. *Tin in Antiquity.* London: Institute of Metals.

Pollard, S. 1966. Neolithic and Dark Age settlements on High Peak, Sidmouth. *Proceedings of the Devon Archaeological Exploration Society* 23: 35-59.

Preston-Jones, A. and Rose, P. 1986. Medieval Cornwall. *Cornish Archaeology* 25: 135-185.

Quinnell, H. 1986. Cornwall during the Iron Age and the Roman period. *Cornish Archaeology* 25: 111-134.

Quinnell, H. 1993. A sense of identity: distinctive Cornish stone artefacts in the Roman and post-Roman periods. *Cornish Archaeology* 32: 29-46.

Quinnell, H. 1995. The pottery, in J. Ratcliffe. Duckpool, Morwenstow: a Romano-British and early medieval industrial site and harbour *Cornish Archaeology* 34: 81-172.

Quinnell, H. 2000. First millennium BC and Roman period ceramics, in P. Herring, *St Michael's Mount, Cornwall. Reports on Archaeological Works, 1995-1998*: 39-46. Truro: Cornwall Archaeological Unit.

Rahtz, P., Woodward, A., Burrow, I., Everton, A., Watts, L., Leach, P., Hirst, S., Fowler, P. and Gardener, K. 1992. *Cadbury Congresbury 1968-73: A Late/Post-Roman Hilltop Settlement in Somerset.* Oxford: British Archaeological Reports British Series 223.

Ratcliffe, J. 1995. Duckpool, Morwenstow: a Romano-British and early medieval industrial site and harbour. *Cornish Archaeology* 34: 80-171.

Reed, S. 2002. *Archaeological survey and recording at*

Meadowsfoot Beach Mothecombe, South Devon. Unpublished report, Exeter Archaeology No.02/29. Exeter, Exeter Archaeology.

Reed, S. 2003. *Archaeological survey and recording at Wembury Bay, Plymouth, Devon.* Exeter: Unpublished Exeter Archaeology Report No. 03.58.

Rose, P. and Preston-Jones, A. 1995. Changes in the Cornish countryside, AD400-1100, in D. Hooke and S. Burnell (eds.), *Landscape and Settlement in Britain AD400-1066*: 51-68. Exeter: University of Exeter.

Saunders, A. and Harris, D. 1982. Excavation at Castle Gotha, St Austell. *Cornish Archaeology* 21: 109-153.

Saunders, C. 1972. The excavations at Grambla, Wendron, 1972: interim report. *Cornish Archaeology* 11: 50-52.

Schweiso, J. 1976. Excavations at Threemilestone round, Kenwyn, Truro. *Cornish Archaeology* 15: 50-67.

Serocold, O., Maynard, G. and Patchett, F. 1949. A dark-age settlement at Trebarveth, St Keverne. *Antiquaries Journal* 29: 169-182.

Sylvester, R. 1981. An excavation on the post-Roman site at Bantham, South Devon. *Devon Archaeological Society Proceedings* 39: 89-118.

Thomas, C. 1968. Grass-marked pottery in Cornwall, in J. Coles and A. Simpson (eds.), *Studies in Ancient Europe*: 311-332. Leicester: Leicester University Press.

Thomas, C. 1973. Parish churchyard, Phillack. *Cornish Archaeology* 12: 59.

Thomas, C. 1981. *A Provisional List of Imported Pottery in Post-Roman Western Britain and Ireland.* Redruth: Institute of Cornish Studies Special Report 7.

Thomas, C. 1988. The context of Tintagel: a new model for the diffusion of post-Roman Mediterranean imports. *Cornish Archaeology* 27: 7-26.

Thomas, C. 1993. *Tintagel: Arthur and Archaeology.* London: Batsford/English Heritage.

Thomas, C. 1994. *And Shall These Mute Stones Speak? Post-Roman Inscriptions in Western Britain.* Cardiff: University of Wales Press.

Thorpe, C. 1997. Ceramics, in R. Harry and C. Morris, Excavations on the Lower Terrace, Site C, Tintagel Island 1990-94. *Antiquaries Journal* 77: 1-143.

Thorpe, C. 2003. *Mullion Church, Cornwall: Archaeological Watching Brief.* Unpublished report, Cornwall Archaeological Unit No. 2003 R004. Truro: CAU.

Threipland, L. 1956. An excavation at St Mawgan-in-Pydar, North Cornwall. *Archaeological Journal* 113: 33-81.

Todd, M. 1983. Lammana. *Cornish Archaeology* 22:122-123.

Turner, S. 2003. Making a Christian landscape: early medieval Cornwall, in M. Carver (ed.), *The Cross Goes North*: 171-194. Woodbridge: York Medieval Press.

Wooding, J. 1996. Cargoes in trade along the western seaboard, in K. Dark (ed.), *External Contacts and the Economy of Late-Roman and Post-Roman Britain*: 67-82. Woodbridge: Boydell.

5: A landscape in transition? Palaeoenvironmental evidence for the end of the 'Romano-British' period in southwest England

Ralph Fyfe and Stephen Rippon

Introduction

The transition from Roman Britain to medieval England has traditionally been studied using a very limited range of documentary sources, and an archaeological record that is at best patchy in its regional coverage and until recently was dominated by funerary evidence. Discussion has, therefore, been dominated by socio-political issues of continuity, conquest, colonisation and acculturation as seen through the relationship between the native Romano-British population and the Anglo-Saxon immigrants. The scarcity of sources, and socio-political focus of this discussion, has resulted in debate being at a highly generalised level, with only very limited consideration of the extent to which there were local differences in how these processes operated. This paper adopts a very different approach in that it starts with the premise that because there was considerable regional variation in the landscape character of Roman Britain, and considerable regional variation in the landscape character of medieval England, there is likely to have been considerable regional variation in the nature of the transition between the two. There is a need to study landscape evolution at the local scale, though the scarcity of distinctive material culture in many regions makes this difficult. It has traditionally been thought that using palaeoenvironmental evidence was similarly limited due to a lack of suitable peat sequences, though this paper aims to show that a shift in focus away from upland blanket mires, whose location remote from areas that were actually settled at the time makes them largely irrelevant to the majority of Roman Britain, towards small lowland valley and spring mires within areas that were occupied does have the potential to shed new light on the end of that period.

The many landscapes of Roman Britain, and their relationships to the many landscapes of medieval England

It is increasingly appreciated that the landscape of Roman Britain showed distinct regional variations in its character, with the degree of complexity going far beyond the traditional, and far too simplistic, divisions between 'upland-lowland', 'military-civilian' and 'villa-native'. Even a cursory examination of a map of Roman Britain shows marked variations in the distribution and character of settlement, most notably perhaps the density of villas (Figure 5.1; e.g. Jones and Mattingly 1990; Ordnance Survey 2001). Regional variations in the social and economic workings of the landscape are similarly reflected in the distribution of certain artefact types, and

schools of mosaicists. Nowhere is this regional variation more pronounced than in the South West, where a line approximately along the watersheds of the Quantock and Blackdown Hills divides the highly Romanised landscape of eastern Somerset and Dorset from the rest of the South West where very little Romanised material culture has been recovered from a rural settlement pattern that retained a largely prehistoric character, in all but the immediate hinterland of the *civitas* capital of *Isca Dumnoniorum*, modern Exeter (Leech 1983; Griffith and Quinnell 1999; Rippon forthcoming). In contrast, highly Romanised eastern Somerset and Dorset was characterised by numerous villas, estate villages and small towns, which in turn contrast with the chalk downlands of Wessex where a still highly Romanised settlement pattern lacks significant numbers of villas, but does have characteristic village-like nucleated rural settlements (e.g. Branigan 1973; Corney 2000; McOmish *et al.* 2002).

Regional variations in the physical fabric of the landscape presumably reflect differences in the underlying social structure, and the Quantock-Blackdown Hills divide presumably represents the boundary between the Iron Age tribal groupings of the Durotriges to the east and the Dumnonii in the South West, the latter retaining an identity until at least the 7th century when the area was absorbed into the Anglo-Saxon kingdom of Wessex (Todd 1987: 205-266). The Quantock-Blackdown Hills boundary was also of significance in the medieval period, marking what was a relatively sharp division between landscapes characterised by dispersed settlement patterns and enclosed field systems to the west, and nucleated villages and regularly arranged open fields to the east that were created around the 10th century (Figure 5.1; Aston and Gerrard 1999; Rippon, in press; Roberts and Wrathmell 2000; 2003). Most research into this 'great re-planning' has focused on changes in the physical fabric of the landscape (*i.e.* settlements and field systems), with the central/midland zone perceived as an aberration in seeing the creation of villages and open fields (Taylor 1983; Williamson 2003). This could imply that areas to the south east, north and west of the 'village zone' might reflect what the landscape would have looked like had this reorganisation not have taken place though this is unlikely to have been the case: firstly, as has been argued, the extent of regional variation in the character of the landscape of Roman Britain is such that no one area can be regarded as 'typical' of the rest of Roman Britain, and secondly, the Midlands were not the only area to have developed regionally distinctive patterns of settlement and agriculture in the medieval period (e.g. Everitt 1986; Gray 1915; Williamson 2003; and see below).

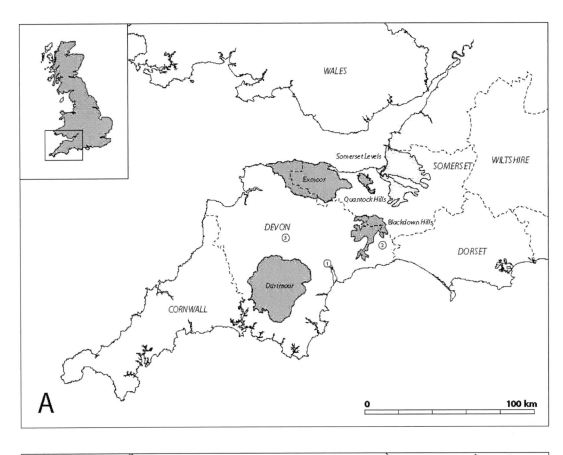

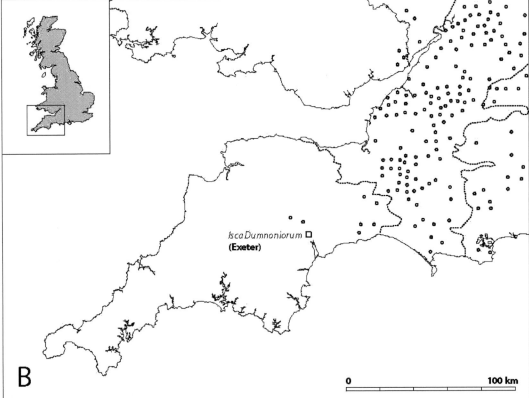

Figure 5.1. A: Southwest England, showing the modern county boundaries and location of areas and lowland pollen sites mentioned in the text (1=Exeter, 2=Aller Farm, 3=Bow). B: Southwest England, showing the distribution of Romano-British villas (Roberts and Wrathmell 2000, Figure 26), and the edge of the 'central province' of medieval nucleated settlement (Roberts and Wrathmell 2000, Figure 1).

The South West is, therefore, a potentially valuable place to study the emergence of regionally distinctive landscapes during the 1st millennium AD in that it represents an area that was unaffected by these three major social forces that shaped the rest of southern Britain: Romanisation, the Anglo-Saxon colonisation, and the creation of villages and open field. However, the South West is a difficult region to study as rural settlements in western Somerset and Devon are associated with very little datable material culture throughout the later prehistoric, Romano-British and early medieval periods. An alternative approach to this problem is to study the emergence of distinctive landscapes by using palaeoenvironmental techniques. Traditionally, however, the deposits that have seen palaeoenvironmental investigation in the South West have been unsuitable for studying this period, as the upper sections of lowland peat sequences (e.g. the Somerset Levels) have been lost to peat cutting and desiccation, leading to a reliance on upland peat sequences which it is argued here are of limited value for understanding changes in the character of the cultural landscape as they lay beyond areas that were actually settled at the time, and at best reflect only a broad regional picture derived from pollen blown in from a wide region (Jacobsen and Bradshaw 1981). Such is the varied topography in the South West, with the resulting differences in resource potential, along with the strong rainfall gradient from the uplands to the lowlands, it is difficult and indeed hazardous to relate the environmental evidence from the uplands to the lowlands (Fyfe *et al.*, in press 1). The landscape of the South West does, however, contain a series of small peat bogs that have previously not been recognised but which do lie within areas that were settled in the later prehistoric, Romano-British and medieval periods and which have produced palaeoenvironmental sequences that allow patterns of landscape management to be reconstructed over the past 2,500 years (Figure 5.2). This paper starts with a summary of previous (upland) work in the region, and then describes the nature of the lowland landscape from these new sites that have been subject to the more recent work. Discussion then focuses on the patterns of agriculture evident in the Roman period to provide the background for an examination of how the landscape responded to the region ceasing to be part of the Roman world. The discussion ends with a consideration of the origins of the medieval landscape, and the extent to which it reflects continuity with the Roman period.

History of palaeoenvironmental research in south west Britain

The earliest palaeoenvironmental research in the South West focussed on the pattern of post-Glacial vegetation development and sea-level changes recorded in the intercalated freshwater peat beds and marine sediments within the low-lying Somerset Levels (Godwin 1941) (Figure 5.1). The majority of this work was focussed on

the prehistoric period, and this emphasis continued into the 1970s through the work of the Somerset Levels Project which focussed on the remains of prehistoric trackways discovered as a result of peat cutting (Coles and Coles 1986). Most of the environmental sequences, however, ended short of the historic period though that from Meare Heath continues through to the end of the first millennium (Beckett and Hibbert 1979).

During the 1960s pioneering baseline palaeo-environmental research began on Dartmoor (Simmons 1964), but due to the lack of lake sediments such as those employed elsewhere in the UK (e.g. Pennington 1970), and the removal and disturbance of sediments through peat extraction and tinning, this research again was concerned mainly with the prehistoric period. Later work on Dartmoor has continued to focus primarily on prehistory, in particular on the relationship between Mesolithic populations and the environment (e.g. Caseldine and Hatton 1993) and the establishment of the Bronze Age field systems (reaves) around the high upland (see reviews in Caseldine and Hatton 1994 and Caseldine 1999). Palaeoenvironmental research also began in the 1970s on Bodmin Moor (Brown 1977), and Exmoor (Merryfield and Moore 1974), although these projects focussed on either early Holocene sequences, or questions concerning the development of blanket peat in the highest uplands. During the 1980s and 1990s greater attention was paid to the post-Roman landscape (e.g. Maguire *et al.* 1983; Austin and Walker 1985; Francis and Slater 1990, 1992; Gearey *et al.* 2000) though still with an emphasis on upland areas. The fortuitous discovery of three peat deposits in the lowlands (Figure 5.1), at Aller Farm, East Devon (Hatton and Caseldine 1992) on the floodplain in Exeter (Caseldine *et al.* 1988), and at Bow, in mid-Devon (Caseldine *et al.* 2000), until recently represented the only lowland post-Roman palaeoenvironmental data in the South West, beyond the Somerset Levels.

It is clear from this brief review that the majority of palaeoenvironmental sequences provide two main problems for analysis of the Romano-British to medieval transition: first the temporal coverage of the sites in that they do not cover the necessary period, and secondly that of spatial distribution of sites: they are overwhelmingly from upland locations beyond the areas actually settled in the Roman and early medieval periods.

The evidence from blanket peat sequences

The analysis of blanket mire sequences on Exmoor, and in particular The Chains (Moore *et al.* 1984), suggests an open pastoral landscape during the Roman period (Figure 5.3). During the 5-6th centuries AD high Exmoor experienced a decline in agricultural activity, and on The Chains, re-establishment of scrubby woodland on the high upland, in particular birch and alder. This decline was characterised by the expansion of heather-heath at

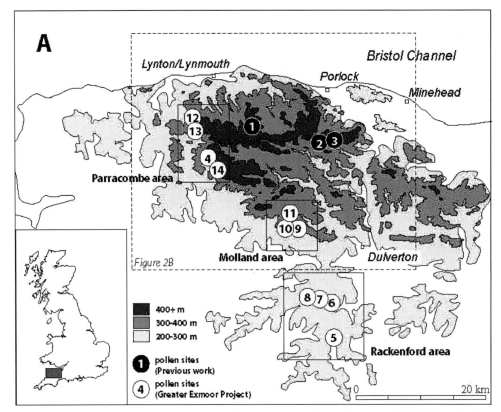

Key to pollen sites: 1: The Chains. 2: Hoar Moor. 3: Codsend Moor. 4: Moles Chamber. 5: Middle North Combe.
6: Lobbs Bog. 7: Windmill Rough. 8: Hares Down. 9: Anstey's Combe. 10: Gourte Mires. 11: Long Breach.
12: Higher Holworthy. 13: Twineford Combe. 14: Sherracombe Ford.

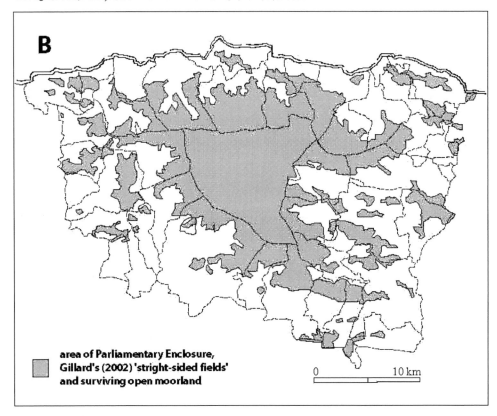

*Figure 5.2. A: Exmoor and Rackenford Moors, showing the location of pollen sites in the Greater Exmoor project and
from previous work. B: The limits of ancient enclosed land on Exmoor (after Gillard 2002).*

nearby Hoar Moor, interpreted as reflecting a reduction in grazing pressure and land management practices during this period (Francis and Slater 1990). On Dartmoor, the general interpretation from the archaeology is that the upland experienced a general retreat of communities to a number of peripheral locations during the first millennium BC, and throughout the Roman and early medieval period was used only for seasonal upland grazing, and although the palaeoenvironmental data for this period is generally poor, it suggests that the uplands were characterised simply by low intensity grazing (Caseldine 1999). Evidence from Bodmin Moor (Gearey *et al.* 2000) and Dartmoor (Austin *et al.* 1980) suggest that the uplands remained part of a seasonal upland grazing system until the 13th-14th centuries AD when settlement expanded onto the uplands, a chronology that is confirmed by reassessment of the pottery evidence from excavated settlements (Allan 1994). Overall, therefore, this limited palaeoenvironmental evidence would appear to support traditional models of the 'marginality' of these upland areas with low intensity of landuse in the Roman and early medieval periods, followed by an expansion of settlement in the High Middle Ages (*c.*13th-14th centuries). Unfortunately, however, this tells us little about how the wider landscape was evolving in the adjacent lowlands from where the colonists presumably came.

The Greater Exmoor Project

In order to understand landscapes in the Roman and medieval periods from palaeoenvironmental evidence there is a need to locate suitable sequences both from areas in the lowlands that were continuously occupied as well as the upland fringes into which settlement expanded at times of high population. In order to achieve this, the Greater Exmoor Project established a study area that extended from mid-Devon (*c.*200 m OD) to the upland fringes of Exmoor (*c.*300-350 m OD) (Figure 5.2), and through an intensive period of fieldwork identified a series of peat bogs which formed over the past 2,500 years. These bogs are not the typical pollen sites that are traditionally employed in palaeoecology (*i.e.* upland blanket mires or raised bogs), but a series of small fens and spring mires, typically 30 to 50 m in width, and which, it can be argued, will provide accurate archives of the local landscape history around each individual site (Jacobsen and Bradshaw 1981; Sugita 1994). Such deposits may have been avoided by palynologists in the past due to the potential over-dominance of their local pollen recruitment (*sensu* Jacobsen and Bradshaw 1981), that is pollen from the site itself rather than the surrounding, extra-local, vegetation, but in this project that potential problem was avoided by using multiple sites in fairly close proximity, i.e. within 1 to 2 km of each other. Each sequence is thought to represent an area of around 1-2 km diameter from the site, and so the comparison of two or three sequences in fairly close proximity allows a broader picture to emerge. A total of

eleven mires were examined in the project, in three clusters: around Rackenford (between 200-250 m OD), Molland Common (300-350 m OD), and Parracombe (300-350 m OD). The sequences from each cluster of sites are reported in detail elsewhere (Rackenford: Fyfe *et al.*, submitted; Molland: Fyfe *et al.*, in press 2; Parracombe: Rippon *et al.*, in prep.) and summarised here for clarity.

The landscape of the lowland and upland fringe during the Romano-British period

It is clear that during the Romano-British period both the lowland and upland fringe around Greater Exmoor were dominated by pastoral activities (Figure 5.3), in a landscape that had been open at least from the middle Bronze Age (Fyfe *et al.*, in press 1). The evidence for arable cultivation is limited: within the Rackenford sequences there are low, yet persistent levels of cereals, with the best representation of these at the lowest lying location, Middle North Combe. Whilst all the Rackenford sites record cereal cultivation with the *region*, the low representation of cereal pollen suggests that cultivation was not being extensively practiced in the immediate proximity of the mires. On the upland fringes, at Molland Common, evidence for cereal cultivation is absent in the Romano-British period, and it seems highly probable that these areas (at around 300-350 m OD) were dominated by a pastoral economy. In both these areas the settlement pattern comprises small enclosed farmsteads, known as hillslope enclosures which elsewhere in Devon are firmly dated between to between the late Prehistoric and early medieval periods. At present there is little evidence for their having been associated with extensive field systems which supports the palaeoenvironmental evidence in suggesting a largely pastoral economy.

Although the landscape is predominantly open, all pollen diagrams record low levels of trees, notably oak and hazel, during the Romano-British period. The evidence from the upland fringe around Molland has allowed some spatial discrimination of land cover types, and strongly suggests woodland is restricted to the steeper-sided valleys, whilst the broad flat interfluves were grazing land (Fyfe *et al.*, in press 2). The data from the Rackenford sites is not suited to such spatial analysis but it is likely that a similar situation occurred there as well, as the sites such as Hares Down and Middle North Combe, which are located in more incised valleys, have better representation of woodland than those at Lobbs Bog and Windmill Rough, which are situated in shallower valleys. Determination of management of woodland or woodland resources is very difficult from pollen data; however, charcoal analysis from two Romano-British iron working sites on the southwest fringes of Exmoor (at Brayford and Sherracombe) have suggested both pollarding and coppicing of oak and hazel was associated with charcoal production (Gale 2003), and it is possible, although not proven, that woodland

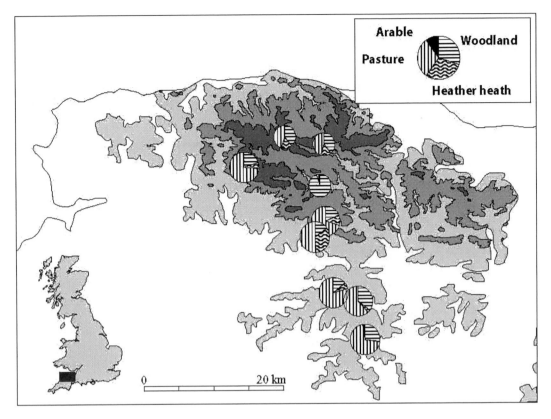

Figure 5.3: The character of the Romano-British landscape in the Greater Exmoor region.
Smaller pie-charts indicate previous work, larger pie-charts the results from the Greater Exmoor project.

management may have been undertaken in the valleys around Molland and Rackenford.

The Roman-Medieval Transition

As described above, the earlier work on the 'traditional' pollen sites - the blanket bogs covering the higher uplands of Exmoor such as on the Chains (Merryfield and Moore 1974) - suggested an abandonment of the high upland during the 5-6th centuries AD. The new sequences obtained from the adjacent upland fringes and lowlands, in contrast, present a very different picture. During the 4th to 6th centuries AD there is very little *significant* change in any of the pollen diagrams from the Greater Exmoor project (Figure 5.4). Minor fluctuations in some of the pollen taxa do occur, but the overwhelming picture is unchanging. This lack of change is an important feature in the data, as it suggests continuity in the prevailing landuse, that is pastoralism predominating alongside small-scale arable in the lowlands, and there is certainly no evidence of woodland regeneration in the landscape.

This pollen evidence suggests clear continuity in the agricultural regimes practiced within the study area, from which it might be inferred that there is unlikely to have been any major dislocation in the physical fabric of the landscape (e.g. desertion or expansion of settlement), or

the tenurial structures within which it was exploited (e.g. the pattern of estates). Considering the very limited degree of Romanisation evident in the landscape of the South West, outside of the immediate hinterland of the *civitas* capital *Isca Dumnoniorum* (Exeter), this should not be surprising: the rural population had not become heavily engaged in the socio-economic systems of Roman Britain and so would be relatively unaffected by their decline.

The later 1st millennium AD: the emergence of the 'historic landscape'

This apparent continuity in landuse in the Greater Exmoor region lasted for several centuries after the end of the Romano-British period until approximately the later 8th century AD around Rackenford, at 200-150 m OD (Fyfe *et al.*, submitted), and by the 10th century around Molland Common at 300-350 m OD (Fyfe *et al.*, in press 2), when the pollen evidence shows a marked increase in the cultivation of cereals in the immediate vicinity of the mires. At the same time indicators of pastoralism continue, and the levels of woodland in the landscape are stable, with no indications of clearance. In the lowlands there is also an increase in heathland within the landscape, which at first sight appears to contradict a model of intensification of landuse represented by the expansion of cereals.

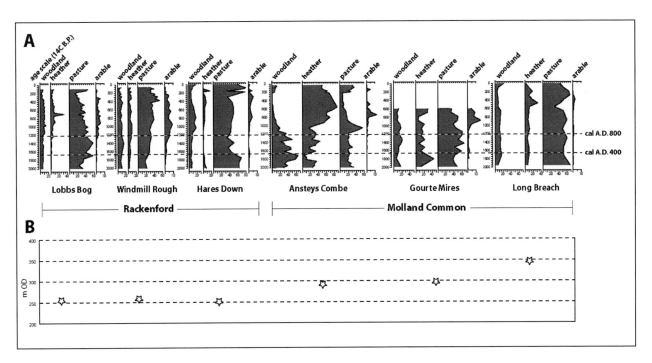

Figure 5.4. A: Summary of pollen work from the Greater Exmoor project. Horizontal axes represent proportion of each vegetation group. B: Altitude of pollen sites in the Greater Exmoor project.

Such a dramatic increase in cereal pollen in the upland fringes such as Molland would traditionally have been interpreted as representing an expansion of settlement into these areas (a traditional 'push into the margins'), though this cannot have been the case; the evidence from the preceding period clearly shows an open and intensively managed landscape, with relatively little woodland and some arable cultivation within the lowlands around Rackenford. Something, however, was causing cereal cultivation to occur in close proximity to the peat bogs for the first time. This may indicate an increase in the density of settlement (internal colonisation), perhaps brought about by rising population, and/or a change in agricultural practice, and it may be that this change in the pollen record might reflect the emergence of a regionally distinctive system of agriculture in the South West, known as convertible husbandry, which is not otherwise documented until the mid-14th century (Hatcher 1988; Fox 1991). Within this system, the land associated with each tenement was arranged in a series of closes, or enclosures. Each close would be cultivated for between 1 and 3 years, before being laid down to grass leys for a long fallow period, of up to 7 years, with cultivation shifting to another close. This system allowed great flexibility as productivity could be individually controlled by the number of closes under an arable crop on each tenement. Fox (1991) suggests that by the 14th century the proportion of land under a crop may have been between 25 and 51%. The date when convertible husbandry was introduced or developed is not documented, but the pollen sequences from the Greater Exmoor region suggests that it may account for the dramatic 8th-10th century increase in cereal pollen for two reasons. Firstly, the amounts of cereal pollen are remarkably high suggesting cultivation

was very close to the peat bogs. For sites such as Lobbs Bog and Windmill Rough in the Rackenford area, which are very peripheral to historic settlement, to have been in an area of permanent cultivation would suggest a remarkably high population/settlement density in the pre-Conquest period, for which there is simply no archaeological evidence: a system of crop/pasture rotation which brought arable cultivation within close proximity of the peat bogs every 4-5 years is a more likely explanation. The second reason why the 8th-10th century pollen change is likely to represent the introduction of convertible husbandry is that there is no other change within these relatively high resolution and continuous sequences that could correspond to its introduction before the 14th century when documentary evidence shows that it certainly existed: the pollen signal from the 8th-10th century is identical to that of the late medieval period by which time convertible husbandry is know to have existed.

The evidence suggests therefore that a rotational system of agriculture is taken up within mid-Devon from around the 8th century (Figure 5.4). The expansion of heather and heath pollen around the Rackenford area may also be indicative of formal enclosure in the landscape, with the segregation of improved closes and rough 'common' grazing land, from which the heath pollen is derived. The data do not suggest any sub-regional agricultural specialisation, with the exception of the high uplands which do not show significant evidence for arable cultivation until the high medieval period, although data is needed from the historically 'richer' agricultural areas such as the Exe valley and the South Hams before this hypothesis can be fully tested.

Conclusions

This paper has examined the contribution that palaeoenvironmental sequences can make to understanding landscape change (or the lack of it) during the Roman to medieval transition, and the origins of the medieval landscape. Such was the regional variation in the character of Roman Britain, and the relatively limited Romanisation in the South West, that care must be taken in extending these results too far, and similar work is required in other lowland areas, but a key *general* theme in the work reported here is that it is possible to obtain palaeoenvironmental sequences from areas that were within that part of the landscape that was settled and farmed during the Roman and medieval periods. The importance of this is most clearly demonstrated by the fact that the results of the datasets from the lowlands and upland fringes of Greater Exmoor reported here are clearly at odds with earlier data from the higher upland blanket mire sequences that lay beyond the limits of Romano-British and medieval settlement, and which can now be seen to be unrepresentative of the wider, settled, landscape.

These upland sequences had suggested that on Exmoor there was a significant contraction of settlement from the higher uplands in the early post-Roman period, while on Dartmoor there was little more than seasonal grazing throughout the later prehistoric and Roman periods until the agricultural expansion into the upland during the 13th century AD. The evidence from the Exmoor upland fringes, in contrast, shows that this 4th-6th century contraction does not extend down as far as 350 m (*i.e.* around Molland Common), and so we can safely assume that during the Romano-British to medieval transition farming and agriculture continued to at least this height. Within the lowland there is no indication for any change until the 8th century AD, when wide-spread arable cultivation is recorded.

Within the lowland/upland fringe landscape there is, in fact, very little evidence for change between the Middle Iron Age and what would traditionally has been called the 'post-Roman' period (e.g. Pearce 1981: 165; Todd 1987: 236). With relatively little engagement of the rural population in the Greater Exmoor region with the 'Roman' world, and virtually no evidence for a change in the patterns of landscape exploitation in the 5th and 6th centuries, the phrase 'post-Roman' is inappropriate for this region. Very little is known about the physical character of the Romano-British landscape in the Greater Exmoor region, though analogy with surveyed and excavated enclosures elsewhere in Devon and west Somerset suggest that a class of site known as hillslope enclosures, of similar character to Cornish 'rounds', continued to be occupied into this period (Griffith 1994; Griffith and Quinnell 1999; Riley and Wilson-North 2001: 55-74; Simpson *et al.* 1989). Relatively few of these enclosures are associated with field systems, confirming the pollen evidence for a predominantly pastoral landscape.

In terms of landscape exploitation, the 'Roman-medieval' transition could be dated as late as the 8th-10th century, when there was certainly a pronounced change in agricultural practice, which may well represent the emergence of a regionally distinctive form of agriculture: convertible husbandry. This also appears to mark a profound change in the physical character of the landscape, with the later prehistoric/Romano-British tradition of small isolated enclosures, with little evidence for associated field systems, being replaced with a the pattern of scattered farmsteads integrated with a near continuous fieldscape that still forms the basis of today's historic landscape. The links between these two landscapes appears negligible: the incidence of hillslope enclosures lying next to medieval farmsteads on Exmoor, which Aston (1983) identified at Bagley and Sweetworthy and is suggestive of continuity, actually appear to have been unique (Riley and Wilson-North 2001: 73-75). In Cornwall (Turner 2003), it appears that a similar change from a landscape associated with isolated enclosures ('rounds') to one of scattered farmsteads, many with *tre-* place-names, in a near-continuous fieldscape may have occurred during or after the 6th/7th centuries. In and around Greater Exmoor there is now a need to test this hypothesis through a programme of excavations on both hillslope enclosures, to see when they were abandoned, and medieval farmsteads to see when they originated: this will be difficult, as much of the 1st millennium AD is aceramic in this region, though the greater use of scientific dating on the latest stratigraphic phases of 'later prehistoric/Romano-British' enclosures (e.g. Simpson *et al.* 1989), and medieval settlements may produce results. Only then, however, we will fully understand the Roman-medieval transition in the South West.

Acknowledgements

This research was funded by a research grant from the Leverhulme Trust [grant number: F/00144/D]. The research has benefited greatly from the collaboration of Tony Brown, and through discussions with Harold Fox and Rob Wilson-North.

Bibliography

Allan, J. 1994. Medieval Pottery and the dating of Deserted Settlements on Dartmoor. *Proceedings of the Devon Archaeological Society* 52: 141-8.

Aston, M. 1983. Deserted Farmsteads on Exmoor and the Lay Subsidy of 1327 in West Somerset. *Proceedings of the Somerset Archaeological and Natural History Society* 127: 74-104.

Aston, M. and Gerrard, C. 1999. 'Unique, traditional and

charming': the Shapwick Project, Somerset. *Antiquaries Journal* 79: 1-58.

Austin D., Daggett, R.H. and Walker, M.J.C. 1980. Farms and fields in Okehampton Park, Devon: the problems of studying a medieval landscape. *Landscape History* 2: 39-57.

Austin, R. and Walker, M.J.C. 1985. A new landscape context for Hound Tor, Devon. *Medieval Archaeology* 29: 147-152.

Beckett, S.C. and Hibbert, F.A. 1979. Vegetational change and the influence of prehistoric man in the Somerset Levels. *New Phytologist* 83: 577-600.

Branigan, K. 1973. *Town and Country: The archaeology of Verulanium and the Roman Chilterns.* London: Spurbooks Ltd.

Brown, A.P. 1977. Late-Devensian and Flandrian vegetational history of Bodmin Moor, Cornwall. *Philosophic Transaction of the Royal Society of London* B276: 251-320.

Caseldine, C.J. 1999. Archaeological and environmental change on Prehistoric Dartmoor – current understandings and future directions. *Journal of Quaternary Science* 14: 575-583.

Caseldine, C.J. and Hatton, J. 1994. Into the mists? Thoughts on the prehistoric and historic environmental history of Dartmoor. *Proceedings of the Devon Archaeological Society* 52: 35-48.

Caseldine, C.J., Coles, B.J., Griffith F.M., and Hatton, J.M. 2000. Conservation or change? Human influence on the mid-Devon landscape, in R.A Nicholson and T.P. O'Connor (ed.), *People as an agent of environmental change*: 60-70. Oxford: Oxbow Books.

Caseldine, C.J., Juggins, S., and Straker, V. 1988. Preliminary palaeoenvironmental analyses of floodplain deposits from a section near the River Exe, in Exeter, Devon, in P. Murphy and C. French (ed.), *The exploitation of wetlands*: 145-162. Oxford: British Archaeological Reports British series 186.

Coles, B. and Coles, J. 1986. *Sweet track to Glastonbury: the Somerset Levels in prehistory.* London: Thames and Hudson.

Corney, M. 2000. Characterising the landscape of Roman Britain: a review of the study of Roman Britain 1975-2000, in D. Hooke (ed.), *Landscape: the richest historical record*: 32-45. Society for Landscape Studies, Supplementary Series 1.

Everitt, A. 1986. *Continuity and Colonization: the evolution of Kentish Settlement.* Leicester: Leicester University Press.

Fox, H.S.A. 1991. Farming practice and techniques, Devon and Cornwall, in E. Miller (ed.), *The Agrarian History of England and Wales, vol 3, 1348-1500*: 303-323. Cambridge: Cambridge University Press.

Francis, P.D. and Slater, D.S. 1990. A record of vegetation and land use change from upland peat deposits on Exmoor. Part 2: Hoar Moor.

Somerset Archaeology and Natural History Society Proceedings 134: 1-25.

Francis, P.D. and Slater, D.S. 1992. A record of vegetation and land use change from upland peat deposits on Exmoor. Part 3: Codsend Moor. *Somerset Archaeology and Natural History Society Proceedings* 136: 9-28.

Fyfe, R.M., Brown, A.G. and Coles, B. in press 1. Mesolithic to Bronze Age vegetation change and human activity in the Exe Valley, Devon, UK. *Proceedings of the Prehistoric Society* 70.

Fyfe, R.M., Brown, A.G. and Rippon, S.J. in press 2. Mid- to late-Holocene vegetation history of Greater Exmoor, UK: estimating the spatial extent of human-induced vegetation change. *Vegetation History and Archaeobotany*.

Fyfe, R.M., Brown, A.G. and Rippon, S.J. submitted. Continuity or change? Environmental evidence from the late prehistoric, "Roman" and medieval period in lowland southwest Britain. *Journal of Archaeological Science*.

Gale, R. 2003. *Sherracombe Ford and Brayford, Exmoor, 2002: The analysis of charcoal from Romano-British iron-working sites.* University of Bristol: Unpublished interim report.

Gearey, B.R., Charman, D.J. and Kent, M. 2000. Palaeoecological Evidence for the Prehistoric Settlement of Bodmin Moor, Cornwall, south west England. Part II: Land Use Changes from the Neolithic to the Present. *Journal of Archaeological Science* 27: 493-508.

Gillard, M.J. 2002. *The medieval landscape of the Exmoor region enclosure and settlement in an upland fringe.* Unpublished PhD thesis, University of Exeter.

Godwin, H. 1941. Studies in the post-glacial history of British vegetation IV: correlations in the Somerset Levels. *New Phytologist* 40: 108-132.

Gray, H.L. 1915. *English field systems.* Cambridge: Cambridge University Press.

Griffith, F.M. 1994. Changing Perceptions of the Context of Prehistoric Dartmoor. *Devon Archaeological Society Proceedings* 52: 85-99.

Griffith, F.M. and Quinnell, H. 1999. Settlement *c*.2500 BC to *c*.AD600, in R. Kain and W. Ravenhill (ed.), *Historical Atlas of South-West England*: 62-68. Exeter: Exeter University Press.

Hatcher, J. 1988. New Settlement: south west England, in H.E. Hallam (ed.), *The Agrarian History of England and Wales, vol 2, 1042-1350*: 234-244. Cambridge: Cambridge University Press.

Hatton, J. and Caseldine, C.J. 1991. Vegetation changes and land use history during the 1st millennium AD at Aller Farm, East Devon as indicated by pollen analysis. *Proceedings of the Devon Archaeological Society* 49: 107-114.

Jacobsen, G.L. and Bradshaw, R.H. 1981. The selection of sites for palaeoecological studies. *Quaternary Research* 16: 80-96.

Jones, B. and Mattingly, D. 1990. *An Atlas of Roman Britain.* Oxford: Blackwell.

Leech, R. 1983. The Roman interlude in the South West: the dynamics of economic and social change in the Romano-British south Somerset and North Dorset, in D. Miles (ed.), *The Romano-British countryside*: 209-268. Oxford: British Archaeological Reports British series 103.

McOmish, D., Field, D. and Brown, G. 2002. *The Field Archaeology of Salisbury Plain.* London: English Heritage.

Merryfield, D.L. and Moore, P.D. 1974. Prehistoric human activity and blanket peat initiation on Exmoor. *Nature* 250: 439-441.

Moore, P.D., Merryfield, D.L. and Price, M.D.R. 1984. The vegetation and development of blanket mires, in P.D. Moore (ed.), *European Mires*: 203-235. London: Academic Press.

Ordnance Survey 2001. *The Ordnance Survey Map of Roman Britain*, 5th Edition. Southamption: Ordnanace Survey.

Pearce, S.M. 1981. *The Archaeology of South West Britain.* London: Collins.

Riley, H. and Wilson-North, R. 2001. *The Field Archaeology of Exmoor.* London: English Heritage.

Rippon, S. 1997. *The Severn estuary: landscape evolution and wetland reclamation.* Leicester: Leicester University Press.

Rippon, S. in press. *Historic Landscape Analysis.* York: Council for British Archaeology.

Rippon, S. forthcoming. Landscapes of pre-medieval occupation, in R. Kain (ed.), *England's landscapes: volume 3 – Landscapes of south west England.* London: English Heritage.

Rippon, S., Fyfe, R.M. and Brown, A.G. in preparation. Medieval and post-medieval landuse and settlement history: a combined landscape, archaeology and palynological approach. *Medieval Archaeology.*

Roberts, B.K. and Wrathmell, S. 2000. *An Atlas of Rural Settlement in England.* London: English Heritage.

Roberts, B.K. and Wrathmell, S. 2003. *Region And Place: A Study of English Rural Settlement.* London: English Heritage.

Simpson, S.J., Griffith, F.M. and Holbrook, N. 1989. The Prehistoric, Roman and Early Post-Roman Site at Hayes farm, Clyst Honiton. *Devon Archaeological Society Proceedings* 47: 1-28.

Simmons, I.G. 1964. Pollen diagrams from Dartmoor. *New Phytologist* 63: 165-180.

Sugita, S. 1994. Pollen representation of vegetation in Quaternary sediments: theory and method in patchy vegetation. *Journal of Ecology* 82: 879-898.

Taylor, C. 1983. *Village and farmstead: a history of rural settlement in England.* London: George Phillip.

Todd, M. 1987. *The South West to AD 1000.* London: Longmans.

Turner, S. 2003. Making a Christian Landscape: Early Medieval Cornwall, in M. Carver (ed.), *The Cross Goes North: Processes of Conversion in Northern Europe, AD 300-1300*: 171-194. York: York Medieval Press.

Williamson, T. 2003. *Shaping medieval landscapes: settlement, society, environment.* Macclesfield: Windgather Press.

6: The Environs of South Cadbury in the Late Antique and Early Medieval Periods

John Davey

Introduction

This paper provides a brief outline of work in progress for my doctoral thesis (Davey in prep.). Much of the work has been undertaken in conjunction with the South Cadbury Environs Project (SCEP). SCEP has hitherto concentrated on the late prehistoric and Romano-British periods (Leach and Tabor 1994: 1). It is the intention of this study to redress the balance in favour of the Late Antique and Early Medieval periods.

Esmonde Cleary has recently made a strong case for studying Late Antiquity as a coherent period spanning the fourth to seventh centuries AD (Esmonde Cleary 2001: 97). In this paper evidence will be presented to demonstrate that in Somerset there is an archaeological horizon beginning in the third century. This represents economic growth and development of the agrarian landscape, elements of which survive to the present day. Thus, for the purposes of this paper, Late Antiquity spans the third to seventh centuries, and Early Medieval the seventh to tenth centuries, at which point the manorial system with its attendant settlement and field systems, was established.

After Alcock's work at Cadbury Castle in the late 1960's and early 1970's (Alcock 1968; 1969; 1970; 1971) it is clear that the Late Antique period is of particular importance in the South Cadbury area. The hillfort was re-fortified and substantial building was undertaken in both the post-Roman and late Saxon periods. There is also clear evidence for high status reoccupation of the hillfort, in the fifth and sixth centuries, through the consumption of goods imported from the Mediterranean in amphorae (Alcock 1995: 30-42). With that established, we can study the environs of South Cadbury, in relation to this important central place, and build up a picture of a sub-Roman estate. It is to the study of this estate and its successors that we must turn if we are to fully understand the role of the hillfort within its proper Late Antique context. Furthermore, it is only when this has been achieved that we can begin to understand in greater detail the role of South Cadbury in the wider context of south west Britain and Europe during the Roman to medieval transition.

This paper has been written with a 'nested' structure. After a brief note concerning methodology, the evidence for a Late Antique and Early Medieval estate centred on South Cadbury is presented. This is followed by a discussion of the settlement patterns existing within such an estate. The field systems attached to these settlements are then examined. Finally the paper explores the social identity of those people living and working in the estate, as expressed through burial practice. These themes are all considered with a view to better understanding, on a regional level, the socio-economic transitions associated with the collapse of Roman administration at the beginning of the 5th century and the establishment of the kingdom of Wessex in Somerset at the end of the 7th century.

Methodology

SCEP is essentially an archaeological project with a landscape focus involving extensive geophysical survey complemented by shovel pitting and test pitting (Tabor 2002: 11-13). However, considering the ephemeral nature of post-Roman and Early Medieval archaeological remains, it has been necessary to target specific fields on the basis of field names or their proximity to known settlement. Furthermore, considering that much of Somerset during the period in question is essentially aceramic, shovel pitting can prove ineffective in dating horizontal phases identified through geophysical survey. For this reason, the fieldwork constitutes geophysical survey and interpretation involving the sorting of horizontal stratigraphy into phases, which can then be sampled through small-scale excavation. This is not guaranteed to date post-Roman phases, it will however, confirm the plan of phases that are stratigraphically later than the ultimate Romano-British phase. In addition, a variety of other techniques have been employed where appropriate. These include shovel pitting, field walking and earthwork survey as well as documentary research, study of aerial photographs and the regressive analysis of cartographic evidence.

The SCEP core study area is an 8km square centred on the hillfort (Leach and Tabor 1995: Figure 1). In Somerset it has long been established that there is significant continuity in the landscape from the Romano-British to the medieval period, notably in settlement patterns (Aston 1989: 19-20), but also in agricultural and political boundaries. Therefore, the SCEP study area has been modified slightly, for this study, to include whole parishes (Figure 6.1).

Estate Boundaries

Cartographic, documentary and place-name evidence have revealed a possible early estate boundary centred on South Cadbury. Figure 6.2 shows that the western parish boundary of Sparkford clearly predates the tenth century manorial boundaries of Weston Bampfylde and Sutton Montis. Similarly, an early boundary to the east composed of the northern part of the eastern boundary of North Cadbury and the eastern boundary of Compton

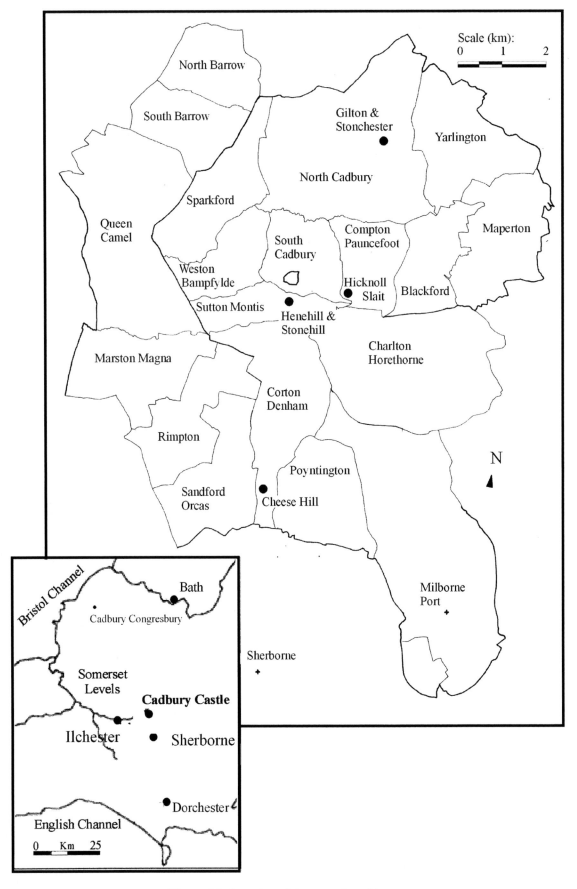

Figure 6.1: Location of sites mentioned in text.

Pauncefoot parishes can be dated to before 1086. In the Somerset Domesday Book a hide at Woolston is recorded as being added to the manor of North Cadbury (Thorn and Thorn 1980: 97c,d). This must be an eastern extension to North Cadbury parish, which masks the earlier, north-south aligned, continuous boundary. North-south alignments are common in SE Somerset and I shall present evidence below to suggest that many of them date from at least the third century AD. The two early boundaries, then, partially enclosing and centred on Cadbury Castle, probably date from the third to tenth centuries. Is this evidence for a *territorium* or estate boundary pertaining to the high status settlement at Cadbury Castle? Caution is required, since third century field alignments are not evidence of third century political boundaries. They could be merely re-used in the tenth century as administrative, i.e. manorial boundaries for the first time. Nevertheless, the two boundaries outlined above clearly predate the tenth century manorial divisions. These early boundaries enclose the Domesday manors of Sparkford, Weston Bampfylde, Sutton Montis, Compton Pauncefoot and Whitcomb as well as North and South Cadbury. The 'tun' place-name elements in this list certainly relate to the central place, South Cadbury. Weston Bampfylde is west of the hillfort and Sutton Montis immediately south. The names Compton and Whitcomb refer to the physical appearance of the manors as viewed from South Cadbury.

A *territorium* boundary has also been proposed for Ilchester (Aston 1985), the eastern boundary of which can be seen on Figure 2. Similarly, the 1086 Somerset-Dorset county boundary is coterminous, in part, with the boundary of the medieval hundred of Sherborne and the *parochia* of Sherborne Minster (Hall 2000: 35-43). It is possible that the county boundary utilised an earlier monastic boundary and represents the northern limit of the Sherborne estate (Figure 6.2). This may have been the 100-hide unit belonging to the church of *Llanprobus*, reputedly given to the new Saxon monastery at Sherborne by Cenwalh in 671, as recorded in a fourteenth century list of the Abbey's holdings (Hall 2000: 11).

Place name and cartographic evidence suggests that the land peripheral to these core estates may have been largely wooded, marshy or unenclosed downland in the Saxon period. It is in these marginal areas that a number of 1-hide units have been identified. Michael Costen was the first to recognise that the tenth century manor of Rimpton was an amalgamation of a number of smaller units, some of which constituted 1 hide. He also suggests that the area around Rimpton and Sandford Orcas '...was made up of several one hide units' (Costen 1985: 21-23). Prior to the tenth century, then, previously marginal land had already been enclosed into 1-hide units, associated with dispersed settlement. Furthermore, Thornton had noted that the parishes of Rimpton, Marston Magna, Trent, and Sandford Orcas seemed to lie outside any neighbouring multiple estate (Thornton 1988: 32-33). This led Hall to suggest that this area represented the

'...fusion of small independent units in an area of late colonisation that was not covered by the Minster system' (Hall 2000: 33). Late, in this context, means tenth century colonisation of wood, marsh or wood-pasture, previously unenclosed and outside the central arable areas of early multiple estates. These units are subsequently amalgamated into larger manors, often associated with a nucleated settlement. Conversely, within the older core estates, manors are created through the subdivision of the larger unit.

Settlement

Dispersed settlement is the normal pattern in Somerset, with only brief interludes of nucleation. One such interlude began in the tenth century and continues to this day, and yet very few parishes in the area contain a single nucleated settlement (Aston 2000: 96). A 1-hide unit still associated with dispersed settlement exists at Holway, now in the parish of Sandford Orcas but formerly a southern extension of Corton Denham parish (Figure 6.2). Evidence for continuity of settlement site has been uncovered here through the joint application of place-name studies, fieldwalking and geophysical survey. Giles Cooper, a member of SCEP, has collected place-names from every tithe map in the study area, and has identified possible indicators of archaeological activity. One of these was a field called Cheese Hill in Holway, known as Chessels by the farmer and indicating a possible Romano-British site (Cooper 2002: 15 and 22). Fieldwalking revealed an extensive scatter of late Romano-British ceramics and building material. This was followed by a geophysical survey, the results of which are displayed in Figure 6.3. There are clearly a number of different phases, apparently starting in the Bronze Age, with the construction of a ring ditch and possible burial mound, on a spur adjacent to a spring (Figure 6.3A). By the Romano-British period this earthwork was still visible as demonstrated by the line of a double ditched track which, although slighting the ring ditch itself, bends to respect the barrow. An irregular hexagonal enclosure was aligned on this track, so shaped to fully enclose the flatter ground at the tip of the spur (Figure 6.3B). At the time of writing this article a small excavation is under way to sample the double ditched track where it is crossed by geophysical anomalies from other phases. This has revealed that the track was actually a well-constructed metalled road. Above the latest road surface is a demolition layer containing large black burnished, dropped flange, rim sherds dating from the third or fourth centuries. The rubble fill of this layer consisted of large faced Inferior Oolite blocks and Lias limestone roof tiles. The Lias tiles lay in discrete patches, often below the masonry suggesting they had slid from a nearby roof to be subsequently covered by tumbling masonry. It seems then that, perhaps during the third century, a metalled road was lined with at least one well-constructed stone building at Holway. The geophysics suggests that by the later Romano-British period more than one building was

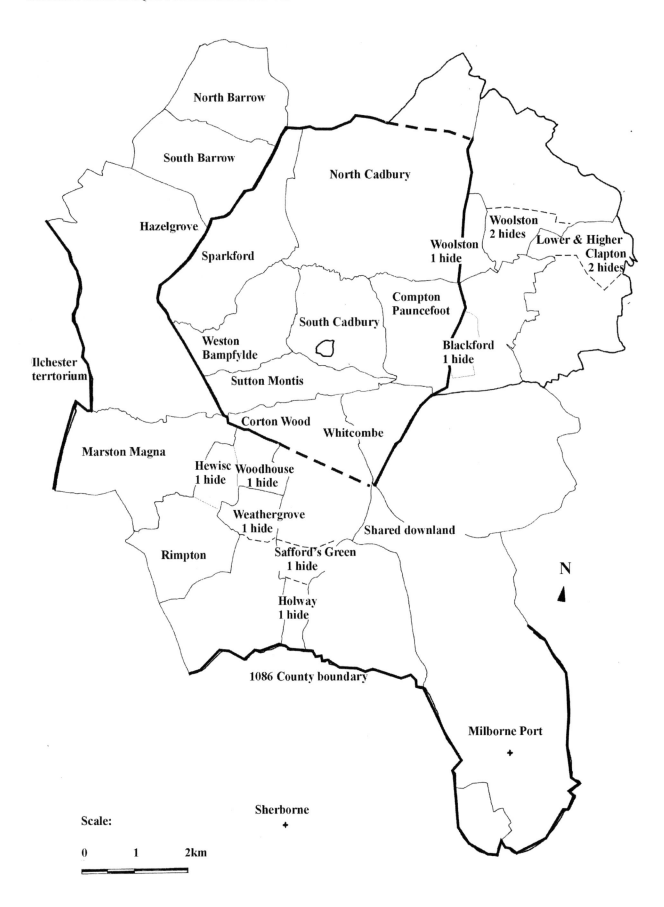

Figure 6.2: Core and periphery in the Late Antique and Early Medieval South Cadbury environs.

present. However, it is not clear whether this settlement was ever more than just a single farmstead with outbuildings (Figure 6.3C). The sequence seems to culminate with a shift of the Romano-British settlement up slope to the site of the medieval and modern hamlet. Only a large, open area excavation could establish the nature, function and interrelationships of the features outlined above. The present small excavation, sampling the various phases revealed through geophysical survey, has not been able to identify any features that are post-Roman. Nevertheless, it appears that there has been continuous settlement at Holway since at least the third century.

One final point of note about the roadway is that it appears to emanate from the modern Holway Lane to the north, which therefore, follows a Romano-British alignment. This is another example of possible third century north-south alignments in the area. These alignments are also utilised by the boundary of the Holway 1-hide unit.

Evidence for another early, dispersed settlement has been recovered during fieldwork carried out by SCEP at fields called Henehill and Stonehill in Sutton Montis (Figure 6.4). Analysis of the medieval pottery from these fields reveals a significant pattern when considered alongside the geophysical survey results. So far no sherds of fifth and sixth century imported pottery have been recovered from fieldwork in the South Cadbury environs. The earliest medieval sherds that have been recovered are tenth century Saxon coarse wares. These have generally been found in close proximity to Saxon manorial centres. However, Henehill and Stonehill present a rare case where tenth century pottery has been found unrelated to nucleated settlements. It seems that a large building, morphologically similar to Roman or post-Roman buildings, aligned on a track from South Cadbury is associated with tenth century pottery. This may represent continuity of dispersed settlement site from the Romano-British to medieval periods, subsequently deserted. Excavation might be able to help clarify this, possibly providing dating evidence for the structure. This dispersed settlement may also have been located within a 1-hide unit composed of the eastern tip of Sutton Montis parish.

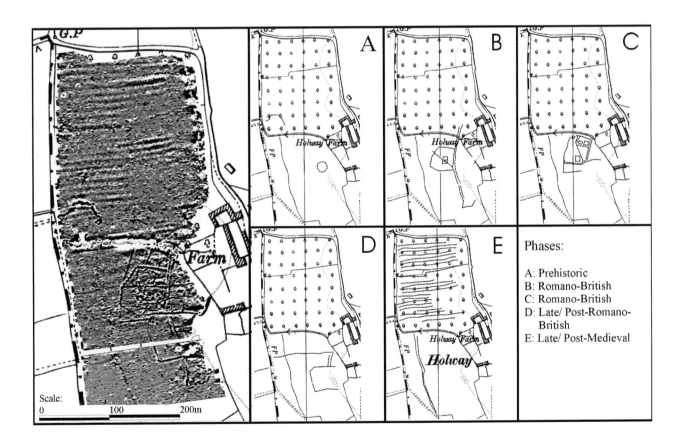

Figure 6.3: Cheese Hill, Holway. Gradiometer survey, results and interpretation.

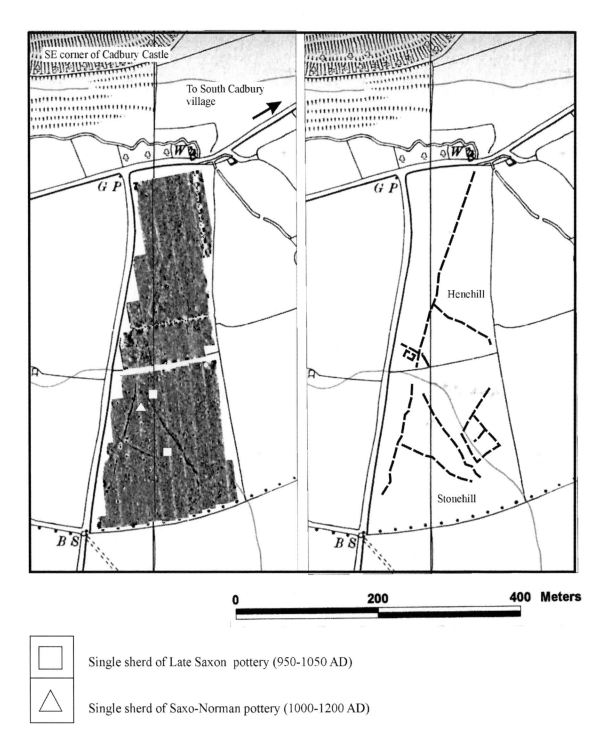

Single sherd of Late Saxon pottery (950-1050 AD)

Single sherd of Saxo-Norman pottery (1000-1200 AD)

Figure 6.4: Gradiometer survey, Henehill and Stonehill, Sutton Montis. Results and interpretation plotted against selected ceramics recovered through shovel pitting.

Field Systems

The results of geophysical survey coupled with excavation indicate that the agrarian landscape was completely reorganised in the third century. The evidence for this comes from a number of sites in the region. Figure 6.5 shows the results of geophysical survey on two fields, Gilton and Stonchester, in North Cadbury. These fields were selected because their names contained the

Roman and Saxon habitative elements, 'tun' and 'chester' in close proximity. It was initially thought that they might provide evidence for continuity of settlement site from the Late Antique to Early Medieval periods. What they actually demonstrate is that modern fields and roads, notably in the tortuous course of Corkscrew Lane, follow earlier field alignments. The field system revealed through this geophysical survey consists of long thin fields with a length to width ratio of 5:1. These strip-like fields have been categorised by Fowler as typically Roman long fields that are frequently superimposed on a pre-existing field system. One particular example excavated in advance of the construction of Heathrow Terminal 5, has been dated to the second to fourth century AD (Fowler 2002: 134-135 and 143-146). The field system in North Cadbury can be dated because an archaeological evaluation was carried out during the construction of the Codford-Ilchester water pipeline (Rawlings 1992). This pipeline is visible on the geophysical plot as a strong linear anomaly just inside and parallel to the western boundary of Gilton. Rawlings recorded a number of ditches perpendicular to the pipe trench, one of which contained exclusively third to fourth century pottery (Rawlings 1992: 41). Although the assemblage was very small, shovel pitting in the adjacent Stonchester also produced almost exclusively Romano-British pottery, with a date range centred on the second and third centuries (Figure 6.5).

Rawlings (1992: 37-38) recorded further late Romano-British, north-south alignments in Ashington near Ilchester. These alignments exist over a wide area and are still utilised by a series of parish and field boundaries between Ilchester and South Cadbury, notably at Limington, Draycott, Ashington and Marston Magna. Similar alignments have been recorded as part of SCEP fieldwork on Sigwells, Charlton Horethorne (Tabor and Johnson 2000: 321-324). The dating of a north-south alignment here to the third and fourth centuries was confirmed in 2002 through excavation (Richard Tabor pers. comm.).

This represents a wide scale reorganisation, or rationalisation, of the agricultural landscape. Obviously, this would have required a strong authority to plan and carry it through. Branigan has suggested that the entire Durotrigian region was under imperial control until the third century when the separate *civitas* of the *Lendinienses* was created with its capital at Ilchester (Branigan 1976: 123-124). Was this landscape revolution the last act of imperial authority or the first act of a new and vibrant *civitas* authority? What is apparent is that the increase in disposable wealth in southeast Somerset in the third century, as evidenced by an upsurge in stone villa construction, coincides with the reorganisation of the agricultural landscape. Many theories have been advance to explain the rise of the stone villa in Somerset in the third century ranging from an influx of wealthy Gauls fleeing trouble on the continent (Branigan 1976: 124-127) to exploitation of the Somerset levels (Leach 1994: 7). However, Roger Leech notes that many stone villas were built on site of wooden precursors and, probably correctly, assigns the rise of the stone villa to a corresponding upturn in the local economy (Leech 1977: 192-195).

Somerset, then, was a thriving place in the Late Antique period, perhaps in contrast to the rest of the empire, which was beset with problems including anarchy, inflation and invasion. As the later empire fragmented in order to survive, satellite economic centres arose resulting in the city of Rome having less of a commanding hold over the economy. In the late fourth century the imperial centre switched to Trier in northeast

Scale:

0   50   100   200m

Figure 6.5: Gradiometer survey, Gilton and Stonechester, North Cadbury. Results and interpretation.

Gaul (Drinkwater and Elton 1992: 1). It may be these factors that allowed regions such as Somerset, previously marginal to the empire, to become economically stronger.

The strength of the Late Antique agrarian economy in Somerset seems to continue into the post-Roman period and beyond as witnessed by extensive examples of third century alignments in the modern landscape. However, it has been noted above that by the Saxon period, there are signs that, in areas peripheral to the core estates of Cadbury, Sherborne and Ilchester, wood, marsh and unenclosed downland dominated. From this under-used land, 1-hide units were enclosed prior to the tenth century, some such as Holway, still using third century alignments. There is another group of one-hide units that have been identified in the South Cadbury area. These are morphologically very distinct in plan, with curved boundaries, often oval in shape. This suggests that there were few physical obstacles to their enclosure when they were established. Their size can vary from 250 to 130 acres, the hide being a measure of tax and not area. There are a few documented examples that are taxed as a hide, notably Hiwisc (Costen 1992: 71-73) and Blackford, but others are fossilised in modern field boundaries at Camel Farm and Wales, Queen Camel, and Sutton Montis (Davey 2002a: 27-30). Morphologically they are similar to, although much larger than, Church Field, Puxton (Rippon 1997). Unfortunately, the presence of residual Romano-British pottery meant that the enclosure could only be dated to between the end of the Romano-British period and the eleventh century (Rippon 1997: 47-51).

It seems, then, that part of the third century field system did fall into disuse in peripheral areas. Parts of this marginal land are enclosed again in a different form before the tenth century. The new enclosures are individual farm units enclosed from wood-pasture in stark contrast to the large scale planning of the third century. In the absence of refined dating this process appears to be a gradual one, possibly connected with demographic changes. It would be dangerous to assume that the abandonment of part of the third century field system is connected to political upheavals in the fifth century. Mike Baillie, through dendrochronology, has identified a dramatic global event affecting vegetation. This narrow tree ring event of AD 540 (Baillie 1999: 9) might provide a better explanation for the reversion of a number of arable fields to wood-pasture.

Burial Rites

Hicknoll Slait is situated on top of the Jurassic limestone scarp, 1km due east of, and overlooking, Cadbury Castle. During the construction of a reservoir in 1966 workmen discovered four burials, although rescue excavations by Leonard Hayward only recorded two *in situ* (Taylor 1967: 67-69). These burials were thought to be part of a seventh century pagan Saxon cemetery after a sugar loaf shield boss and spearhead were recovered from the spoil heap. As such it would have represented the westernmost expansion of the pagan Saxon burial tradition. However, it has not been possible to locate any notes that may have been made during the excavations and, of the material assemblage, only the shield boss could be found in Somerset County Museum, Taunton. Therefore, and considering the proximity of the site to Cadbury Castle, it was decided to conduct a properly controlled and recorded excavation in 2001 (Davey 2002b).

Two further well-preserved burials were uncovered in 2001 (Figure 6.6). The second to be found had been laid in the supine position and oriented northwest to southeast with the head to the northwest. However, there were signs of robbing, the neck vertebrae and right hand were disarticulated. Flecks of copper and a fragment of a blue glass bead were found near the skull. The specialist report on the glass bead is still pending. However, preliminary analysis suggests it may have been an heirloom in continual use since the Roman period.

The first burial to be found was perhaps the more interesting. At first sight he appeared to have been laid in the supine position, but had actually been laid on his side and slumped on to his back during back filling. A chunk of flint (Figure 6.7) was placed in this individual's mouth and all of the neck vertebrae and the skull were undisturbed. Thus the flint could not be intrusive. A similar deposit was found in a fourth century context from a cemetery at Crowmarsh in Oxfordshire. Here, Martin Henig and Paul Booth suggested that the deposition was meant to stand for the payment of Charon's fee (Henig and Booth 2000: 133). It is interesting that the burial at Crowmarsh has the flint clearly visible between the teeth whereas at Hicknoll Slait the flint was hidden from the view of mourners inside a closed mouth. This might be explained by the fact that there may have been a Christian element to the cemetery at Hicknoll Slait, three of the four burials recovered in 1966, were aligned west-east and were unadorned (Taylor 1967: 67-69). It is possible, therefore, that ostentatious payments to Charon were frowned upon at this time. However, it must be noted that rare examples of burial with pebbles placed in the mouth are known from late Saxon Christian contexts at Raunds (Boddington 1996: 41-42) and St.Nicholas Shambles (Schofield 1988: 25). A knife was also found on the hip of this burial. This type of knife (Dover type 2) has been dated to AD 475-700 at Dover (Evison 1987: 115), although at Cannington in Somerset, a burial containing one of these knives was dated by radiocarbon to cal. AD 535-660 (Rahtz *et al.* 2000: 326 and 454). Knife burials are also well attested from Romano-British contexts notably at Ilchester (Leach 1982: 255-256) and Poundbury (Farwell and Molleson 1993: 230-233). At Ulwell near Swanage in Dorset a 7th century cemetery, in which one burial was accompanied by a knife, was considered to represent '...the survival of Romano-British traditions in an area where former Roman economic influence...had been strong' (Cox 1988: 46).

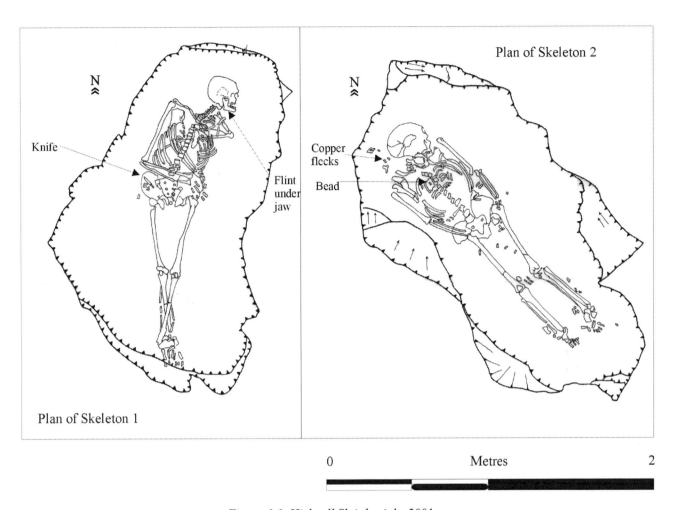

Figure 6.6: Hicknoll Slait burials, 2001.

Figure 6.7: Hicknoll Slait 2001, skeleton 1. Flint in situ.

It appears, then, that at Hicknoll Slait we have a sixth to seventh century cemetery exhibiting a mixture of Romano-British and Saxon burial customs. Helen Geake has suggested that by the seventh century, neighbouring and competing kingdoms were adopting similar material culture (Geake 1999: 203). Strontium isotope analysis has been conducted on teeth from both burials. The results are given below:

$$Skeleton\ 1:\ 87Sr/86Sr = 0.70997$$
$$Skeleton\ 2:\ 87Sr/86Sr = 0.70979$$

These readings are very similar and consistent with Mesozoic geology in Southern England, although they are a little more radiogenic than typical chalk signatures (Paul Budd pers. comm.). This suggests that the individuals buried at Hicknoll Slait were not Saxon incomers from the Wessex chalk downs but rather were brought up locally to South Cadbury. The results of Oxygen isotope analysis are still pending. It seems that this cemetery is more akin to the indigenous cemetery at Cannington, which displayed both Romano-British and Saxon traits. The occurrence of Saxon type grave goods at Hicknoll Slait can be attributed to acculturation rather than invasion.

Summary

The Late Antique period in the South Cadbury environs is initially one of economic strength. This is demonstrated through the restructuring of the agrarian landscape and construction of stone buildings in the third century. To some extent third century field alignments and settlement patterns continue into the medieval period and beyond. The evidence for this comes from settlement sites such as Holway and Henehill as well as field alignments and political boundaries throughout the region between Ilchester and South Cadbury. However, coupled with this is the reversion of some marginal land to unenclosed wood, marsh or downland. This change probably occurs at some time between the fifth and seventh centuries and it is not clear whether the principal cause be the collapse of central Roman authority at the beginning of the fifth century, or climatic disaster in the middle of the sixth century. A shift of central place from Ilchester to Cadbury Castle in the middle of the fifth century is coupled with the continued conspicuous consumption of imported goods into the middle of the sixth century. This suggests that the true situation cannot be simply ascribed to a monocausal explanation.

By the beginning of the seventh century then, the landscape of southeast Somerset consists of core estates separated by marginal land. Between the seventh and tenth centuries the marginal land is progressively enclosed into family units or hides associated with dispersed settlement. During the tenth century we see the subdivision of the large estates and the amalgamation of the smaller hide units into the medieval manorial system.

This system is associated with nucleated settlement, though in Somerset, the majority of settlement remains dispersed.

Conclusions

In Somerset, the received wisdom has been that a protracted sub-Roman period preceded Saxon invasions in the seventh century, as described by the *Anglo-Saxon Chronicle*. The problems inherent in using this ninth century work as source for the post-Roman period are well known (for instance Yorke 1993). A more useful perspective is to use the results of archaeological research to examine the transformation of this region in the Late Antique period. In the South Cadbury environs there appear to be two significant 'events' visible in the archaeological record during this period.

The third century rationalisation of the agricultural landscape as witnessed by the wholesale planned reorganisation of field systems associated with increased wealth, as invested in villa construction.

The fifth century saw the collapse of complex administrative structures and an associated shift of high status settlement to Cadbury Castle occurred in the middle of the century. At the same time there is broad continuity in agricultural practice. In this respect, the limited environmental evidence available for the region supports the archaeological evidence from the South Cadbury environs. Apart from a possible retreat from marginal land, the environmental evidence indicates that there is no decline in agricultural activity from the fourth to fifth centuries (Dark 1996: 35-50). Similarly, the evidence from the South Cadbury environs suggests that, although there may have been some desertion in the fifth century, notably at Sigwells (Leach and Tabor 1994: 7) the majority of rural settlement sites display evidence of continuity at least into the medieval period.

The first event, then, is economic and the second is political. It is clear from this study, however, that political change does not necessarily mean social upheaval. The northern and southern Durotrigian *civitates* were in a strong economic position at the turn of the fifth century. This is clear from the continuity of agriculture, settlement and perhaps even pottery production (Gerrard, this volume) at least until AD 450. An agricultural surplus must have continued to be produced into the fifth and sixth centuries in order to enable long distance exchange of commodities and luxury items such as wine and oil.

It seems that the Durotrigians maintained a strong cultural identity throughout the Roman period. In the ultimate pre-Roman Iron Age phases at Sigwells, one mile south east of Cadbury Castle, the ritual deposition of bovine mandibles and limestones burnt red was common. In the Romano-British and post-Romano-British phases at Castle Farm, South Cadbury, bovine mandibles are also deposited, this time associated with upturned broken bases of Black Burnished pottery as well as large red stones. Perhaps, then, on the collapse of central authority in Britain, some time in the fifth century, the Durotrigian *civitas*, having retained a strong identity, was able to assume regional autonomy without the need for social upheaval. In this scenario the reoccupation of Cadbury Castle in the middle of the fifth century might be seen as a symbolic separation from Roman authority and a link to the Durotrigian past rather than a response to external stress. In reality it was probably a response to both of these factors.

It is impossible to say at what point the Late Antique period came to a close in the South Cadbury area. The evidence from Hicknoll Slait indicates that by the seventh century the people of South Cadbury were embracing a new set of cultural values consisting of a mixture of the old Romano-British and new Saxon cultural traits. So, regardless of what may be written in the pseudo-historical *Anglo-Saxon Chronicle* about the battle of Pen and the subsequent conquest of the West Country, the most decisive event may have been the peaceful emergence of a new cultural identity in the seventh century. It is at this point perhaps, that the Late Antique world of Somerset passed into the new medieval order.

This slow process of acculturation suggests that, if any truth can be gleaned from the *Anglo-Saxon Chronicle*, the emphasis on military conquest is certainly misleading. Nevertheless, The approximate date for the West Saxon absorption of Somerset is broadly correct. It is clear from a variety of documentary sources that by the seventh century Ine, king of Wessex, and the Saxon 'Roman' church, through Bishop Aldhelm, were very active in Somerset.

Acknowledgements

This study has been funded through the Tratman scholarship and the Arts and Humanities Research Board to whom I am grateful. I am also grateful to the Maltwood fund for supporting the Strontium and Oxygen isotope analysis on the skeletons from Hicknoll Slait.

Thanks to my colleagues from the South Cadbury Environs Project, Dr. Richard Tabor and Giles Cooper, for their help and advice. Thanks to Richard Wykes, Mark Morgan, Peter Sherwin, John Ferdinando, Sarah Reeves, James Gerrard, Ian Milstead, and many others for their help in the field. Thanks also to Roger and Dave Yeomans of Holway Farm, Sandford Orcas; Archie Montgomery of Home Farm, North Cadbury; John Stokes of North Cadbury; and Greg Hitchins of Compton Castle for permission to carry out fieldwork on their land. Finally, thanks to Professor Mick Aston, Teresa Hall, James Gerrard and Rob Collins for reading through and commenting on draughts of this paper.

Bibliography

Alcock, L. 1968. Excavations at South Cadbury Castle, 1967: a summary report. *Antiquaries Journal* 48: 6-17.

Alcock, L. 1969. Excavations at South Cadbury Castle, 1968: a summary report. *Antiquaries Journal* 49: 30-40.

Alcock, L. 1970. Excavations at South Cadbury Castle, 1969: a summary report. *Antiquaries Journal* 50: 14-25.

Alcock, L. 1971. Excavations at South Cadbury Castle, 1970. *Antiquaries Journal* 51: 1-7.

Alcock, L. 1995. *Cadbury Castle, Somerset. The Early Medieval Archaeology*. Cardiff: University of Wales.

Aston, M. 1985. *Interpreting the Landscape*. London: Batsford.

Aston, M. 1989. The Development of Medieval Rural Settlement in Somerset, in R. Higham (ed.), *Landscape and Townscape in the South West*: 19-40. Exeter: University of Exeter.

Aston, M. 2000. Medieval Rural Settlement, in C. Webster (ed.), *Somerset Archaeology: Papers to Mark 150 Years of the Somerset Archaeological and Natural History Society*: 93-98. Taunton: Somerset County Council.

Baillie, M. 1999. *Exodus to Arthur*. London: Batsford.

Boddington, A. 1996. *Raunds Furnells, the Anglo-Saxon Church and Churchyard*. London: English Heritage.

Branigan, K. 1976. Villa Settlement in the West Country, in K. Branigan and P. Fowler (eds.), *The Roman West Country: Classical Culture and Celtic Society*: 20-41. Newton Abbot.

Cooper, G. 2002. Fieldname Survey, in R. Tabor (ed.), *South Cadbury Environs Project. Interim fieldwork report, 1998-2001*: 15-25. Bristol: University of Bristol.

Costen, M. 1985. Rimpton in Somerset: a Late Saxon estate. *Southern History* 6: 13-24.

Costen, M. 1992. Huish and Worth: Old English survivals in a later landscape. *Anglo-Saxon Studies in Archaeology and History* 5: 65-83.

Cox, P. 1988. A Seventh Century Inhumation Cemetery at Shepherd's Farm, Ulwell near Swanage, Dorset. *Proceedings of the Dorset Natural history and Archaeological Society* 110: 37-47.

Dark, S.P. 1996. Palaeoecological Evidence for Landscape Continuity and Change in Britain ca. AD 400-800, in K. Dark (ed), *External Contacts and the Economy of Late Roman and Post-Roman Britain*: 23-51. Woodbridge: Boydell.

Davey, J. 2002a. The Early Medieval Period, in R. Tabor (ed.), *South Cadbury Environs Project. Interim fieldwork report, 1998-2001*: 25-31. Bristol, University of Bristol.

Davey, J. 2002b. Hicknoll Slait 2001, in R. Tabor (ed.), *South Cadbury Environs Project. Interim* fieldwork report, 1998-2001,80-9915-25. Bristol: University of Bristol.

Davey, J. in prep. *The Roman to Medieval transtion: the view from South Cadbury*. University of Bristol Ph.D. thesis (provisional title).

Drinkwater, J. and Elton, H. 1992. *Fifth Century Gaul: A Crisis of Identity?* Cambridge: Cambridge University Press.

Esmonde Cleary, S. 2001. The Roman to Medieval Transition, in S. James and M. Millet (eds.), *Britons and Romans: advancing an archaeological agenda*: 90-97. London: Council for British Archaeology Research Report 125.

Evison, V. 1987. *Dover: the Buckland Anglo-Saxon Cemetery*. London: Historical Buildings and Monuments Commission of England, Archaeological Report 3.

Farwell, D. and Molleson, T. 1993. *Poundbury Volume II: the cemeteries*. Dorchester: Dorset Natural History and Archaeological Society Monograph 11.

Fowler, J. 1951. *Mediaeval Sherborne*. Dorchester: Longmans.

Fowler, P. 2002. *Farming in the First Millennium AD*. Cambridge: Cambridge University Press.

Geake, H. 1999. Invisible Kingdoms: the use of Grave Goods in Seventh Century England. *Anglo-Saxon Studies in Archaeology and History* 10: 203-215.

Hall, TA. 2000. *Minster Churches in the Dorset Landscape*. Oxford: British Archaeological Reports British Series 304.

Henig, M. and Booth, P. 2000. *Roman Oxfordshire*. Stroud: Sutton.

Leach, P. 1982. *Ilchester Volume 1: excavations 1974-5*. Bristol: Western Archaeological Trust.

Leach, P. 1994. *Ilchester Volume 2: archaeology, excavations and fieldwork to 1984*. Sheffield: Sheffield Excavation Reports 2.

Leach, P. and Tabor, R. 1994. *The South Cadbury Environs Project Fieldwork Report 1994*. Birmingham: Birmingham University Field Archaeology Unit Report 327.

Leach, P and Tabor, R. 1995. *The South Cadbury Environs Project Fieldwork Report 1995*. Birmingham: Birmingham University Field Archaeology Unit Report 374.

Leech, R. 1977. *Romano-British Rural Settlement in South Somerset and North Dorset*. Unpublished PhD. Thesis, University of Bristol.

Rahtz, P. Hirst, S. and Wright, S. 2000. *Cannington Cemetery*. London: Britannia Monograph Series 17.

Rawlings, M. 1992. Romano-British Sites Observed Along the Codford to Ilchester Water Pipeline. *Proceedings of the Somerset Archaeological and Natural History Society* 136: 29-60.

Rippon, S. 1997. Roman and Medieval Settlement on the North Somerset Levels: survey and excavation at Banwell and Puxton, 1996. *Archaeology in the Severn Estuary* 7: 39-52.

Schofield, J. 1988. The Cemetery of St. Nicholas Shambles, in W. White (ed.), *The Cemetery of St. Nicholas Shambles*: 7-27. London: London Archaeological and Museums Archive Service.

Tabor, R. and Johnson, P. 2000. Sigwells, Somerset, England: Regional Application and Interpretation of Geophysical Survey. *Antiquity* 74: 319-25.

Taylor, R. 1967. An Anglo-Saxon Cemetery at Compton Pauncefoot. *Proceedings of the Somerset Archaeological and Natural History Society* 111: 67-9.

Thorn, C. and Thorn, F. 1980. *Domesday Book, Somerset*. Chichester: Phillimore.

Thornton, CC. 1988. *The Demesne of Rimpton, 938 to 1412: A Study in Economic Development*. Unpublished University of Leicester PhD. thesis.

Yorke, B. 1993. Fact or Fiction? The written evidence for the fifth and sixth centuries AD. *Anglo-Saxon Studies in Archaeology and History* 6: 45-50

7: Roman Estates to English Parishes?
The Legacy of Desmond Bonney Reconsidered

Simon Draper

Introduction

The antiquity of boundaries and estates is an enduring source of contention in English landscape history. The writings of Desmond Bonney on the subject are well known and have set the tone for lively national debate. In recent years, interest in the detail of Bonney's arguments has faded, leaving academic opinion on the worth of his research divided. This paper seeks to move the debate forward by re-examining the Wiltshire evidence that featured so heavily in Bonney's seminal discussions. The incidence of 'pagan' Saxon burials on parish boundaries is reconsidered in the light of new research that questions the dating of many such burials. Evidence is also found for a close relationship between Anglo-Saxon burials, boundaries and routeways, which, it is argued, provides an alternative explanation for the phenomenon of early medieval boundary burial. Lastly, Bonney's arguments concerning parish boundaries and Roman roads in Wiltshire are scrutinised. The conclusions reached are twofold. Firstly, Bonney's claims for the deep antiquity of some boundaries, as argued from the Wiltshire evidence, can no longer be shown to have an evidential basis. Secondly, the creation of such boundaries may just as easily be placed in the context of the later Anglo-Saxon centuries, rather than the prehistoric or Roman past.

Boundaries and Burials: Changing Views

Desmond Bonney is rightly acknowledged as the chief protagonist of the long-running academic debate concerning the antiquity of estates and their boundaries in southern England. His three articles in the 1960s and 1970s (Bonney 1966; 1972; 1979), which built on foundations laid by Frederic Seebohm (1883) and H.P.R. Finberg (1955), have been continually discussed since publication, seemingly without consensus. Like Seebohm and Finberg, Bonney believed that a number of nineteenth-century ecclesiastical parishes, which often correspond to estates defined in Anglo-Saxon charters, may be hailed as the direct successors of prehistoric and Romano-British territories that had passed through the period of Late Antiquity virtually unscathed. Although many strands of evidence were cited in support of this scenario, Bonney mainly focused on the apparent coincidence between 'pagan' Saxon burial sites and parish boundaries, as defined on nineteenth-century tithe maps.

In his first article (1966), Bonney studied the locations of sixty-nine Wiltshire burial sites (occurring as cemeteries, primary and secondary barrows and graves), which were all believed to date from the 'pagan' Saxon period (c.AD 400-700). Of these sixty-nine, he found that twenty (28.6%) lay directly on parish boundaries, whilst a further ten (14.3%) were situated within 500ft (152m) of a boundary (Bonney 1966: 27). To Bonney, this was no coincidence: 'they surely indicate that those boundaries, as boundaries, were in being as early as the pagan Saxon period and they imply the existence of a settled landscape clearly divided among the settlements at a time prior to any documentary evidence for such' (Bonney 1966: 28).

Spurred on by his initial findings, Bonney later extended his study of burials and boundaries to other parts of the country, noting significant correlations in Hampshire, Dorset, Berkshire, Lincolnshire and Cambridgeshire (Bonney 1972: 171-172). He also examined Late Saxon charter bounds in Wiltshire, Dorset and Hampshire, discovering twenty-nine occurrences of the terms 'burials' or 'heathen burials', which he interpreted as further evidence for 'pagan' Saxon burials located on estate boundaries (Bonney 1979: 45-47). Not surprisingly, Bonney's concluding thoughts remained unchanged: in fact, he now felt confident enough to suggest that 'some boundaries, and therefore even estates or land-units, have had a continuous existence since Roman and earlier times' (Bonney 1972: 184).

Bonney's observations did not remain unchallenged for long. Ann Goodier (1984) and Martin Welch (1985) published notable critiques of his work in the 1980s. However, whilst both authors set out to question the validity of Bonney's claims, the factual basis of his original work in Wiltshire was left largely unscrutinised. Welch (1985: 20) merely concluded that burials on boundaries were most likely convenient landmarks adopted for later boundaries, whilst Goodier (1984: 6-7) actually found herself agreeing with Bonney that the number of burials coinciding with parish boundaries was indeed statistically significant and merited further explanation.

Since the 1980s, there has been a surprising reluctance amongst archaeologists and landscape historians to engage critically with the details of the debate. Instead, only passing reference is given to Bonney's work and, even then, it is usually only to register either deep mistrust (e.g. Blair 1991: 18; Klingelhöfer 1992: 46; Tingle 1991: 79-81) or broad support (e.g. Aston 1985: 39-40; Corney 2000: 35; Fowler 2000: 230). This reluctance to become involved is perhaps best represented in a recent remark by Della Hooke (1998: 67), who simply states that 'unfortunately there is insufficient data for a sound statistical analysis of burial/boundary location to be made and the argument remains open'.

Hooke's comment, however, fails to take account of recent developments in Anglo-Saxon burial archaeology. In a review of the evidence for the burial of criminals and social outcasts in the later Anglo-Saxon period, Andrew Reynolds has concluded that some burials considered to be 'pagan' Saxon in origin are, in fact, later burials of eighth- to eleventh-century date. Many of these appear to be deliberately located on or close to estate boundaries, perhaps to emphasise the social exclusion of the individuals concerned. It now seems that included within this category are the numerous charter references to 'burials' and 'heathen burials' earlier used by Bonney to argue for 'pagan' Saxon burial on boundaries (Reynolds 2002; *contra* Bonney 1979).

In addition, recent work by a number of specialists has added to the growing suspicion that many burials once classified as 'pagan' Saxon in date are not what they seem to be. For example, there is mounting evidence in support of a seventh- to ninth-century date for a group of cemeteries whose unaccompanied burials are virtually indistinguishable from those of so-called 'pagan' Saxon cemeteries (Lucy and Reynolds 2002: 4; Reynolds 2002: 185-186). Clearly, the potential implications of these discoveries for the 'Bonney debate' are enormous and it is now apparent that Bonney's original work in Wiltshire is in urgent need of reassessment.

Burials, Boundaries and Routeways in Wiltshire

At the end of his 1966 article, Bonney included an appendix of thirty burial sites in Wiltshire that were located 'on' or 'very near' (*i.e.* within 152m of) parish boundaries (Table 7.1; Bonney 1966: 28-29). In order to acquire the necessary data for these burials, Bonney relied on the information supplied by Audrey Meaney in her seminal *Gazetteer of Early Anglo-Saxon Burial Sites* (1964). As Martin Tingle (1991: 79) has recently highlighted, however, the problems inherent in the Wiltshire entries of Meaney's *Gazetteer* are not trivial:

> Of the 82 burials listed for the county of Wiltshire ... the vast majority were identified in the eighteenth and nineteenth centuries. Only 46 of the 82 are inhumations associated with Anglo-Saxon metalwork. The others are made up of 15 secondary barrow inhumations and flat burials without identifying grave goods and the remaining 21 composed of stray finds of metalwork said to represent ploughed out burials, hearsay accounts of finds and unlocated burials. In the light of more recent work on prehistoric burial practice it is likely that some of the unaccompanied burials have been mis-identified, especially those originally dated by racial characteristics deduced from the shape of their skulls.

Just one example of a burial site in the county that causes concern is the group of unaccompanied inhumations found close to the Crofton Pumping Station in Great

Bedwyn parish in 1892. This site features in two of Bonney's articles as a 'pagan' Saxon cemetery occurring on a parish boundary (Bonney 1966: 28; 1979: 47); however, it should be noted that no grave goods have ever been found here and the original excavator also noted large numbers of flint implements in the field (Tingle 1991: 79-80). Furthermore, aerial photography and fieldwork has revealed the presence of a substantial Neolithic causewayed enclosure immediately adjacent to the burial site (Chandler 2001: 120; Tingle 1991: 81). Needless to say, the case for these burials being Anglo-Saxon in date is by no means proven.

Another unaccompanied burial deposit in Bonney's appendix that requires review is that at Newtown Plantation in Heytesbury, which lies on a hundred boundary and consists of three human skulls and a headless skeleton (Meaney 1964: 269). It is clear that these are not 'normal' interments and the likelihood must surely be that this was an execution burial of later Anglo-Saxon date, comparable to those studied elsewhere in Wessex by Andrew Reynolds (1998). A skull found in the Ell Barrow in Wilsford parish (also close to a hundred boundary) was noted to have a probable sword wound (Meaney 1964: 267) and the possibility must remain that some of the other unaccompanied interments listed by Bonney, especially those inserted into prehistoric barrows on or close to major boundaries, may be Late Saxon execution burials (Reynolds 1999: 108).

In light of the above examples, it may be concluded that the corpus of evidence cited by Bonney for the association of 'pagan' Saxon burials and parish boundaries is left considerably weakened as a whole. It is further undermined when it is realised that many Anglo-Saxon burials in Wiltshire only lie on or close to parish boundaries because the boundaries in question follow rivers and other watercourses. A prime example is the secondary interment in a Neolithic long barrow at Sherrington in the Wylye valley (Figure 7.1). The barrow here is located only 50m from the River Wylye, which not only forms the parish boundary between Sherrington and Codford, but also neighbouring Boyton and Upton Lovell. Clearly, a natural feature as prominent as a river would have made an obvious choice for a territorial marker at any point in time and the fact that a Saxon burial is located here surely tells us little about the dating of either this particular boundary or others in the surrounding region.

Perhaps of greater significance is the fact that the Sherrington barrow is clearly visible from both the Wylye river and the current A36 trunk road, which is likely to be the modern successor of an earlier long-distance valley route (Cossons 1959: 254). The barrow may have served as a landmark for many generations of travellers, passing by either on foot or by boat. The Sherrington burial, however, is not alone in being visually prominent from long-distance routeways. If the locations of all thirty

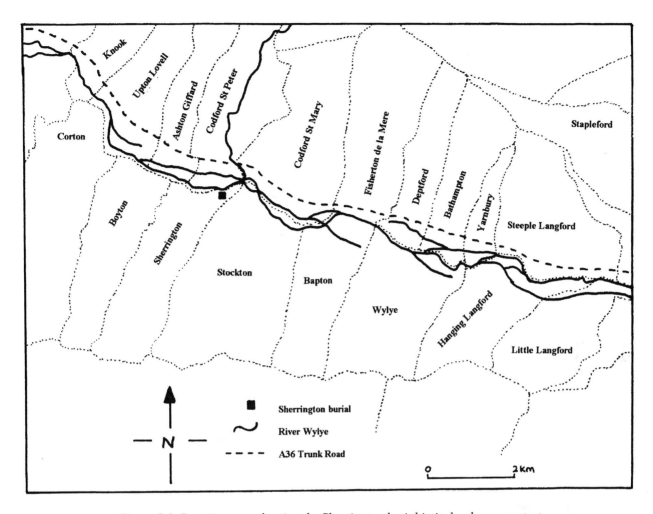

Figure 7.1: Location map showing the Sherrington burial in its landscape context.

burials occurring on or close to parish boundaries in Wiltshire are studied in relation to known principal trackways in the county, a clear pattern begins to emerge (Figure 7.2): it is noticeable that fifteen sites (50% of the sample) are situated less than 100m from a significant long-distance routeway.

Admittedly, the fact that Saxon burials frequently occur close to roads, tracks and rivers is no revelation. Howard Williams has already observed that many high-status seventh-century barrow burials in southern England are deliberately situated so as to be easily referenced by passing travellers, thereby enhancing the status of the individuals buried (Williams 1999: 75). Andrew Reynolds has also stressed the connection between execution sites and trackways (Reynolds 1999: 109) and the sight of corpses hanging from a gallows would undoubtedly have made a stark visual impression on travellers passing by. In Wiltshire, the correlation between Anglo-Saxon burials and routeways runs particularly deep. Returning to the graph (Figure 7.2), it is apparent that all thirty burial sites lie within 1km of a major routeway, six (20%) of which are associated with Roman roads and one (3%) of which (Sherrington) is located beside the navigable River Wylye. Significantly,

twenty-three (77%) occur in association with other ancient long-distance through-routes – a category which here includes ridgeways, drove-roads and current A roads.

Perhaps the most striking example of the link between burials and routeways may be found at West Overton on the Marlborough Downs (Figure 7.3). Here, sixth-century secondary interments have been found in three unusual Roman tombs, marked 6, 6a and 7 on the map, and four further intrusive sixth-century burials have been found in a Bronze Age barrow, marked 6b (Eagles 1986; Fowler 2000: 53). The significance of this place is that it lies at the crossroads of the Great Ridgeway, which here forms the boundary between West Overton and Avebury parishes, and the Roman road between Bath and Mildenhall. This was clearly an important spot, both in the Roman and Anglo-Saxon periods and, in my opinion, it is this crossroad location that governed the siting of these burials, not the fact that a parish boundary passes close by.

With this in mind, it may be noted that the West Overton burials appear prominently in Bonney's articles by virtue of the fact that the parish boundary here chooses to

Burial	Burial Type	Grave goods	Grid Reference	Routeway	Distance from Routeway	Distance from Boundary
Petersfinger	cemetery	Yes	SU 163293	A36 River Avon	<100m 750m	<100m
Barbury Castle	?burial	Yes	SU 150763	Smeathe's Ridge Great Ridgeway	<100m 400m	<100m
Crofton	Graves	No	SU 261623	Burbage road Margary 43	<100m 300m	<100m
Heytesbury	graves	No	ST 920428	A36 River Wylye	<100m 350m	<100m
Savernake Hospital	single grave	Yes	SU 207686	A4 Margary 43/44	<100m 1000m	<100m
Stanton Fitzwarren	single grave	Yes	SU 188905	A361 B4019	300m 1100m	<100m
Witherington	single grave	Yes	SU 185252	Clearbury track Witherington road	<100m 300m	<100m
Middle Down	primary barrow	Yes	ST 967252	Salisbury Way Ansty/Alvediston road	<100m 500m	<100m
Roundway Hill	primary barrow	Yes	SU 019643	Wansdyke Ridgeway A361	750m 1000m	<100m
Coombe Bissett	primary barrow	Yes	SU 104281	Salisbury Way Margary 4c	<100m <100m	<100m
Boscombe Down	secondary barrow	Yes	SU 177400	Margary 44	900m	<100m
Clyffe Pypard	secondary barrow	Yes	SU 090772	Clyffe Pypard Ridgeway	<100m	<100m
Ell Barrow	secondary barrow	No	SU 073513	Devizes/Old Sarum track	250m	<100m
Great Botley Copse 1	secondary barrow	Yes	SU 293600	Margary 43	700m	<100m
Great Botley Copse 2	?secondary barrow	No	SU 293603	Margary 43	900m	<100m
King Barrow	secondary barrow	Yes	ST 897444	Great Ridgeway A36	250m 300m	<100m
Kill Barrow	?secondary barrow	No	SU 000478	Imber/Old Sarum track	<100m	<100m
Winterbourne Stoke 1	?secondary barrow	Yes	SU 104422	Harrow Way (A303) Devizes/Old Sarum (A360)	500m 600m	<100m
Winterbourne Stoke 2	?secondary barrow	No	SU 101416	Harrow Way (A303) Devizes/Old Sarum (A360)	150m 150m	<100m
Winterslow Hut	secondary barrow	Yes	SU 228353	Porton road Lunway (A30)	250m 750m	<100m
Basset Down	cemetery	Yes	SU 115799	Clyffe Pypard Ridgeway Salt Way (B4005)	<100m 250m	150m
North Newnton	single grave	Yes	SU 132570	A345 Rushall road	<100m <100m	100m
Codford St Peter 1	?primary barrow	No	ST 979426	Chitterne road	300m	150m
Ford Down	primary barrow	Yes	SU 172332	Margary 45a A338	150m 150m	100m
Codford St Peter 2	secondary barrow	Yes	ST 980428	Chitterne road	350m	150m
Everleigh	?secondary barrow	No	SU 184560	Pewsey road A342	750m 1250m	150m
Roundway Down	secondary barrow	Yes	SU 006647	Wansdyke Ridgeway	<100m	<100m
Sherrington	secondary barrow	Yes	ST 968391	River Wylye Codford/Sherrington road	<100m 200m	<100m
West Overton	secondary barrow	Yes	SU 119683	Great Ridgeway Margary 53	100m 100m	100m
Ansty	secondary barrow	Yes	ST 967254	Salisbury Way Ansty/Alvediston road	<100m 400m	<100m

Table 7.1: Topographical affinities of 'pagan' Saxon burials on or close to parish boundaries in Wiltshire (see Margary 1955 for Roman road classifications).

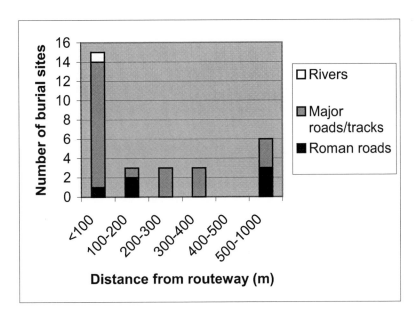

Figure 7.2: Graph showing the correlation between burial sites listed in Table 1 and their nearest routeways.

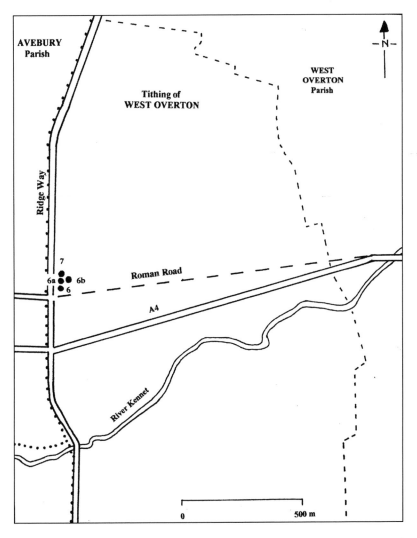

Figure 7.3: Location map of Anglo-Saxon burials in West Overton showing their proximity to the intersection of the Great Ridgeway and the Roman road and also the parish boundary between West Overton and Avebury. After Eagles.

follow the Great Ridgeway route. In fact, the boundaries of no fewer than ten parishes in northern Wiltshire follow the Ridgeway over a distance of some 10km. This tendency for boundaries to follow routeways is one that has often been overlooked in the past, but it is of the utmost importance to the present debate. Peter Fowler has recently considered the antiquity of many of the trackways crossing the Marlborough Downs and the conclusion that he reaches is that many, if not all of them, are 'ancient' in origin; in other words, they date from the prehistoric period or the earliest centuries AD (Fowler 1998: 40). Indeed, he (2000: 257) writes:

> In practical terms, when it came to defining long-term boundaries, it would have been extremely convenient to begin to follow lines already being etched into human consciousness as well as into the land. In part at least, what emerge as the tithings are the shape they are, with their boundaries where they are, because of the lie of the drove-ways around which they tended to arrange themselves.

Seen in these terms, it is perhaps no great surprise that so many parish and tithing boundaries in Wiltshire follow stretches of roads and tracks. A large proportion of the county is characterised by upland chalk, stretching from Mere in the southwest to Baydon in the northeast, and the importance of drove-ways in defining the parish shapes here is immediately apparent at even the most cursory glance of a modern 1:25,000 scale map. Indeed, the characteristic 'strip' parishes of Wiltshire, stretching from the valley floors to the high downland, must surely owe their origins to the transhumant economy (Bettey 2000: 35-36; Fowler 2000: 257; Hooke 1998: 74). This landscape zone is also where the vast majority (all but four) of Bonney's 'pagan' Saxon burial sites are located. Clearly, in such circumstances the chances of a burial coinciding with a boundary that happens to follow a routeway must be high. Routeways, therefore, are undoubtedly primal features in the landscape of chalkland Wiltshire and their presence provided an obvious template for the boundaries of parishes and estates.

An Alternative Model for Parish Boundary Formation

When were the boundaries of parishes recorded on nineteenth-century maps first laid out? Although none of the evidence discussed so far rules out a degree of survival from prehistoric or Roman territories, an alternative sequence of events can nevertheless be put forward which explains all the relevant elements not in terms of ancient land-units, but in terms of a later Saxon origin for parish boundary formation.

Stage 1: Long-distance routes and more localised drove-ways are established in the prehistoric, Romano-British and immediate post-Roman periods (before c.AD 450).

Stage 2: Some routeways, many of which have prehistoric barrows located close by, are chosen as focal points for mainly high-status burials (c.AD 450–700).

Stage 3: A number of routeways are chosen as obvious and convenient boundaries for newly created estates, some of which are defined in charters (c.AD 600–1100).

Stage 4: Criminals and outcasts are buried close to the boundaries of established estates in order to emphasise their exclusion from society (c.AD 750–1150).

As with all models, there are clear limitations. Admittedly, not all of the boundaries associated with burials follow obvious routeways; although it should be noted that there may be a great deal of truth in Martin Welch's suggestion that barrows and other visible burial markers were simply adopted as obvious landmarks for later boundaries (Welch 1985: 21). Furthermore, there is no easy way in which the model can be *proven* beyond doubt; although it should be pointed out that there is similarly no way of proving the alternative scenario (*i.e.* Roman estate continuity) since Bonney's evidence has now been found wanting. What is attractive about the above model, however, is that it establishes for the first time important links between routeways, burials and boundaries that not only make the theoretical likelihood of an Anglo-Saxon burial occurring on a boundary significantly greater, but also mean that such boundaries no longer have to be seen as relics from the distant past. In proposing this model, therefore, I have opened up a valid alternative to the continuity argument. I have not ruled out the possibility that some prehistoric and Roman boundaries did survive into the post-Roman period; however, I have suggested that a later origin for the majority of parish boundaries is perhaps more likely. Indeed, it is possible that most are a product of what Andrew Reynolds has termed the 'New Geography' of the later Anglo-Saxon centuries (Reynolds 2002: 188).

Early Boundaries in Wessex?

So far, this paper has focused primarily on Desmond Bonney's thoughts concerning 'pagan' Saxon burials and boundaries in Wiltshire. However, in his second article, entitled *Early Boundaries in Wessex*, Bonney constructed a second unrelated argument for the antiquity of estates in the county based on the relationship between parish boundaries and linear features, such as Roman roads and earthwork ditches (Bonney 1972: 173-85). The argument ran as follows. In some parts of Wiltshire, Roman roads are followed for many miles by parish boundaries, whilst in other parts of the county the boundaries seem to ignore the Roman road network altogether, choosing instead to stick to the lines of linear earthworks that may be prehistoric in origin. Logically, where a parish boundary faithfully follows a Roman road, it must post-date the construction of the road: however, is the reverse true? If parish boundaries ignore Roman roads, can we conclude that the boundaries are themselves pre-Roman in date?

Bonney believed that we could. He likened the construction of Roman roads in these circumstances to the driving of nineteenth-century railways across the countryside, '...cutting, but certainly not altering, the boundaries of most estates...' (Bonney 1972: 181).

Since Bonney's work on Roman roads and boundaries, a similar logical reasoning has been applied to other areas of the English landscape where Roman roads are seemingly ignored by parish boundaries. In Somerset, for example, Roger Leech has drawn attention to the fact that many parishes seem to cross the Fosse Way Roman road south of Ilchester, leading him to suggest that some of these estates were in place by the first century AD (Leech 1982: 235-6). A similar situation has been observed in Gloucestershire by Katherine Barker (1985) and Susan Pearce (1982). In East Anglia, however, Tom Williamson (1986) has used the same basic argument to argue against Bonney. Here, Roman roads appear to carve through extensive rectilinear field systems, the boundaries of which must, as a result, pre-date the construction of the roads. However, when Williamson superimposed the parish boundaries on the surviving pattern of prehistoric and Romano-British fields, little similarity was found: 'in short', he wrote, 'the boundaries appear to have been imposed upon an earlier landscape' (Williamson 1986:

246). Williamson, therefore, regarded parish units in East Anglia as an essentially Middle to Late Saxon creation.

In Wiltshire, there are a number of reasons for believing that the pattern of parishes and boundaries is similarly later Anglo-Saxon in date. When the supporting evidence in Bonney's 1972 paper is examined in greater detail, it is immediately apparent that all is not what it seems. Three areas of the county on which Bonney focused particular attention were Chittoe, the Grovely Ridge and Hippenscombe (Bonney 1972: 176-83). In all these places, Bonney attempted to explain why certain boundaries did not follow Roman roads. At Chittoe, for example, the former chapelry attached to Bishops Cannings parish extended both north and south of the road from Bath to Mildenhall, unlike neighbouring parishes to the east and west (Figure 7.4). Similarly, along the Grovely Ridge and at Hippenscombe, boundaries followed linear earthworks rather than parallel Roman roads. The conclusion Bonney came to was that the boundaries here must all pre-date construction of the Roman roads. There is one important factor, however, linking all three places that he failed to take into account: they all lie in densely wooded parts of the county that once formed the hearts of medieval royal forests.

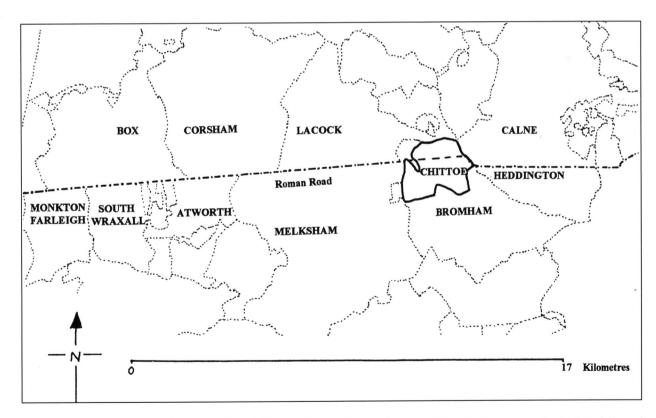

Figure 7.4: Location map of the chapelry of Chittoe showing its position straddling the Roman road, which is followed by parish boundaries both to the east and west of Chittoe. After Bonney.

Chittoe, whose very name has recently been reinterpreted as a Brittonic survival meaning 'great or thick wood' (Coates 2000: 88), once lay at the core of Pewsham Forest and constituted an area of woodland that had probably been allocated to Bishops Cannings by Domesday (Costen 1994: 104). The Grovely Ridge, meanwhile, stretching between the Wylye and Nadder valleys, once formed the rump of Grovely Forest, whilst Hippenscombe was situated at the heart of Chute Forest, whose name again (like Chittoe) contains the Brittonic element cęd, meaning 'wood' (Coates 2000: 88). Significantly, the place-name Pertwood, to the west of Grovely Forest, may also contain a Brittonic element meaning 'wood' (Gover et al. 1939: 176) and this evidence gives us good grounds for believing that all three locations were densely wooded by the later Anglo-Saxon period.

The significance of this point is that Roman roads, especially if they had ceased to function as such, could easily have become 'lost' in the undergrowth of woodland by the time estate boundaries were being formulated in the later Anglo-Saxon centuries. Bonney even admits that the Grovely Ridge road 'appears never to have been more than a slight earthwork ... and today it survives only intermittently' (Bonney 1972: 179). In such circumstances, the most sensible option would surely

have been either to divert around the edge of the woodland, as seems to have been the case at Chittoe, or to follow a more prominent feature in the landscape, such as the existing linear earthworks along the Grovely Ridge and at Hippenscombe. The deviations from Roman roads in these three locations can satisfactorily be explained as practical responses in the Anglo-Saxon period to difficult circumstances on the ground and there is no reason to postulate the existence of these boundaries before the eighth or ninth centuries.

One final area of Wiltshire where Bonney envisaged the long-term survival of ancient land-units is in the vicinity of the East Wansdyke (Figure 7.5). This prominent linear earthwork, which stretches for over 20km across the downs of central Wiltshire, is almost completely ignored by parish boundaries in the region. This fact led Bonney to suggest that the boundaries here must pre-date the construction of Wansdyke itself and, since it is traditionally interpreted as an early post-Roman earthwork, possibly constructed in the 490s (Fowler 2001: 196), his conclusion was 'that the pattern of estates as reflected in the parish boundaries is ... not later than the fifth or sixth centuries' (Bonney 1972: 176).

Bonney's reasoning, however, relied on the assumption that no later boundary would have ignored the line of

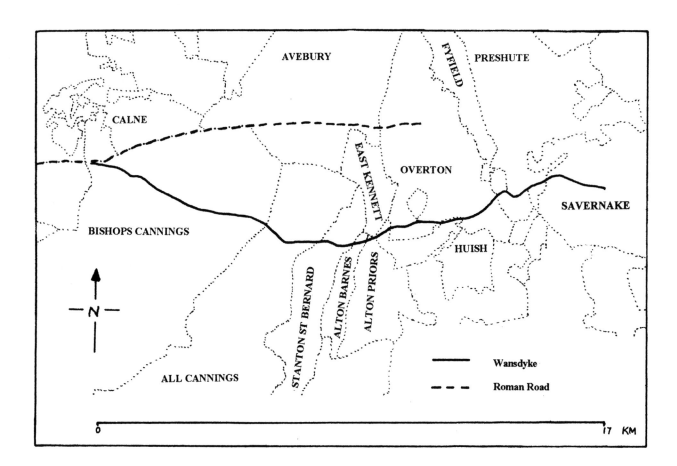

Figure 7.5: Location map showing parish boundaries crossing the East Wansdyke. After Bonney.

Wansdyke; but could it not be the case that the parishes were established at a time when Wansdyke had lost its military and political significance? The valuable sheep pastures of Bishops Cannings, All Cannings and Stanton St Bernard that are located to the north of Wansdyke are known to be linked to their parent settlements by ancient drove-ways, crossing
the earthwork through a series of breaches, or 'gates'. As Peter Fowler (2001) has recently established, there was clearly extensive movement across the line of Wansdyke on a north-south axis, even when the earthwork was functional, and we should not place too much emphasis on the notion that this was a Dark Age 'iron curtain': even Hadrian's Wall contained a number of gateways in its length, through which travellers could proceed in a northerly or southerly direction (Breeze and Dobson 1987; see also Collins this volume). Like other areas of chalk downland, the Wansdyke ridge is characterised both physically and economically by its framework of drove-ways. Consequently, it may be argued that these tracks would have been the preferred choice for the boundaries of newly defined Middle or Late Saxon estates, rather than the arbitrary line of a redundant earthwork.

Conclusion

The aim of this paper has been to demonstrate that the evidence cited by Bonney for the 'deep' antiquity of parish boundaries in Wiltshire cannot be read at face value. Many, if not all, of the examples used are open to reinterpretation and it is just as easy to fit the evidence into a Middle or Late Saxon context, rather than a prehistoric or Romano-British one. Through an analysis of the Anglo-Saxon burials, boundaries and routeways, I have not only proposed a relationship between these three landscape elements, but also I been able to construct an alternative model for parish boundary formation. I offer this model not as a definitive account of what actually took place in the landscape, but as a working hypothesis, to be openly challenged and contested. In this way, I hope to invigorate a debate that is still as relevant today as it was when Desmond Bonney first put pen to paper, over thirty years ago.

Acknowledgements

This paper was originally presented on 14th June 2003 at the 'Debating Late Antiquity' conference at the University of York. I am grateful to all the delegates who asked questions and made comments, in addition to Professor Matthew Johnson, Dr Chris Gerrard and Dr Sam Lucy, who took the time to read and comment on various drafts. I would also like to thank the Arts and Humanities Research Board for funding my studies. Any errors are, of course, my own.

Bibliography

Aston, M. 1985. *Interpreting the Landscape*. London: Routledge.

Barker, K. 1985. Institution and landscape in early medieval Wessex: Aldhelm of Malmesbury, Sherborne and *Selwoodshire*. *Proceedings of the Dorset Natural History and Archaeological* 106: 33-42.

Bettey, J. 2000. Downlands, in J. Thirsk (ed.), *The English Rural Landscape*: 27-49. Oxford: Oxford University Press.

Blair, J. 1991. *Early Medieval Surrey: Landholding, Church and Settlement before 1300*. Stroud: Alan Sutton.

Bonney, D. 1966. Pagan Saxon burials and boundaries in Wiltshire. *Wiltshire Archaeological and Natural History Magazine* 61: 25-30.

Bonney, D. 1972. Early boundaries in Wessex, in P. Fowler (ed.), *Archaeology and the Landscape: Essays for L.V. Grinsell*: 168-186. London: John Baker.

Bonney, D. 1979. Early boundaries and estates in southern England, in P. Sawyer (ed.), *English Medieval Settlement*: 41-51. London: Edward Arnold.

Breeze, A. and Dobson, B. 1987. *Hadrian's Wall*. Harmondsworth: Penguin.

Chandler, J. 2001. *Marlborough and Eastern Wiltshire*. East Knoyle: Hobnob Press.

Coates, R. 2000. Chittoe, Wiltshire, in R. Coates and A. Breeze (eds.), *Celtic Voices, English Places: Studies of the Celtic Impact on Place-Names in England*: 88-9. Stamford: Shaun Tyas.

Corney, M. 2000. Characterising the landscape of Roman Britain: a review of the study of Roman Britain 1975-2000, in D. Hooke (ed.), *Landscape: The Richest Historical Record*: 33-45. Birmingham: Society for Landscape Studies Supplementary Series 1.

Cossons, A. 1959. Roads, in E. Crittal (ed.), *The Victoria County History of Wiltshire*, volume 4: 254-71. London: Oxford University Press.

Costen, M. 1994. Settlement in Wessex in the tenth century: the charter evidence, in M. Aston and C. Lewis (eds.), *The Medieval Landscape of Wessex*: 97-113. Oxford: Oxbow.

Eagles, B. 1986. Pagan Anglo-Saxon burials at West Overton. *Wiltshire Archaeological and Natural History Magazine* 80: 103-19.

Finberg, H. 1955. *Roman and Saxon Withington: A Study of Continuity*. Leicester: Leicester University Press.

Fowler, P. 1998. Moving through the landscape, in P. Everson and T. Williamson (eds.). *The Archaeology of Landscape*: 25-41. Manchester: Manchester University Press.

Fowler, P. 2000. *Landscape Plotted and Pieced: Landscape History and Local Archaeology in*

Fyfield and Overton, Wiltshire. London: Society of Antiquaries Research Report 64.

Fowler, P. 2001. Wansdyke in the woods: an unfinished Roman military earthwork for a non-event, in P. Ellis (ed.), *Roman Wiltshire and After: Papers in Honour of Ken Annable*: 179-198. Devizes: Wiltshire Archaeological and Natural History Society.

Goodier, A. 1984. The formation of boundaries in Anglo-Saxon England: a statistical study. *Medieval Archaeology* 28: 1-21.

Gover, J., Mawer, A. and Stenton, F. 1939. *The Place-Names of Wiltshire.* Cambridge: Cambridge University Press.

Hooke, D. 1998. *The Landscape of Anglo-Saxon England.* London: Leicester University Press.

Klingelhöfer, E. 1992. *Manor, Vill and Hundred: The Development of Rural Institutions in Early Medieval Hampshire.* Toronto: Pontifical Institute of Medieval Studies, Studies and Texts 112.

Leech, R. 1982. The Roman interlude in the south-west: the dynamics of economics and social change in Romano-British southern Somerset and northern Dorset, in D. Miles (ed.), *The Romano-British Countryside: Studies in Rural Settlement and Economy*: 209-267. Oxford: British Archaeological Reports, British Series 103.

Lucy, S. and Reynolds, A. 2002. Burial in early medieval England and Wales: past, present and future, in S. Lucy and A. Reynolds (eds.), *Burial in Early Medieval England and Wales*: 1-23. London: Society for Medieval Archaeology, Monograph 17.

Margary, I. 1955. *Roman Roads in Britain.* Volume 1. London: Phoenix.

Meaney, A. 1964. *A Gazetteer of Early Anglo-Saxon Burial Sites.* London: Allen and Unwin.

Pearce, S. 1982. Estates and church sites in Dorset and Gloucestershire: the emergence of a Christian society, in S. Pearce (ed.), *The Early Church in Western Britain and Ireland,* 117-43. Oxford: British Archaeological Reports, British Series 102.

Reynolds, A. 1998. *Anglo-Saxon Law in the Landscape.* University of London Ph.D. thesis.

Reynolds, A. 1999. *Later Anglo-Saxon England: Life and Landscape.* Stroud: Tempus.

Reynolds, A. 2002. Burials, boundaries and charters in Anglo-Saxon England: a reassessment, in S. Lucy and A. Reynolds (eds.), *Burial in Early Medieval England and Wales*: 171-194. London: Society for Medieval Archaeology, Monograph 17.

Seebohm, F. 1883. *The English Village Community.* London: Longmans.

Tingle, M. 1991. *The Vale of the White Horse Survey.* Oxford: British Archaeological Reports, British Series 218.

Welch, M. 1985. Rural settlement patterns in the early and middle Anglo-Saxon periods. *Landscape History* 7: 13-25.

Williams, H. 1999. Placing the dead: investigating the location of wealthy barrow burials in seventh century England, in M. Rundkvist (ed.), *Grave Matters: Eight Studies of First Millennium AD Burials in Crimea, England and Southern Scandinavia*: 57-86. Oxford: British Archaeological Reports, International Series 781.

Williamson, T. 1986. Parish boundaries and early fields: continuity and discontinuity. *Journal of Historical Geography* 12(3): 241-8.

8: How late is late? Pottery and the fifth century in southwest Britain

James Gerrard

Introduction

The modern counties of Somerset and Dorset, which approximate to the *civitas* of the Durotriges, offer an unrivalled opportunity to investigate the transformation of Roman Britain. The reasons for this are twofold. Firstly, the Durotrigian *civitas* is an area of highly visible Romano-British settlement that has been well studied (e.g. Leech 1977). Secondly, this is one of the few areas of the lowland, 'Romanized' zone which appears to have maintained an independence from 'Germanic' ideology for at least two centuries after the traditional end of Roman Britain. Here, if anywhere, we might expect to be able to investigate a 'Late Antique' society.

Any investigation of the immediate post-Roman period in Somerset and Dorset is hamstrung by the bane of all archaeologists working on the fifth and sixth centuries: a lack of diagnostic material culture. With the exception of a few brooches, a fifth or sixth century site in the southwest can only be identified if imported Mediterranean pottery is recovered or if radiocarbon determinations are undertaken. To date these methods have revealed a handful of sites, mainly reoccupied hillforts like Cadbury Castle (Alcock 1995) or Cadbury-Congresbury (Rahtz *et al.* 1993), and the occasional cemetery of which Cannington (Rahtz *et al.* 2000) and Poundbury (Sparey-Green 1987, this volume) are the prime examples. The problem is essentially one of archaeological visibility (see Davey, this volume). The fourth century with its suite of 'Roman' material culture can be easily identified. High status sites of the period AD 475-550, the date of the imported Mediterranean pottery, can also occasionally be identified. But if we want to compare the fourth with the late fifth century the difficulties begin. In essence such an exercise is meaningless because our fifth century dataset is so slim. We would not dream of describing fourth century Britain just from the evidence of its towns. The town (and we assume that this was the same for a hillfort) was at the heart of a highly complex and sophisticated society. However, we know virtually nothing of fifth century society, especially at its lower levels. This paper does not add materially to our knowledge of fifth century societies. Such an aim would be beyond its scope. Instead it attempts to show a way through which such societies can be identified. Once the identification has been achieved, then and only then, can we become "students of the process" (Rahtz 1988: 130) and achieve a greater understanding of the Late Antique world in Somerset and Dorset.

It has been suggested that this paper will attempt to provide a means through which the archaeologically invisible fifth century can be identified in the Durotrigian *civitas*. This can be achieved through the identification of possible fifth century ceramic types in otherwise morphologically Late Roman (*i.e.* fourth century) assemblages. As any student of the fifth century will know it is widely accepted that following the 'end' of Roman Britain pottery production ceased (for instance Esmonde-Cleary 1989: 154; Faulkner 2001: 147-148). The following discussion argues that this interpretation is fundamentally flawed theoretically and that it is difficult to maintain in the face of empirical data derived from a series of different excavations in Somerset and Dorset.

Pottery and the paucity of theory

The Roman period in Britain still remains, despite the best efforts of the Theoretical Roman Archaeology Conference, a problematic arena for the theoretical archaeologist. With only a few notable exceptions Romano-British pottery studies, a relatively specialist sub-discipline, has been and to a large extent remains theoretically moribund (Monaghan 1995). The majority of Romano-British pottery specialists work in the commercial sphere where opportunities to wax lyrical about theoretical issues are largely swamped by the pressing need to produce the required report by the required deadline. Nevertheless archaeological theory and historiography can cast a useful light on the end of Roman Britain and its pottery production.

A western worldview sees the present at the end of a long progression of linear time (Murray 1999). That time is divided into slices labelled as periods. Such a statement may seem banal but it is ultimately at the core of many of the issues in this volume. 'Late Antiquity', after all, is being used here as a label for a transitional period (see Faulkner this volume). These period labels are the language that we use to understand the past. The Bronze Age or the Roman period may mean something different to each individual 'user' but they also have broad connotations which all would agree on. They have become a shorthand for a suite of material culture. For Roman Britain this material culture might include Samian, coins, roads, towns, villas and forts (Haverfield 1912, Millett 1990). Such a list is more than reminiscent of Childe's (1929) famous description of an archaeological culture as:

certain types of remains – pots, implements, ornaments, burial sites, house forms – constantly recurring together.

This is not an attempt to describe every archaeologist (myself included!) of Roman Britain as a Culture Historian. Instead it is an attempt to demonstrate the difficulties in reconciling material culture with a sharply defined historic period like Roman Britain (AD 43-AD 410). Take, for instance, the following quotation made by Gillam (1976: 59) on the end of Black Burnished production in Roman Britain:

> the production of BB1 never ceased until Britain ceased to be Roman.

What this statement is actually saying is that Roman Britain is defined through its pottery. Without Black Burnished ware Britain is not Roman. To assert such a claim is patently ridiculous and this reading of Gillam is perhaps unfair. Nevertheless at the end of a period the Culture History school needs the material culture of one period to be replaced by another. That is the definition of change. In Britain, 'Anglo-Saxon' material culture heralds this change, except in those areas where it is absent. Equally if 'Romano-British' pottery dates to after the Honorian rescript, a reference which some would argue may refer to Italy (e.g. Thompson 1983), how can it be 'Roman'? The answer is, of course, it cannot. But then our convenient model, which integrates history with archaeology, begins to disintegrate.

Fortunately, or unfortunately depending on one's point of view, a combination of factors merge in the early fifth century, which enable us to retain our neat model of Roman Britain. In AD 403 the mint of Rome produced a bronze coin bearing the legend VRBS ROMA FELIX. This coin, a replacement for the earlier SALVS REIPUBLICAE issues of Honorius and Arcadius, does not reach Britain (Brickstock 2000: 35). The cessation of copper alloy coin supply to the British Diocese reverberates across modern accounts of the end of Roman Britain. It is, for those who wish to see a rapid 'end', a graphic demonstration of Roman Britain's impending apocalypse. More importantly this event robs us of our most prolific intrinsically dateable artefacts.

The absence of coinage is the single most important factor that bedevils our understanding of the fifth century. Without coins a group of fifth century pottery can, at best, be labelled as 'after AD 400' or 'AD 400+'. As Whyman (1993: 64) has noted this means that:

> the whole of the fifth century is compressed into the first three decades or less, drawn as if by a magnet to the last horizon of coin dated assemblages.

In reality a coin of the House of Theodosius (AD 388-402) provides nothing more than a *terminus post quem* for a deposit. A piece of pottery stratified above such a coin could have been dropped in AD 390, 490 or 1990! (Barker 1993: 205-206, 224-229). Obviously the same logic applies to an earlier coin. Pottery above a coin of AD 350 could, for instance, date to AD 355 or 455. There is, in the absence of other data, no way of discriminating between these two alternatives. This is not just a hypothetical issue. Ryan (1988) has provided statistical data that highlights the very real problems encountered in using fourth century coins as dating evidence. He took the issue date of the latest coin in a deposit and compared it with other coins in the same context. This demonstrated that the age of a fourth century coin at deposition fluctuated considerably (Ryan 1988: Fig 5.13) but was on average 43.6 years ±10.9 years older than the date of its minting (Ryan 1988: 135). Thus a deposit containing coins of AD350 could feasibly not have been deposited until AD390. This obviously has important ramifications for the dating of material culture, especially pottery, by its association with coins.

All works on the end of Roman Britain acknowledge that there is a serious difficulty in dating the early fifth century. However, the disappearance of coinage is also seen as an archaeological confirmation of the historical 'end'. Pottery, coins and 'the end' were most successfully united at the end of the 1970s, a decade which saw tremendous leaps forward in Romano-British pottery studies. On the back of New Archaeology scientific and statistical techniques began to be applied to Late Roman pottery. Economics was now at the forefront of discussion (Fulford 1975; Young 1977). Yet there was still, perhaps unsurprisingly, a paucity of theory applied to this dataset. The newly quantified distributions of Late Roman pottery were interpreted as the product of a capitalist free market. A successful producer, such as the Oxford kilns, was seen as successful because it had access to riverine transport routes and could therefore transport its goods more cheaply than its rivals or alternatively, it had a greater productive capacity, making more pots cheaper than its competitors and flooding the market place with them. This model is essentially a formalist attempt to explain the past. The economics of the past are seen as being broadly similar to modern economic systems. Fulford (1979) united this 'formalist' model of the Late Roman economy with the coin evidence to provide an explanation for the end of Roman pottery production in Britain. He hypothesised (Fulford 1979: 129) in an influential article that:

> it is… fair to argue that the disappearance of coin as a medium of exchange would erode the basis for the continued existence of… potteries.

This, coupled with a disintegrating security situation in the early fifth century, would have caused the market economy to implode and exchange over any distance to cease. Pottery production, without the consumers to sustain it, would end and we would be left with a largely aceramic fifth century (Fulford 1979). In short a new argument had been constructed which merely reinforced the connection between the 'end' of Roman Britain and its material culture.

A deconstruction of Fulford's (1979) model is beyond the scope of this present paper (Gerrard, in prep.). However, if we examine the central tenet of the model, namely that the late Roman economy was articulated through a 'free market' and coin based exchange, then we can cause enough damage to it to remove it as an obstacle to the hypothesis that pottery production continued into the fifth century.

In a 'free market' the market is driven by demand. Demand, in turn, can be stimulated or depressed by the cost of an item. The formalist arguments advanced by Fulford (1975) and others argue that one of the major factors in the cost of a late Roman pot is the distance it has travelled from source to consumer. Following Duncan Jones' (1974: 366-369) calculations a pot transported by water should be cheaper than one travelling by road. Therefore a successful late Roman pottery producer will be situated on a river or maritime communications route. This hypothesis was 'proven' archaeologically through a study of the interaction of the Oxford and New Forest kilns in southern England (Fulford and Hodder 1975). They demonstrated that the Oxford kilns, which had access to the Thames, were more 'successful' than their competitors in the New Forest. If we ignore the fact that these industries almost certainly were not in competition, as they mainly produced mutually exclusive vessel forms (Gerrard 2001; Millett 1990: 172), then we can take the concept of 'cheap transportation routes' and use it to demonstrate the late Roman economy was not a 'free market'.

If the late Roman economy was a 'free market' in which entrepreneurial potters competed for a slice of market share, then we would expect products of kilns situated on rivers or coastlines to utilise these 'cheap routes'. A number of pottery kilns manifestly fail to do this however. Returning briefly to the New Forest producers we need to ask why a production centre situated so close to the south coast failed to utilise the English Channel to capture coastal markets (Holbrook and Bidwell 1991: 81). Similarly, Black Burnished ware, produced on the Poole Harbour littoral in south-east Dorset, accounts for less than twenty percent of a Roman period assemblage in the Solent area while accounting for an equal percentage in the upper Severn Valley around Wroxeter (Allen and Fulford 1996: Fig 8). The Solent should, on the model outlined above, be saturated with Black Burnished products. Finally, in the north of Britain an explanation for why Crambeck ware fails to exploit coastal communications to access markets south of the Humber along the east coast is needed (Evans 1989: 76). This list could be extended *ad infinitum*. However, the examples listed suffice to demonstrate that a 'free market', in which a cheaply transported pot was more desirable than an expensively transported pot, does not seem to have existed in the fourth century.

If we remove the notion of a 'free market' and replace it with an alternative economic model then we can view the 'end' of Roman pottery production in Britain through a different lens. The vast bulk of Late Roman pottery production appears to have taken place in what we would consider marginal areas: heathland and estuarine environments. Are these landscapes as marginal as they at first appear though? Black Burnished production in Poole Harbour is associated with a wide variety of other economic activities including salt production (e.g. Allen and Fulford 1996: 268). Similar connections between Romano-British pottery producers and salt extraction can be seen in the Thames estuary (Pollard 1988: 194-195) and have been suggested in the north in the Humber region (Whyman 2001: 253). If instead of seeing the pots as the commodity we view them as packaging or indicators of archaeologically invisible products (such as salt or foodstuffs), then our questions can be framed differently. Wickham (1984) has highlighted that the disintegration of the Western Empire was a period in which the successors to imperial authority attempt to secure control over resources. The early fifth century in Britain surely saw the emergent, independent post-Roman political elites scrambling to secure resources. Such a scramble would have diverse effects - some destructive and some constructive. If pottery production was associated with resource extraction and its articulation then we do not need to see it ending abruptly in the early fifth century. Instead there may have been a much longer, drawn out process stretching beyond the Honorian Armageddon in AD 410. The challenge is demonstrating this empirically.

Black Burnished ware and the fifth century

The focus of this paper has been defined as the Durotrigian *civitas*, approximating to the modern counties of Somerset and Dorset, in south-western England. Within this region one type of Romano-British pottery, produced in south-east Dorset, appears to have been pre-eminent: Black Burnished ware.

All authorities are agreed that South-East Dorset Black Burnished ware (SEDBB1) had its roots in the Late Iron Age 'Durotrigian' production around Poole Harbour. The Roman conquest of the West Country saw the establishment of a 'Vexillation' fortress at Lake Farm in Dorset and this installation was linked by road to a 'supply port' on Poole Harbour at Hamworthy. It is not surprising to find SEDBB1, or perhaps the commodities with which it was associated, rapidly coming to the attention on the Roman army. A relationship between Poole Harbour, its resources and pottery developed with *Legio* II and SEDBB1 ultimately became a major supplier to the northern frontier zone. By the second half of the fourth century SEDBB1 had been replaced in the north by so-called Huntcliff or Calcite Gritted Wares (Gillam 1976: 59; Whyman 2001: 256). After this date Black Burnished ware became 'restricted' to its earlier

'Durotrigian core' in the south-west. This is usually seen as the beginning of the end for SEDBB1 as its 'market share' went into terminal decline. The model outlined in the preceding discussion provides an alternative view though. SEDBB1 and the commodities, like salt (e.g. Allen and Fulford 1996: 268), with which it was associated, can be seen as being retained and used in the south-west rather than being siphoned off to the distant north. Here, I would argue, we can see ability of the Roman state to enforce long-standing obligations in the diocese decreasing.

In AD 400 Black Burnished ware was still circulating in the area of its 'traditional' distribution. For the purposes of this paper we need to establish the production of the ware beyond this date. Before tackling the pottery itself it is worth reviewing briefly the evidence for post-Roman activity in the production zone. Dark (2000: 108) has drawn attention to two 'Frankish' beads of sixth century date which were loosely associated with a timber building at the Black Burnished production site of Ower, Dorset (Woodward 1987: 64, 100-101). Other finds associated with this structure included 'Late Roman' pottery and kiln furniture while another building nearby yielded an Arcadian coin (post AD 383) in a later excavation (Cox and Hearne 1991: 157). A parallel can be drawn with another Black Burnished production site at Worgret, near Wareham. Excavations at this site recovered a bead of possible sixth century date as well as a Valentinianic coin (Hearne and Smith 1991: 91-92). While this evidence is far from conclusive it is provocative and an explanation is needed for the occurrence of these beads in an area of Dorset, which is otherwise lacking in 'Dark Age' material (Hinton 2002: 86-87).

The theoretical arguments outlined above and the hints of post-Roman activity on Black Burnished production sites combine to suggest that Black Burnished production may have continued beyond AD 410. If this was the case then we can hope to identify attributes, which might point to a pottery assemblage's fifth century date. In fact some progress has already been made towards this aim.

Dorchester, Dorset (*Durnovaria*), the 'cantonal' capital of the Durotriges, has seen a number of large scale excavations of deeply stratified urban sites. One of the most significant of these excavations took place between 1981 and 1984 at Greyhound Yard (Woodward *et al.* 1993). The resulting analysis of over forty-two thousand sherds of Black Burnished ware was an enormous task. It culminated with the publication of a major type series of over sixty vessel forms. One of the forms identified at Greyhound Yard is of specific interest to this paper. It was labelled 'Type 18' (Fig. 8.1), and defined (Seager-Smith and Davies 1993: 233) as a:

> Round-bodied, open bowl with everted rim and flat base; rim/neck/shoulder slipped and/or burnished; lower zone heavily wiped; narrow decorated band of diagonal lines, top right to lower left around girth.

Seager-Smith and Davies (1993: 233) drew attention to a number of 'Late Roman' parallels for this form from sites around Dorchester and suggested a third to fourth century date with the possibility that it might continue into the sub-Roman period. Other researchers have also commented upon the apparent 'lateness' of this form, most notably Holbrook and Bidwell (1991: 103), Sparey Green (1996: 123 and fn 7) and Lyne (2003: 71). Despite this there has been no overall synthesis that has looked specifically at this vessel form. It is hoped that the following discussion will rectify this situation.

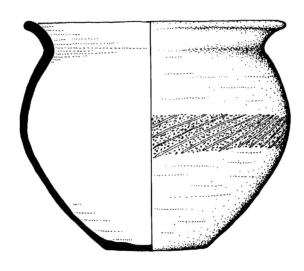

Fig. 8.1: A Type 18 bowl from Poundbury, Dorset (after Sparey-Green 1987: Fig. 88.41).

Before the distribution and dating of the Type 18 bowl can be considered some attention must be turned to the difficult issue of definition. Obviously Seager-Smith and Davies' (1993: 233) definition provides a starting point and Type 18 vessels labelled as such by Seager-Smith have been classed as 'definite' occurrences. Other sherds have been published which conform to the description and these have been also been included as definite examples. However, occasionally sites have produced only small sherds decorated with diagonal burnished lines, or the vessel form is correct but the published fabric description is ambiguous. These sherds have been classed as 'probable'. This distinction highlights the difficulties inherent in identifying this form. The identification of a Type 18 bowl is dependent on a large proportion of its vessel form being intact. A small sherd is indistinguishable from a fragment of Type 2 or Type 3 jar. Even the band of diagonal burnished lines is not sufficient to point to the presence of a Type 18 bowl as jars can also, on occasion, be decorated with this motif. Thus the identification of a Type 18 bowl is unfortunately dependent on the excavation of deposits containing either large sherds or alternatively (and less convincingly) groups of sherds decorated with just diagonal burnished lines.

The dating evidence for all of the reported Type 18 vessels has been summarised in Table 8.1. Obviously one of the main concerns of this study is dating and therefore considerable care has been exercised in constructing this table. The dates have, where possible, been described as coin based *termini post quos*. This is either derived from a coin in the underlying deposit or for a coin in the same context as the sherd being discussed. Where this has proved impossible to extract from the published report or alternatively where satisfactory contextual information does not exist then the excavator's phasing or description of the deposit has been given. Thus a sherd will ideally be dated to after AD 388-402 but it might be listed simply as coming from a 'Late Roman layer' with no further information available in the publication.

Although Table 8.1 provides a very useful summary of the dating evidence for each of the 'definite' and

Site Number and O.S. grid reference	Site name	Type of site	Definite or probable Type 18 vessel	Excavator's date for the context or phase	Reference
1. SY690900	Dorchester: Greyhound Yard (2 vessels)	Urban	Definite	AD350-450	Seager-Smith and Davies 1993: 233
2. SY690900	Dorchester: Hospital	Urban	Definite	very late Roman demolition rubble	Greene 1993: 89,100 and Fig. 19.32
3. SY690900	Dorchester: Library site, Colliton Park	Urban	Definite	post *c*.AD350	Aitken and Aitken 1982: 97, 104, 112 and Fig17.6
4. SY690900	Dorchester: bath house (2 vessels)	Urban	Definite	post *c*.AD388-402	Andrews forthcoming
5. SY680920	Poundbury, Dorset	Cemetery / settlement	Definite	probably post AD364-378 v. late Roman / early fifth century	Davies and Hawkes 1987: 124, 128 and Fig 88.41; Sparey-Green 1987: 63; 1996, 123
6. SY702899	Alington Avenue	Settlement	Definite	fourth century?	Seager-Smith 2002a: Table 18
7. ST500280	Worth Matravers, Dorset	Settlement	Definite	fourth century?	Seager-Smith 2002b: 53
8. ST500280	Worgret, Dorset	Industrial	Definite	late fourth century	Hearne 1991: 79, 88 and Fig. 13.30
9. SY935867	Redcliff, Dorset	Industrial	Definite	fourth century	Lyne 2003: 71 and Fig. 13.97
10. SX960880	Exeter, Devon	Urban	Definite	late fourth / early fifth century	Holbrook and Bidwell 1991: 103 and Fig. 29.21.1-3
11. ST500280	Catsgore: Catsgore (2 vessels)	Settlement	Definite	post *c*.AD360	Leech 1982: 166, 68, 22 and Fig. 109.422-3
12. ST500280	Catsgore: Well	Settlement	Definite	post *c*.AD364-378	Ellis undated: 25, 12, Fig. 11.13
13. ST480303	Bradley Hill, Somerset (2 vessels)	Settlement	Definite	post *c*.AD350 and post *c*.AD388-402	Leech 1981: 243,192, 243, 189 and Figs 22.50 and 23.122
14. ST450430	Brue Valley Mound XXXVII, Somerset	Industrial	Probable	fourth century	Leech 1977: 43 and Fig. 27.4
15. ST450430	High Ham, Somerset	Villa	Probable	unstratified probably late Roman	Leech 1977: 119 and Fig. 116.2
16. ST250400	Cannington, Somerset	Cemetery	Probable	loosely associated with Str 2. third to eighth century	Fulford and Williams 2000: 292-293
17. ST620430	Shepton Mallet, Somerset	Settlement / urban	Probable	Period 5 *c*.AD330-450	Evans 2001: 151 and 157; Leach and Evans 2001, 71-73
18. ST750640	Bath, Somerset	Temple / urban	Probable	post *c*.AD388-402	Cunliffe and Davenport 1985: 154-158 and Fig. 90.115
19. ST820760	Nettleton, Somerset	Temple / settlement	Probable	post *c*.AD388-402	Wedlake 1982: 87, 254 and Fig. 112.474
20. SU642535	Oakridge: well, Hampshire	Rural	Probable	Post *c*.AD364-367. Associated with late buckle.	Oliver 1992: 86, Fig 12.80

Table 8.1: Contextual data for Type 18 vessels

'probable' Type 18 sherds listed it does not take into account some of the more general aspects of the archaeological sequences on these sites. As an example of some of the subtle and not so subtle archaeological nuances which need to be considered a sub-sample of the sites listed will be discussed more generally. At Poundbury the Type 18 vessel was recovered from a pit, which may have formed a structural element of a late or early post-Roman timber building (Fig. 8.2). The pit seems to have been cut through a cobbled spread that sealed a Valentinianic coin. At Catsgore the Type 18 sherds came from 'occupation' layers sealing buildings in Complex 3. One of the buildings sealed coins of c.AD360 while other buildings in the complex produced Theodosian coins and Late Roman 'military' type metalwork (Leech 1982: 22). The site at Bradley Hill, not far distant from Catsgore, produced a clipped *siliqua* of Arcadius. Clipped coins are a facet of Britain's very Late Roman coin hoards such as Hoxne (Burnett 1984). In this

context it is interesting to note that two other items of material culture on this site point to post-Roman activity. The first is a small penannular brooch, thought by the excavator to be of first century date. It seems to be a Fowler D7, a type which Snape (1992) has argued might be of 'very late or sub-Roman' date. The second item is a glass bead from an inhumation burial. This artefact was best paralleled in fifth century Gallic contexts. Finally, we have the probable Type 18 vessel sherds from the inner precinct of the Temple of Sulis-Minerva at Bath. These sherds came from Period 5e, which contained a late 'military' type belt-fitting. The preceding period (5d) contained Theodosian coins. The excavators suggested that Period 5 at Bath could be very extended even stretching into the sixth century (Cunliffe and Davenport 1985: 74-75). This 'whistle stop' tour of only a handful of the sites listed on Table 8.1 hopefully gives a flavour of the 'very late' nature of some of these deposits and their associated Type 18 sherds.

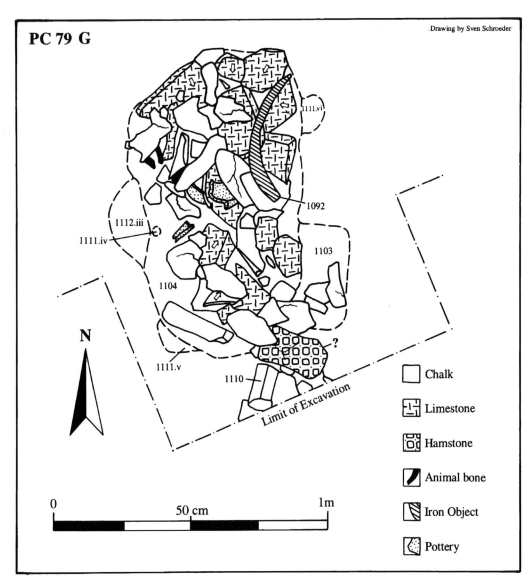

Fig 8.2: A Type 18 bowl fragment and iron scythe in the fill of a late pit at Poundbury (after an unpublished plan in the Dorset County Museum).

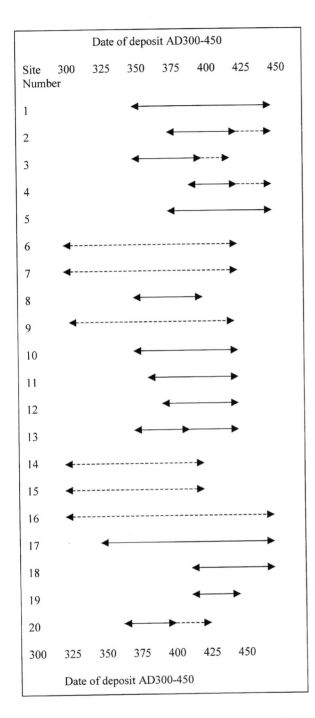

Fig. 8.3: The possible date ranges for the contexts Type 18 bowls are found in. Solid bars indicate definite ranges, dashed probable.

The problem for a study of this nature is reconciling the coin based *termini post quos* with less quantifiable data, such as an excavator's thoughts on the duration of a stratigraphic sequence. Fig. 8.3 is an attempt to undertake this challenge. A solid bar denotes a coin based *terminus post quem* or firm stratigraphic evidence of activity. A broken bar points to possible activity. Some will no doubt argue that such a diagram of 'date ranges' is methodologically flawed, based as it is on circumstantial

evidence. Yet that circumstantial evidence is the best that we have in the absence of coinage and radiocarbon assays and it should not be dismissed.

Taking the dating evidence presented in Table 8.1 it is clear that Type 18 bowls are a very late Roman Black Burnished form. The earliest evidence for the date of their production is provided by the absence of any examples from the northern frontier. This suggests a date of *c.*AD 350 for the start of production although a date after *c.*AD 375 is not impossible given the vagaries of coin based dating. The longevity of their production after AD 400 will be contentious. However, their occurrence in demonstrably post-Roman deposits is highly significant and points to their deposition in the first half of the fifth century. A programme of radiocarbon dating is currently underway on faunal material from deposits associated with probable Type 18 sherds at Bath. This may enable the tentative chronology outlined here to be refined in due course.

Perhaps of greater significance is the distribution of the bowl forms (Fig. 8.4). It includes most of the area nominally assigned to the 'Durotrigian *civitas*' with the occasional outlier. This suggests that during the currency of Type 18 bowls Black Burnished ware was still being transported over considerable distances. If the late and post-Roman date of these vessels is accepted then it also suggests that the late fourth century economic networks did not suddenly collapse in the early fifth. This leads us to an issue of even greater importance. The Type 18 bowl is a late form and it is also found with other Black Burnished vessel forms (Fig. 8.5). These include jars (Types 2 and 3), 'dog dishes' (Type 20) and dropped flange bowls (Type 25). If one accepts the late and immediately post-Roman date for Type 18 bowls then such a date also has to be assigned to these other vessels, the standard components of 'Late Roman' Black Burnished ware.

Conclusions

This paper has ranged widely from the historiography of Romano-British studies to specific facets of an unusual Black Burnished vessel form. The historiographical discussion has argued that our perceptions of the end of Roman Britain and its highly integrated market economy are inherently flawed. This flawed theory, when combined with the severe dating problems in the period, have foreshortened the use of Romano-British pottery and brought material culture falsely into line with the historical record. Whether the theoretical arguments presented here are accepted or not, the empirical study of the Type 18 bowl surely presents a body of data that points to Black Burnished ware's fifth century credentials. Hopefully, this synthesis will serve to highlight the importance of these pots and stimulate debate and interest in them and the supposed 'end' of

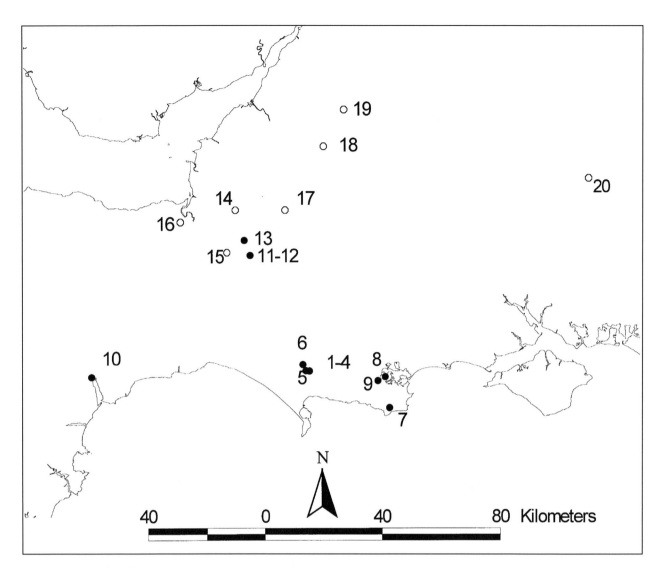

Fig. 8.4: A distribution map of Type 18 vessels in Britain. Filled circles represent definite examples, empty circles represent probable. For site numbers, see Table 8.1.

Black Burnished ware production. I hope that this study and others like it will offer new avenues through which Late Antiquity can be explored in south western Britain and other regions.

with permission. Sven Schroeder prepared Figures 8.1, 8.2 and 8.5.

Acknowledgements

I would like to record my thanks to Steve Roskams (University of York), Rachael Seager-Smith (Wessex Archaeology) and Christopher Sparey-Green (Canterbury Archaeological Trust) as well as numerous participants at the conference who influenced the arguments contained within this paper. I would also like to record my thanks to Dr. David Petts for highlighting the Fowler D7 brooch at Bradley Hill and Dr Margaret Snape for commenting on it. Any errors and misconceptions remain my own.

This paper was written during a period of research funded by the Arts and Humanities Research Board and it contains maps based on copyright digital map data owned and supplied by Harper Collins Cartographic and is used

Bibliography

Aitken, G. and Aitken, N. 1982. Excavations on the Library Site, Colliton Park, Dorchester, 1961-3. *Proceedings of the Dorset Natural History and Archaeological Society* 104: 93-126.

Alcock, L. 1995. *Cadbury Castle, Somerset: the early mediaeval archaeology.* Cardiff: Cardiff University Press.

Allen, J. and Fulford, M. 1996. The distribution of South-East Dorset Black Burnished Category 1 pottery in South-West Britain. *Britannia* 27: 223-282.

Andrews, G. forthcoming. The pottery, in D. Batchelor, *Excavations at the Bath House, Dorchester.*

Barker, P. 1993. *Techniques of Archaeological Excavation.* London: Batsford.

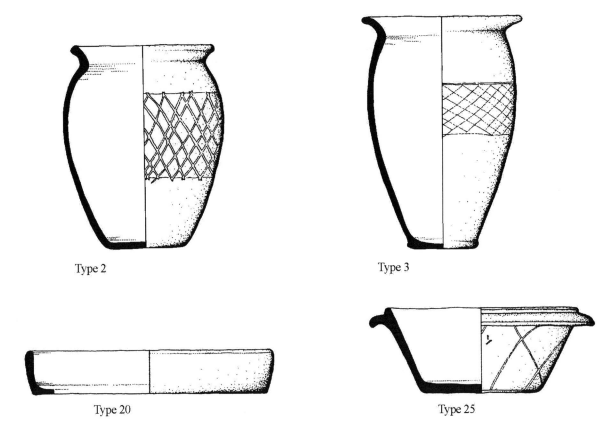

Type 2

Type 3

Type 20

Type 25

Fig. 8.5: Types 2, 3, 20 and 25 Black Burnished vessels (after Seager-Smith and Davies 1993: Figs. 122 and 123).

Brickstock, R. 2000. Coin supply in the north in the late Roman period, in T. Wilmott and P. Wilson (ed.), *The Late Roman Transition in the North*: 33-37. Oxford: British Archaeological Reports British Series 299.

Burnett, A. 1984. Clipped *siliqua* and the end of Roman Britain. *Britannia* 15: 163-168.

Childe, V. 1929. *The Danube in Prehistory*. Oxford: Oxford University Press.

Cox, P. and Hearne, C. 1991. *Redeemed from the Heath: the archaeology of the Wytch Farm oilfield (1987-90)*. Dorchester: Dorset Natural History and Archaeological Society Monograph 9.

Cunliffe, B. and Davenport, P. 1985. *Excavations at the Temple of Sulis Minerva, Bath Volume I: the site*. Oxford: Oxford University Committee for Archaeology Monograph 7.

Dark, K. 2000. *Britain and the End of the Roman Empire*. Stroud: Tempus.

Davies, S. and Hawkes, J. 1987. The Iron Age and Romano-British coarse pottery, in C. Sparey-Green, *Excavations at Poundbury Vol I: the settlements*: 123-128. Dorchester: Dorset Natural History and Archaeological Society Monograph 7.

Duncan Jones, R. 1974. *The Economy of the Roman Empire*. Cambridge: Cambridge University Press.

Ellis, S. undated. *Catsgore 1979: further excavation of the Romano-British village*. Bristol: Western Archaeological Trust.

Esmonde-Cleary, S. 1989. *The Ending of Roman Britain*. London: Routledge.

Evans, J. 1989. Crambeck: the development of a major northern pottery industry, in P. Wilson (ed.), *Crambeck Roman Pottery Industry*: 43-90. Leeds: Yorkshire Archaeological Society.

Evans, J. 2001. The Roman Pottery, in P. Leach and J. Evans, *Excavation of a Romano-British Roadside Settlement in Somerset: Fosse Lane, Shepton Mallet 1990*: 107-169. London: Britannia Monograph 18.

Faulkner, N. 2001. *The Decline and Fall of Roman Britain*. Stroud: Tempus.

Fulford, M. 1975. *New Forest Roman Pottery*. Oxford: British Archaeological Reports British Series 17.

Fulford, M. 1979. Pottery production and the end of Roman Britain: the case against continuity, in P. Casey (ed.), *The End of Roman* Britain: 120-132. Oxford: British Archaeological Reports British Series 71.

Fulford, M. and Hodder, I. 1975. A regression analysis of some late Romano-British pottery: a case study. *Oxoniensia* 39: 26-33.

Fulford, M. and Williams, D. 2000. Fabric H, black-burnished ware, in P. Rahtz *et al.*, *Cannington*

Cemetery: 292-293. London: Britannia Monograph 17.

Gerrard, J. 2001. Pots for cash? A critique of the role of the 'free market' in the late Roman economy, in M. Carruthers *et al.* (eds.), *Proceedings of the Eleventh Theoretical Roman Archaeology Conference*: 13-23. Oxford: Oxbow.

Gerrard, J. in prep. *Late Roman Britain in Transition: a ceramic perspective from south western Britain.* University of York Ph.D. Thesis (provisional title).

Gillam, J. 1976. Coarse fumed ware in northern Britain and beyond. *Glasgow Archaeological Journal* 4: 57-80.

Greene, J. 1993. Excavations at Dorchester Hospital (Site C), Dorchester, Dorset. *Proceedings of the Dorset Natural History and Archaeological Society* 115: 71-100.

Haverfield, F. 1912. *The Romanization of Roman Britain.* Oxford: Clarendon.

Hearne, C. 1991. Local coarse wares: Black Burnished wares (BB1), in C. Hearne and R. Smith, A Late Iron Age settlement and Romano-British Black Burnished Ware (BB1) production site at Worgret, near Wareham, Dorset (1986-7). *Proceedings of the Dorset Natural History and Archaeological Society* 113: 55-106.

Hearne, C. and Smith R. 1991. A Late Iron Age settlement and Romano-British Black Burnished Ware (BB1) production site at Worgret, near Wareham, Dorset (1986-7). *Proceedings of the Dorset Natural History and Archaeological Society* 113: 55-106.

Hinton, D. 2002. The Isle of Purbeck from the Norman Conquest to the Black Death, in D. Hinton (ed.), *Purbeck Papers*: 84-117. Oxford: Oxbow.

Holbrook, N. and Bidwell, P. 1991. *Roman Finds from Exeter.* Exeter: Exeter Archaeological Report 4.

Leach, P. and Evans, J. 2001. *Fosse Lane, Shepton Mallet 1990.* London: Britannia Monograph Series 18.

Leech, R. 1977. *Romano-British Rural Settlement in South Somerset and North Dorset.* Unpublished University of Bristol Ph.D. thesis.

Leech, R. 1981. The excavation of a Romano-British farmstead and cemetery on Bradley Hill, Somerton, Somerset. *Britannia* 12: 177-252.

Leech, R. 1982. *Excavations at Catsgore 1970-73.* Bristol: Western Archaeological Trust.

Lyne, M. 2003. The Late Iron Age and Romano-British pottery production sites at Redcliff, Arne and Stoborough. *Proceedings of the Dorset Natural History and Archaeological Society* 124: 45-99

Millett, M. 1990. *The Romanization of Britain.* Cambridge: Cambridge University Press.

Monaghan, J. 1995. Roman pottery research for the 1990s, in P. Rush (ed.), *Proceedings of the Second Theoretical Archaeology Conference*: 148-157. Avebury: World Archaeology Series 4.

Murray, T. 1999. *Time and Archaeology.* London: Routledge.

Oliver, M. 1992. Excavation of an Iron Age and Romano-british settlement site at Oakridge, Basingstoke, Hampshire, 1965-1966. *Proceedings of the Hampshire Field Club Archaeological Society* 48: 55-94.

Pollard, R. 1988. *The Roman Pottery of Kent.* Gloucester: Kent Archaeological Society Monograph 5.

Rahtz, P. *et al.* 1993. *Cadbury-Congresbury 1968-73: a late/post Roman hilltop settlement in Somerset.* Oxford: British Archaeological Reports British Series 223.

Rahtz, P. 2001. *Living Archaeology.* Stroud: Tempus.

Rahtz, P., Hirst, S. and Wright, S. 2000. *Cannington Cemetery.* London: Britannia Monograph Series 17.

Ryan, N. 1988. *Fourth Century Coin Finds from Roman Britain: a computer analysis.* Oxford: British Archaeological Reports British Series 183.

Seager-Smith, R. 2002a. Late Iron Age and Romano-British pottery, in S. Davies *et al.*, *Excavations at Alington Avenue, Fordington, Dorchester, Dorset 1984-87*: 93-106. Dorchester: Dorset Natural History and Archaeological Society Monograph 15.

Seager-Smith, R. 2002b. The pottery, in D. Hinton (ed.), *Purbeck Papers*: 45-56. Oxford: Oxbow.

Seager-Smith, R. and Davies, S. 1993. Roman Pottery, in P. Woodward *et al.*, *Excavations at Greyhound Yard, Dorchester 1981-4*: 202-299. Dorchester: Dorset Natural History and Archaeological Society Monograph 12.

Snape, M. 1992. Sub-Roman brooches from Roman sites on the northern frontier. *Archaeologia Aeliana Fifth Series* 20: 158-159.

Sparey-Green, C. 1987. *Excavations at Poundbury Vol I: the settlements.* Dorchester: Dorset Natural History and Archaeological Society Monograph 7.

Sparey-Green, C. 1996. Poundbury, Dorset: settlement and economy in Late and Post Roman Britain, in K. Dark (ed.), *External Contacts and the Economy of Late and Post Roman Britain*: 121-152. Oxford: Boydell Press.

Thompson, E. 1983. Fifth century facts? *Britannia* 14: 272-274.

Wedlake, W. 1982. *The Excavation of the Shrine of Apollo at Nettleton, Wiltshire, 1956-1971.* London: Society of Antiquaries of London Research Report 40.

Whyman, M. 1993. Invisible people? Material culture in 'Dark Age' Yorkshire, in M. Carver (ed*.), In Search of Cult: archaeological investigations in honour of Philip Rahtz*: 61-68. Woodbridge: Boydell.

Whyman, M. 2001. *Late Roman Britain in Transition: a ceramic perspective from East Yorkshire.* University of York Ph.D. Thesis.

Wickham, C. 1984. The other transition from ancient world to feudalism. *Past and Present* 103: 3-36.

Woodward, P. 1987. *Romano-British Industries in Purbeck*. Dorchester: Dorset Natural History and Archaeological Society Monograph 6.

Woodward, P., Davies, S. and Graham, A. 1993. *Excavations at Greyhound Yard, Dorchester 1981-4*. Dorchester: Dorset Natural History and Archaeological Society Monograph 12.

Young, C. 1977. *The Roman Pottery of the Oxford Region*. Oxford: British Archaeological Reports British Series 43.

9: Burial in Western Britain AD 400-800:
Late Antique or Early Medieval?

David Petts

The debate about the nature of British society, particularly western British society, in the 5th and 6th centuries is extensive. Generally speaking, it is possible to characterise two broad positions. Some see the end of Roman society in Britain as being 'nasty, brutish and short', arguing that the end of Roman political control in the early 5th century led to the removal of crucial aspects of the late governmental and fiscal infrastructure leading to a rapid collapse of what they characterise as the distinctly Roman social formations that linked Britain with the rest of the Western Empire (e.g. Esmonde Cleary 1989). Others have argued that whilst direct Roman political control ended in the early 5th century successor polities rapidly took up the reins of power (e.g. Dark 1994). Whilst the governing infrastructures may have been devolved to a regional or even sub-regional level they still survived in a form that might be seen as Roman in the broadest sense. This body of opinion has also stressed the Roman cultural inheritance of 5th century Britain, emphasizing both the continuity of aspects of 4th century Romano-British society and the maintenance of socio-cultural links with the Western Empire into the 5th century.

The notion of Late Antiquity has obviously appealed more to those in the latter camp than in the former. At its very broadest, Late Antiquity can be understood as the period from the traditional end of the Classical world in AD 284 with the end of the Principate and the beginning of the Dominate under Diocletian to the 7th century, which saw the rise of the Islam and the concomitant Arabic expansion; events which saw the final destruction of any Byzantine hopes of a reconquest of the West and its ultimate reduction to a Balkan rump. This 400 year period was also characterised by a fundamentally important social process, the move to monotheism, specifically Christianity, and more importantly the rise of the Church as a powerful corporate body. The entire relationship between state and religion was heavily reworked in this period. Partly as a consequence of the increasingly difficult relations (theologically, politically and, of course, physically) between the Western and Eastern churches the Christian world underwent a first 'Reformation' in the 7th/8th century leading to the formation of a distinctly Western European Christendom and marking the end of Late Antiquity (Brown 1978; Brown 1995)

This blurring of Late Antiquity as a simple chronological period and as one that described the rise of Christendom has led to a lack of clarity in the debate. Amongst many scholars, Late Antiquity has been used as a term that compliments Early Medieval – another term which can be used both to describe a chronological period (c.AD 400-

1000) and a cultural development (the rise of kings and kingdoms who traced their origins to the influx of non-Roman tribes from beyond the *limes* in the 4th and 5th century).

For many working on 4th to 6th century Britain the use of these terms tends to fall along academic boundaries. Many Romanists (and this is certainly a generalisation) see culture and society in 5th century Britain as very different from that found in the heyday of Roman Britain (usually characterised as fairly distinct package of villas, towns, temples and forts; see Faulkner, this volume). Scholars working primarily on Anglo-Saxon archaeology also see the material culture and social organisation of their areas of study as having clear links with Germanic cultures (though the extent to which this is caused by mass migration is another hotly contested topic). The notion of Late Antiquity and Roman continuity is perhaps most supported amongst those whose primary field of study is western Britain. This is perhaps because Christianity survived most strongly in this area and it is in the Church that we see most clearly both continuity of a Roman institution and continued links with the Roman Empire (attested textually, epigraphically and archaeologically).

Increasingly, there are wider calls for the term Late Antiquity to be used when studying Britain, even from scholars who have not traditionally been aligned with the 'continuity' school (e.g. Esmonde Cleary 2001: 97). Esmonde Cleary has pointed out that the use of the term has two advantages. It is an 'integrative discourse' bringing together many variables in the study of the period, crucially including archaeological and documentary evidence. Secondly, the Late Antique world is a large one, spreading from the Tigris to Thames, and it 're-integrates Britain with what is going on in the Continent' (Esmonde Cleary 2001:97). This paper attempts to place the burial rites found in late Roman and Early Medieval Western Britain in the context of this Late Antique world. It is up to the reader to decide whether the subject benefits from placing the evidence in this framework.

Burial in Western Britain

The 4th century

By the 4th century two broad burial traditions can be recognised in the archaeological record of Western Britain (Fig. 9.1). One (Group 1) is characterised by a west-east alignment, an extended body position and very few grave goods. Amongst this group an increasing use

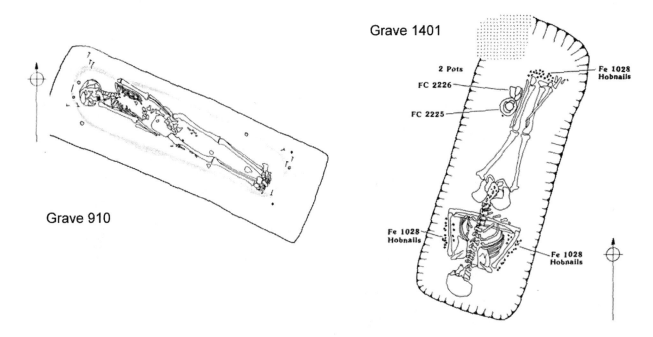

Figure 9.1: Typical Group 1 (left) and Group 2 (right) graves from Poundbury, Dorset (after Farwell and Molleson 1993).

of stone-lined graves and stone coffins can also be found. Some burials in this category were also placed, either individually or in groups, in small rectangular mausolea or grave enclosures. Good examples of such burials can be found at the Poundbury cemetery in Dorchester (Dorset), Ashton (Northants.) and Ilchester (Somerset) (Philpott 1991: 226-227).

Burials in the other group (Group 2) were more commonly placed on a north-south alignment, and frequently contained a range of grave goods, such as pottery vessels, coins, hobnailed shoes and boots and, for women in particular, a large number of low value jewellery items, such as bracelets, armlets and hairpins (Philpott 1991: 224-225). There was also a wider variety of burial position with crouched and prone burials being not uncommon. Another unusual rite found in this group of burials is post-mortem, ritual decapitation (Harman *et al.* 1981).

Although there are some occasional overlaps between these two contemporary burial practices, statistical work on these burials by Lucas Quensel-von Kalbern has shown that these mortuary rites were very distinct (Quensel-von Kalbern 2000). This analysis focused only attributes of the individual graves, but this clear distinction between the burial rites was also played out in their spatial organisation. Burials of the first group are often laid out neatly in rows, usually running north south. The graves show little evidence of intercutting; instead the individual graves clearly respect each other. These cemeteries have been termed 'managed cemeteries' by Charles Thomas (Thomas 1981: 232). They contrast with burials from the second group, which often show different patterns of organisation. For example, groups of

such burials may often cluster around a central burial. In general less emphasis is placed on the overall layout of the cemetery, but instead organisation and careful consideration of their physical relationship occurs at the level of individual clusters of graves. These patterns are not completely exclusive; in some cases cemeteries with graves which belong primarily to the first group and contain mainly well-ordered graves also include one or two clusters of the graves of the second group.

This can be seen at the cemetery at Poundbury, Dorchester (Farwell and Molleson 1993; see also Sparey-Green, this volume). This cemetery is of great importance in the study of Roman burial practice in Britain. Standing between the River Frome and a main road leading northwest from the town of *Durnovaria*, over 1400 burials were found during archaeological investigations between 1964 and 1980. Although a few late Iron Age and early Roman burials were discovered, most of the graves belong to the Late Roman period. The main body of the burials in the cemetery consisted of a group of around 1100 burials aligned west-east. Most of these were buried in wooden coffins and grave goods were largely absent. A number of burials were also buried in lead-lined or stone coffins. Included in this main group were the remains of at least eight stone built mausolea, decorated internally with painted plaster. These graves were well organised in north-south rows. Even the mausolea were integrated into this overall plan.

However, around the edges of this central cemetery a number of different groups of graves could be recognised. Some, such as the graves to the east of the main cemetery were aligned north-south and contained many grave goods. Grave goods were also common in the west-east aligned graves to the north of the main site, and in a number of other peripheral grave groups. To the southwest a number of roughly rectangular ditched enclosures were recorded. Unlike the mausolea, which contained several burials, possibly family groups, these enclosures contained only one central grave. In this they have stronger parallels with the ditched enclosures from the Lankhills cemetery at Winchester (Clarke 1979). Here, the central graves contained burials accompanied by high-status, and probably official, belt sets.

At Butt Road, Colchester, the cemetery stands to the southwest of the important Roman town of Camulodunum (Crummy *et al*. 1993). In Period 1, phase 3, probably dating to the early 4th century AD, a cemetery of burials aligned north-south was laid out over a site where a number of even earlier burials, including some cremations, had been placed sometime between the end

of the 1st century AD and the early 3rd century AD. Just over half of these early 4th century graves were accompanied by grave goods, including pottery vessels, personal adornments, such as armlets, and shoes. A number of clusters of graves could be recognised, and it was suggested that they might have been family groups.

Sometime between 320 and 340 the cemetery underwent a major reorganisation. Over 650 burials were placed in the new cemetery. Most were contained in timber coffins, though some were also placed in lead coffins. The burials from this phase were uniformly arranged broadly west-east, in rough north-south rows. Unlike graves from the preceding period, very few grave goods were found. The followers of this rite had enough power to prevent or at least discourage a continuation of early burial rites; forcing people to either convert to the new rite or bury their dead in an alternative site.

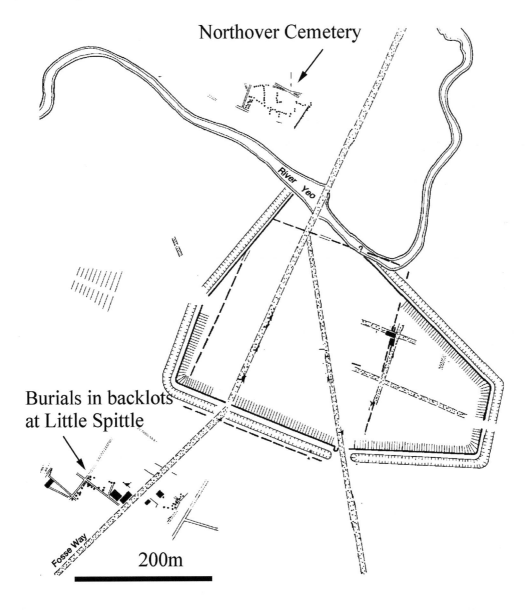

Figure 9.2: Spatial distinction of late Roman burial types: the cemeteries at Ilchester, Somerset (after Burnham and Wacher 1990).

The spatial separation within individual cemeteries, such as Poundbury, can also be seen within larger settlements. For example, at Ilchester (Somerset) two contemporary cemeteries have been recognised (Fig. 9.2) (Leach 1982). To the north of the town was the Northover cemetery; it was situated on the Foss Way which cuts through the town, just outside the North gate. The cemetery appears to have been founded *a novo* in the 4th century. Unfortunately the archaeological work on this site has been limited to a campaign of evaluation trenches. However, it appears that site was situated in an enclosure, with the southern boundary defined by the River Yeo and the eastern boundary defined by the Foss Way. During the process of evaluation only eight burials were excavated completely; however, other grave cuts were identified and the excavator suggested that up to 1500 burials could lie within the site. The graves were predominantly aligned west-north-west/east-south-east, although there were slight variations around this point, and there may have been some organisation into rows. Amongst graves identified was a double grave containing two lead coffins interred next to each other, another similar grave contained two stone coffins made from the local Ham Hill stone, with lead linings. At least three more stone coffins are known from the site, as well as fragments of at least five other lead coffins. Although the site certainly started sometime in the mid 4th century there is no firm date for the cessation of inhumation. The excavator suggests that it may well have been in use into the 5th century. To the south of the town were a series of Group 2 burials. Rather than being placed within an organised cemetery these were buried in the scattered groups in the backyards of a series of buildings placed along the Foss Way as it ran south from the town.

A similar pattern of the two burial rites existing at the same time can also be seen at nearby Shepton Mallet (Leach 2001). Here, excavations have shown the two different burial traditions in operation in adjacent enclosures. The main group consisted of seventeen burials aligned west-east; one burial in this group was placed in a lead coffin. However, elsewhere the burials were placed on a north-south alignment, some were buried face down and others were decapitated. The burials of this small community were split roughly equally between the two rites, which may have implications for the number of Christians in the locality.

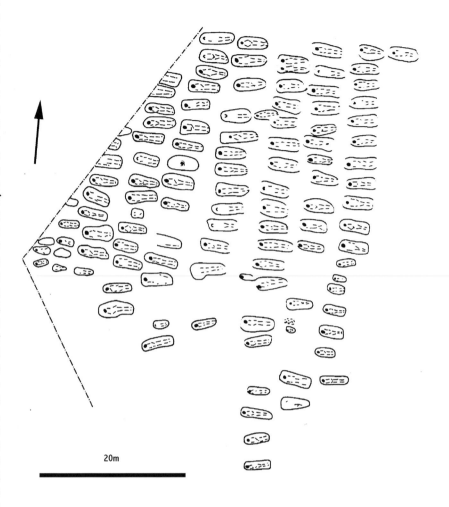

Figure 9.3: Roman 'managed' cemeteries: Ashton, Northants.

This pattern is not limited to the southwest of England. A similar situation has been found at Ashton (Northants.) (Fig. 9.3) (Frere 1984: 300; 1985: 288). Again there is a formal cemetery of west-east burials, which stands to the southwest of the town. Over 170 graves have been identified, and they indicate a high degree of organisation with the graves arranged in rows. The burials were laid out on their backs with no grave-goods, except two Constantinian coins associated with a young child. There were possible boundaries to the cemeteries to the east and north. There was skeletal evidence for the burial of children, infants and neonates. The dates for the cemetery are uncertain, but it seems to start some time in the early/mid 4th century. Other burials, some decapitated and many with grave goods were found elsewhere in the town, but mainly associated with individual roadside properties and enclosures. This spatial separation of the two burial rites has even been found within the same cemetery. At Poundbury, burials containing such rites as decapitation and prone burial were placed in peripheral areas of the managed cemetery.

Into the 5ᵗʰ century...

In the 5ᵗʰ century AD there are clear changes in the burial rites practiced in western Britain, though it is not clear precisely how they relate to the events surrounding the end of Roman political control around AD 410. These changes can be best understood by looking at the trajectories of the two broad burial rites outlined above.

The Group 1 tradition (west-east graves with very few grave-goods) undoubtedly continued to be widely used in the 5ᵗʰ and 6ᵗʰ centuries. Since Philip Rahtz's first exposition of what he called 'sub-Roman' burial rites (Rahtz 1968) a series of 5ᵗʰ to 7ᵗʰ century cemeteries have been excavated in Western Britain and Wales, including Cannington (Somerset), Henley Wood (Somerset), Vicarage Orchard Garden, Caerwent (Gwent) and Llandough (Vale of Glamorgan) (Rahtz *et al.* 2000; Watts and Leach 1996; Campbell and Macdonald 1993; Thomas and Holbrook 1995). Although many of these appear to have had their origin in the late Roman period they continue into the 6ᵗʰ/7ᵗʰ century and beyond. These are dominated by typical Group 1 graves. It is important not to pretend that these grave-goods are completely absent – the occasional object, such as a knife, are found in the burials, but the overall total is very different from Roman Group 2 burials or contemporary Anglo-Saxon burials further to the east.

However, one of the biggest challenges for archaeologists is identifying these small, Early Medieval cemeteries. The lack of grave-goods or other diagnostic dating criteria make it hard to correctly date such burials, as the broad west-east alignment and lack of grave-goods is known in other periods, including the Iron Age and mid to late Anglo-Saxon period (Geake 1992).

Geographically these burial sites are not found throughout south-west England and Wales but are limited to some of the areas of the province of Britannia Prima which had been most heavily Romanised in the 3ʳᵈ and 4ᵗʰ centuries AD, namely Somerset, Dorset and southeast Wales. These are all areas which had been heavily agriculturally exploited and in which large villa-estates were common. As in the 4ᵗʰ century, many of these cemeteries showed a degree of cemetery management. The graves were placed, more or less approximately, in rows. There are occasional focal graves, such as at Cannington, where slab-marked Grave Mound FT 26 initiated a small sequence of grave clustering around it (Rahtz *et al.* 2000: 124). However, the overwhelming impression gained in inspecting the plans of these cemeteries is a high degree of uniformity in the burial rite.

Further to the west in the more peripheral areas of the province in Wales and Cornwall the pattern of burial shows more variation. An increasing number of cemeteries are attested archaeologically in these areas (Petts 2001; Preston-Jones 1992; Nowakowski and

Thomas 1990; 1991; Murphy 1992; James 1987). It is clear that the dominant form of burial was again typical of Group 1 graves – the west-east alignment predominates and grave goods are largely absent. However, rather than this being an indicator of continuity in burial practice from the late Roman period this is instead an new introduction. Little is known about burial practice in Roman Wales and Cornwall, particularly away from the occasional Roman military sites. However, what little we do know suggests that simple cremation was probably used. There is no evidence that the inhumation practices discussed above were common in the late Roman period. Instead the advent of Group 1 burials is a clear indicator of an important shift in burial practices.

Differences can also be seen in the spatial organisation of these cemeteries. Clustered cemeteries are characterised by the presence of several groups of burials, usually containing between five and ten burials. They are distinguished from focal grave groups, by a lack of central focal burials around which the other burials are placed. In focal cemeteries the central graves are often emphasised through some form of above ground elaboration of the grave. At Tandderwen square barrows are used (Brassil *et al.* 1992), at Plas Gogerddan (Murphy 1992) the focal graves are placed in small rectangular fenced enclosures (Fig. 9.4) and at Kenn (Weddell 2000) the focal graves are within similar rectangular fenced or hedged enclosures.

A final, yet crucial, difference in the burial rite in these far south-western areas is the presence of an epigraphic tradition. The carved burial memorials of western and northern Britain are one of the most instantly recognisable aspects of the material culture of these regions in the Early Medieval period (Knight 1992). They are clearly derived from two distinct epigraphic traditions. The presence of ogham on many stones, particularly in southwest Wales and to a lesser extent in Cornwall is a clear indicator of southwestern Irish influence, and it is not surprising to find historical evidence for Irish immigration into these areas. However, a relatively small number of these stones are purely ogham-inscribed. Most carved stones are bilingual or purely in Latin. The range of formula used, particularly *Hic Iacit* (and its insular variant *Hic Iacet*), show clear parallels with the wider epigraphic tradition of the Western Roman Empire. Although Jeremy Knight has suggested that the main locus of parallels for these inscriptions could be placed in western Gaul (Knight 1992; 1996), Mark Handley has recently shown that the formula borrowed were found widely distributed across Western Europe and North Africa (Handley 2001). A final important point to note is that despite the occasional outlier (e.g. Silchester – Fulford *et al.* 2000; Wroxeter – Wright and Jackson 1968) this type of 5ᵗʰ century epigraphy was not used in the more distinctly sub-Roman areas of England. No convincing 5ᵗʰ-7ᵗʰ century epigraphy has been found in Dorset, Somerset east of the River Parrett and little in southeastern Wales. This suggest that

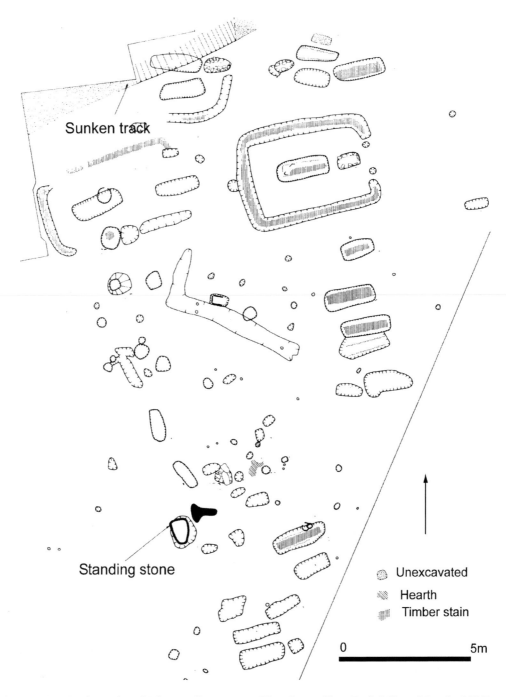

Sunken track

Standing stone

Unexcavated
Hearth
Timber stain

0   5m

Figure 9.4: Early medieval 'clustered' cemetery: Plas Gogerddan, Dyfed (from Murphy 1992).

the borrowing was taken direct from the Continent rather than *via* elsewhere in England. This, of course, raises the possibility that as the Group 1 burial rite was a seemingly also a contemporaneous introduction that it too may also have come from the Continent. It is at this point that we finally turn to the wider European burial evidence.

What's happening on the Continent?

If we are going to talk about the western British burial traditions in the 4th-6th century AD as being distinctly 'Late Antique', then it is important to understand contemporary burial practices elsewhere in the late Roman world. In northern Gaul the broad burial pattern appears to be similar to that in late Roman Britain, though here there appears to be a greater predominance of the grave-good rich Group 2 burials (Van Ossell 1993; Halsall 1992; Halsall 2000). This burial rite appears to have had a significant impact on the early 5th century *reheingraber* burials, which has traditionally been seen as being primarily a Germanic introduction. However, a reanalysis by Guy Halsall has shown the importance of the pre-existing late Roman rite (Halsall 1992). The belt-buckle sets which had long been seen as of Germanic workmanship are now better understood as typical Late Roman metalwork. Halsall detached his interpretation of the burial evidence from the prevailing 'ethnic' models and instead saw them as being caused by the high levels of tension and competition within late 4th and early 5th century society in northern Gaul. In contrast, he noted, these accompanied burials were not found south of the Loire, where the transition from Roman rule to Germanic kingship was more seamless.

However, despite the focus on these accompanied burials, graves more typical of the Romano-British Group 1 burials are known both north and south of the Loire. In the northwest of Gaul, in Brittany, the Group 1 tradition continued from the 4th century into the 5th and 6th century (Guigon 1994; Gailliu 1989: 59, 75). The burials are commonly aligned west-east and have few, if any, grave goods. A good example of such a site is Plomeur (Morbihan), where the graves are surrounded by stone cists (Guigon 1994: 47) It is thought that these burials date from the 5th/6th century onwards As in the western area of Britain these Breton cemeteries also utilised funerary epigraphy. These stones seem to have had closer stylistic affinities with the insular stones than contemporary Gaulish memorials.

Similar Group 1 burials are found spread widely across the rest of France. A cemetery at Faverdines (Cher) began in the earlier Roman period, but by the 4th century the cremation rite was succeeded by a series of west-east aligned burials in wooden coffins with no grave-goods (Fourleau-Bardaji et al. 1993). The rural cemetery at Pignans, Saint-Roche (Provence) was very similar in form, also of 4th and early 5th century date (Fig. 9.5) (Gébara and Pasqualini 1993: 355-357). Like many other 5th and 6th century AD cemeteries, some of the graves were placed in tile (tegula) 'tents' – these appear to be a local adaptation to the wider tendency to place burials in stone-lined graves. The rural church site at Saint-Maurice, Briord (Ain) is larger in size (Duvall 1998: 200-203). As at Faverdines, there was a phase of earlier cremations, but these were succeeded by Group 1 burials of 4th to 7th century AD date. Although better known for the huge number of Merovingian period stone coffins found at the site, the cemetery at Civaux (Poitou-Charentes) originated as a typical late Roman Group 1 cemetery (James 1977: 174-176, 421).

This type of burial is not just found in rural sites. Indeed, a half-hour browsing through the volumes of the Noël Duval's magisterial *Les premiers monuments chrétiens de la France* (1995) will bring to light many urban cemeteries of 4th-7th century date, often associated with churches, containing burials of this type. For example, the church of St. Georges, Vienne (Jannet-Vallat 1996) was associated with burials of this type, some in graves lined with stone or covered by large fragments of amphora. These dated, broadly to the 6th and 7th century. In Lyons many burials were found associated with the excavated

church sites, such as St. Just and St. Laurent (Reynaud 1998: 203-221). Although burial at these sites carry on beyond the 7th century AD, graves from the 3rd to 6th century are characterised by an emphasis on lining the burial, using stone coffins, tegulae and amphora. A similar Late Antique emphasis on this kind of grave lining has also been recognised elsewhere in the southeast of the country (Collardelle et al. 1996).

Further south in the Mediterranean these simple graves are found in Sardinia, such as at San Cromiazo, Villaspeciosa (Halsall 1995: 24) where they were associated with an early church building. Moving westwards into Spain similar burials can be found. For example, similar burials were found at Tarragona in the cemeteries at Parc de la Ciutat (TED'A 1987) and the Fabrica de Tabacos (Serra Vilaro 1928). In North Africa, these Group 1 burials also dominated in the Roman period. Several cemeteries have been found at Carthage. Over 50 burials were uncovered in excavations on the Theodosian Wall cemetery, many in tile and brick cists (Ellis et al. 1988). A similar cemetery of Vandalic date was found elsewhere in the city (Stevens 1995). The same burial tradition, using amphorae and tegula tents to protect the body has been discovered elsewhere in Tunisia, such as at Leptiminus (Ben Lazreg and Mattingley 1992). Further to the west similar graves have been found at Lambaesis, where sometime after AD 350 parts of the former military camp became a cemetery (Roskams 1995). Tegula tent burials were also observed by the author placed within the courtyards of suburban houses at nearby Timgad.

This quick 'Cook's Tour' of the burial rites of 4th-7th century Western Europe has focused on the evidence for Group 1 burials. As in England, there was also a parallel burial rite broadly derived from the burial rites of incoming Germanic groups. Despite a huge amount of regional variation, these burials rites, whether Anglo-Saxon, Merovingian, Visigothic or Vandalic all show some similarities. Most notably are their conformity to what Guy Halsall has called the 'usual gender rule' (Halsall 1995: 78). This is the tendency for some males to be buried with weapons; swords and shields for the richest, but spears and knives being more common. Meanwhile, women tend to be buried with a range of jewellery, usually in a position within the grave suggesting that they were worn on the body. As noted earlier, Halsall (1992) suggested that in northeast Gaul there is good evidence to suggest a late Roman influence on these burials. There are other hints of cross-fertilisation between these two ostensibly distinct rites, such as the use of stone sarcophagi and coffins made from plaster. Although the Late Antique period saw a flourishing of almost baroquely carved stone coffins in southern Gaul (e.g. Février 1991) – the practice of using elaborately decorated coffins, often made from plaster and cast from moulds, was taken up by the Merovingians (Delahaye and Périn 1991).

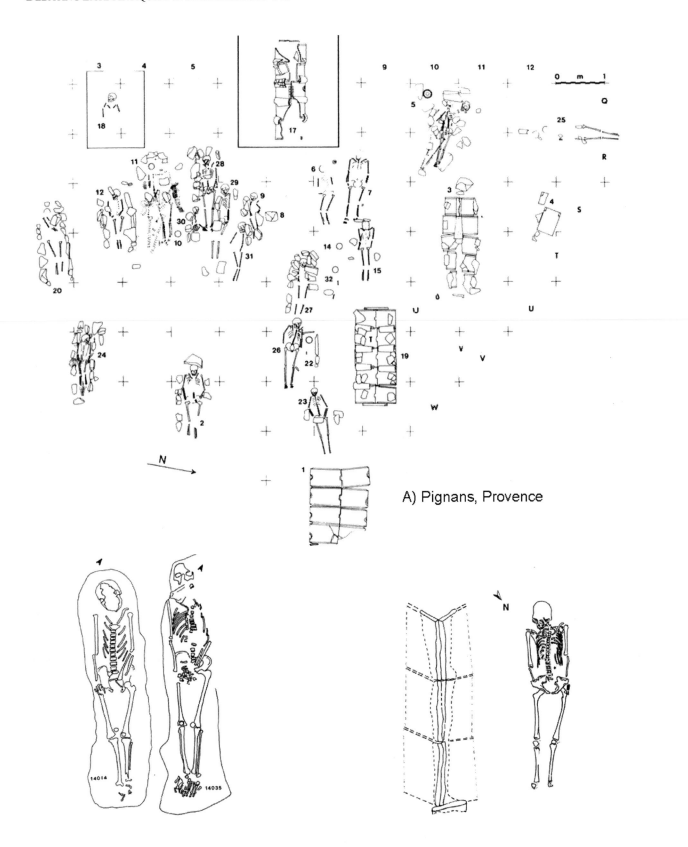

A) Pignans, Provence

b) Burials from the Theodosian Wall Cemetery, Carthage (Tunisia)

c) Burials from Leptiminus (Tunisia)

Figure 9.5: Late Antique burials in the Western Empire: a) from Gébara and Pasqulini 1993, b) based on Humphrey 1988, c) based on Ben Lasreg and Mattingley 1992.

Thus in the later Western Roman Empire, as in insular Britain, it appears possible to recognise two broad burial rites: Group 1 graves are aligned west-east, have few grave-goods and show evidence for an interest in protecting the body by use of coffins, cists and grave linings. In contrast, Group 2 burials are dug on a range of alignments and contain large numbers of grave-goods, usually following the 'usual gender rule'. In this respect, the evidence for Britain in the late Roman and Early Medieval periods clearly mirror contemporary burial rites in Western Europe. The distinction between the Group 1 burials in western Britain and the accompanied burials of Anglo-Saxon England was typical of the situation found on the Continent.

Conclusions

To briefly summarise, the burial rites in western Britain in the 5th-7th century certainly show distinct continuity from one of the two main late Romano-British burial rites. However, the Romano-British burial rite does not appear to survive in this area into the Early Medieval material. There are, however, hints that it went on to have some influence on the new Germanic style burial traditions which developed in eastern England.

This western British burial should not just be seen as the dying embers of a late Roman burial tradition, reflecting a sub-Roman conservatism. Instead, the evidence from the Continent shows that these burials are typical of one of the more widely spread 5th/6th century burial rites found in the Western Empire and its successor states. The possibility that this is merely a case of fortuitous parallel evolution rather than a product of direct communication between the mainland and the Insular West is refuted by the clear evidence that the Early Medieval epigraphic tradition is a clear 5th century introduction, borrowing directly from Gaul, North Africa and Spain. This archaeological evidence for continued communication between the two areas is buttressed by ample historical evidence for continued trade, social and political relationships between insular Britain and the rest of Europe (e.g. Thomas 1990; Knight 1996; Wooding 1996).

So is this a Late Antique burial rite? As always with such matters it depends upon the definition of Late Antique chosen. Nonetheless, we see here a burial rite that is widely spread across the area that would become Western Christendom, and appears to have been used primarily by communities of Christians. It appears to contrast with a distinct, furnished burial rite used primarily by incoming Germanic migrants and the social groups who associated themselves with them. These two rites are contemporary, so the term 'Late Antique' should certainly not be used as a simple period definition. However, the work of Peter Brown and others has shown that in the 5th-7th century there was a certain common Christian culture that permeated many areas of Western Europe. Whilst some aspects of this may have been restricted to the educated echelons of society, elements of this culture package, such as religious worship and burial practice appears to have become widely spread throughout all strata of society. The evidence shows that there was of course wide regional variation, but the common thread was strong. To label this rite as 'Christian' whilst broadly true would lead to problems; burial traditions in the Christian areas of the Eastern Empire were very different (Kyriakakis 1974), and the placement of grave-goods, particularly pottery vessels was common.

This paper, and indeed the conference at which it was presented, had the express intention of exploring whether the notion of Late Antiquity was a useful one when writing about the archaeology of the transition from Roman to Early Medieval Britain. Whilst, terms such as Late Antiquity are ultimately just labels, they do have a greater power. By helping to shape our frames of reference and connecting the evidence with alternate discourses in the archaeology of the period, they have the potential to open up the way in which we talk about the past. This paper has shown that if we look at the burial rites of 4th-7th western Britain in the context of the wider Roman world, we can start to recognise a wider *koine* or community of burial in the late Western Roman Empire. There are of course, many variations and counter-currents within the archaeological record, but despite this it is clear that these traditions are part of a vibrant and developing Late Antique burial rite and not the moribund and conservative rites of an isolated sub-Roman polity.

Bibliography

Ben Lazreg, N. and Mattingley, D. 1992. *Leptiminus (Lamta): A Roman Port City in Tunisia Report No.1.* Ann Arbor: Journal of Roman Archaeology Supplementary Series 4.

Brassil, K., Owen, W. and Britnell, W. 1992. Prehistoric and early medieval cemeteries at Tandderwen, near Denbigh, Clwyd. *Archaeological Journal* 148: 46–97.

Brown, P. 1978. *The Making of Late Antiquity.* Harvard.

Brown, P. 1995. *The Rise of Western Christendom: Triumph and Diversity 200-1000.* Oxford.

Burnham, B. and Wacher, J. 1990. *The 'Small Towns' of Roman Britain.* London: Batsford.

Campbell, E. and Macdonald, P. 1993. Excavations at Caerwent Vicarage Orchard Garden 1973: an extra-mural post-Roman Cemetery. *Archaeologia Cambrensis* 142: 74–98.

Clarke, G. 1979. *Pre-Roman and Roman Winchester - Part ii: The Roman Cemetery at Lankhills.* Oxford.

Colardelle, M., Démians D'Archimbaud and Raynaud, C. 1996. Typo-chronologie des Sépultures du Bas-Empire à la fin du Moyen-Age dans le Sud-Est de la Gaule, in H. Galinié and E. Zadora-Rio (eds.), *Archaeologie du Cimietière Chrétien:*

270-99. Tours: 11ᵉ Supplément à la Revue Archéologique du Centre de la France.

Crummy, N. and Crossan, C. 1993. Excavations at Butt Road Roman Cemetery, 1976–9, 1986 and 1989, in N. Crummy, P. Crummy and C. Crossan, *Colchester Archaeological Report 9: Excavations of Roman and Later Cemeteries, Churches and Monastic sites in Colchester*: 4–163. Colchester.

Dark, K. 1992. Epigraphic, art-historical and historical approaches to the chronology of class 1 inscribed stones, in N. Edwards and A. Lane (eds.), *The Early Church in Wales and the West*: 51-61. Oxford: Oxbow Monograph 16.

Dark, K. 1994. *Civitas to Kingdom.* Leicester.

Delahaye, G-R and Périn, P. 1991. Les sarcophages mérovingien, in N. Duval (ed.), *Naissance des arts Chrétiens. Atlas des Monuments Palaéochrétiens de la France*: 288-306. Paris.

Duval, N. 1995-8. *Les premiers monuments chrétiens de la France.* Paris.

Ellis, S., Humphreys, J. and Marshall, J. 1988. The Theodosian Wall and the Cemetery 1982-3, in H. Humphrey (ed.), *The Circus and Byzantine Cemetery at Carthage Vol.1*: 179-257. Ann Arbor.

Esmonde Cleary, S. 1989. *The Ending of Roman Britain.* London.

Esmonde Cleary, S. 2001. The Roman to medieval transition, in S. James and M. Millett (eds.), *Britons and Romans: Advancing an archaeological agenda*: 90-97. London: Council for British Archaeology Research Report 125.

Farwell, D. and Molleson, T. 1993. *Poundbury Volume 2: The Cemeteries.* Dorchester: Dorset Natural History and Archaeological Society Monograph Series 11.

Gébara, C. and Pasqualini, M. 1993. Sepultures et cimetières ruraux en Provence orientale a l'epoque gallo-romain, in A. Ferdiere (ed.), *Monde de Mort, monde des vivants en Gaule rurale*: 341-66. Tours.

Février, P. 1991. Les sacrophages décorés du Midi, in N. Duval (ed.), *Naissance des arts Chrétiens. Atlas des Monuments Palaéochrétiens de la France*: 270-287. Paris.

Fourleau-Bardaji, A-M., Marinval, P., Ruas, M-P. and Marguerie, D. 1993. La nécropole gallo-romaine des Vernes à Faverdines (Cher), in A. Ferdière, *Monde de Mort, monde des vivants en Gaule rurale*: 265-271. Tours.

Frere, S. 1984. Roman Britain in 1983. *Britannia* 15: 265–332.

Frere, S. 1985. Roman Britain in 1984. *Britannia* 16: 251–317.

Fulford, M., Handley, M. and Clarke, A. 2000. A New Date for Ogham: the Silchester Ogham Stone Rehabilited. *Medieval Archaeology* 44: 1-23.

Gailliou, P. 1989. *Les Tombes Romaines d'Armorique.* Paris.

Geake, H., 1992. Burial practice in seventh- and eighth-century England, in M. Carver (ed.), *The Age of Sutton Hoo*: 83-94. Woodbridge.

Guigon, P. 1994. *Les Sépultures du Haut Moyen-Age en Bretagne.* Rennes, Patrimoine Archéologique de Bretagne.

Halsall, G. 1992. The origins of the *Reheingräberzivilisation*: forty years on, in J. Drinkwater and H. Elton (eds.), *Fifth-Century Gaul: A Crisis of Identity*: 196-207. Cambridge.

Halsall, G. 1995. *Early medieval Cemeteries: An Introduction to Burial Archaeology in the Post-Roman West.* Glasgow.

Halsall, G. 2000. Burial customs around the North Sea, in A. Pentz, *The Kings of the North Sea.* Newcastle.

Handley, M. 2001. The Origins of Christian commemoration in late Antique Britain. *Early Medieval Europe* 10 (2): 177-99.

Harman, M., Molleson, T. and Price, J. 1981. Burials, bodies and beheadings in Romano-British and Anglo-Saxon cemeteries. *Bulletin of the British Museum: Natural History (Geology)* 35/3: 145–88.

James, E. 1977. *The Merovingian archaeology of south-west Gaul.* Oxford: British Archaeological Reports International Series 82.

James, H. 1987. Excavations at Caer, Bayvil, 1979. *Archaeologia Cambrensis* 136: 51–76.

Jannet-Vallat, M. 1996. L'organisation spatiale des cimetières Saint-Pierre et Saint-Georges de Vienne (IVᵉ-XVIIIᵉ siècle), in H. Galinié and E. Zadora-Rio (eds.), *Archaeologie du Cimietière Chrétien*: 125-37. Tours: 11ᵉ Supplément à la Revue Archéologique du Centre de la France.

Knight, J.K. 1992. The Early Christian Latin Inscriptions of Britain and Gaul: Chronology and Context, in N. Edwards and A. Lane (eds.), *The Early Church in Wales and the West*: 45-51. Oxford: Oxbow Monograph 16.

Knight, J.K. 1996. Seasoned with Salt: Insular-Gallic contacts in the early memorial stones and cross-slabs, in K. Dark (ed.), *External Contacts and the Economy of Late Roman and Post-Roman Britain*: 109-120. Woodbridge.

Kyriakakis, J. 1974. Byzantine burial customs. *Greek Orthodox Theological Review* 19: 37–72.

Leach, P. 1982. *Ilchester Volume 1: Excavations 1974–5.* Bristol.

Leach, P. 2001. *Excavation of a Romano-British roadside settlement in Somerset: Fosse Lane, Shepton Mallet, 1990.* London.

Murphy, K. 1992. Plas Gogerddan, Dyfed: A Multiperiod Burial and Ritual Site. *Archaeological Journal* 149: 1–39.

Nowakowski, J. and Thomas, C. 1990. *Excavations at Tintagel Parish Churchyard, Cornwall, Spring 1990: Interim Report.* Truro.

Nowakowski, J.A. and Thomas, C. 1991. *Grave News from Tintagel: An Illustrated Account of*

Archaeological Excavations at Tintagel Churchyard Cornwall 1991. Truro.

Petts, D. 2001. *Burial, religion and identity in sub-Roman and early medieval Britain: AD 400–800.* Unpublished University of Reading Ph.D thesis.

Philpott, R. 1991. *Burial Practices in Roman Britain: A Survey of Grave Treatment and Furnishing.* Oxford: British Archaeological Reports British Series 219.

Preston-Jones, A. 1992. Decoding Cornish Churchyards, in N. Edwards and A. Lane (eds.), *The Early Church in Wales and the West*: 104-124. Oxford: Oxbow Monograph 16.

Quensel-von Kalbern, L. 2000. Putting Late Roman Burial Practice (from Britain) in context, in J. Pearce, M. Millett and M. Struck (eds.), B*urial, Society and Context in the Roman World*: 217-230. Oxford.

Rahtz, P. 1968. Sub-Roman Cemeteries, in M. Barley and R. Hanson (eds.), *Christianity in Britain 300–700*: 193-195. Leicester.

Rahtz, P. Hirst, S. and Wright, S. 2000. *Cannington Cemetery.* London: Britannia Monograph Series 17.

Reynaud, J. 1998. *Lugdunum Christianum: Lyon du IVe au Ville. Topographie, necropolis et edifices religeux.* Paris: Document d'archéologie Française 69.

Roskams, S. 1995. Late- and post-Roman Lambaesis: recent work within the 'Camp de l'Est', in T. Wiedeman (ed.), *North Africa from Antiquity to Islam*: 25-29. Bristol.

Serra Vilaró, J. 1928. *Excacaviones en la necrópolis romano-cristiana de Tarragona: memoria.* Madrid.

Stevens, S. 1995. A Late Roman Urban Population in a Cemetery of Vandalic date at Carthage. *Journal of Roman Archaeology* 8: 263–271

TED'A. 1987. *Els Enteraments del Parc de la Ciutat: La Problemàtica Funerària de Tàrraco: Memòires d'Excavació 1 Taller Escola D'Arqueologia.* Tarragona.

Thomas, A. and Holbrook, N. 1995. *Excavations at Great House Farm, Llandough, Cardiff, South Glamorgan: A Preliminary Report.* Cirencester.

Thomas, C. 1981. *Christianity in Roman Britain to AD500.* London.

Thomas, C. 1990. *Gallici Nautae de Galliarum Provinciis* – A Sixth / Seventh Century Trade with Gaul Reconsidered. *Medieval Archaeology* 34: 1-26.

Van Ossel, P. 1993. L'occupation des campagnes dans le nord de la Gaule Durant l'antiquité tardive: l'apport des cimetières, in A. Ferdière (ed.), *Monde de Mort, monde des vivants en Gaule rurale*: 185-96. Tours.

Watts, L. and Leach, P. 1996. *Henley Wood: The Romano-British Temples and a Post-Roman Cemetery: Excavations by E Greenfield and others between 1960–68.* London: CBA Research Report 99.

Weddell, P. 2000. The Excavation of a Post-Roman Cemetery Near Kenn. *Proceedings of the Devon Archaeological Society* 58: 93-126.

Wooding, J. 1996. *Communications and Commerce along the Western Sealines AD400-800.* Oxford: British Archaeological Reports International Series 654.

Wright, R.P. and Jackson, K.H. 1968. A late inscription from Wroxeter. *Aniquaries Journal* 48: 296–301.

10: Artefacts in Early Medieval graves: A new perspective

Howard Williams

Introduction

As ethnographies frequently show, there are innumerable reasons why mourners might place artefacts in the graves of the dead (Ucko 1969). Yet in the last two decades, early medieval archaeologists and historians have developed a broad theoretical consensus to explain the practices of furnished burial found across Anglo-Saxon England and Merovingian Gaul between the fifth and seventh centuries AD. Whereas the burial of grave-goods has been traditionally addressed in terms of chronology, ethnic groups and religious beliefs, recent approaches have focused on the social, symbolic and ideological interpretations of early medieval graves.

This paper will review some of the key themes of these recent studies of early medieval mortuary archaeology. It will be argued that recent studies of early medieval social structure, symbolism and ideology have offered many new insights and have numerous theoretical strengths over earlier culture-historic and processual paradigms. However, the paper aims to demonstrate that this current orthodoxy conceals some inherent theoretical weaknesses. In particular, it is suggested that studies of grave goods need to reconsidered in the light of recent discussions of personhood and social memory. As a case study for developing this idea, a new interpretation of the artefacts placed in early Anglo-Saxon cremation burials will be presented. The frequent burial of toilet implements (tweezers, shears and razors either buried singly or in combinations) and bone and antler combs had mnemonic as well as symbolic roles in the post-cremation rites. Rather than primarily acting as a symbolic 'text' intended to be displayed and 'read' by mourners, these small and relatively unobtrusive items functioned in bodily presentation and maintenance through their use to arrange, pluck and cut hair. These were items linked to the shifting biography of the deceased during their life cycle and subsequently connected in mortuary practices with the reconstitution of a new 'body' for the deceased following death. In this sense, their addition to the post-cremation burial deposit was concerned with the fragmentation and transformation of the deceased's personhood in dual strategies of selective remembering and forgetting in which their symbolic associations focused on transforming rather than displaying identities.

Theorising Early Medieval Burial – the last twenty-five years

Following trends in prehistoric archaeology, the late 1970s and 1980s saw the influence of processual or 'New' archaeology upon early medieval archaeology.

These new approaches perceived graves as a valuable source of evidence for reconstructing the changing socio-economic organisation and complexity of past societies. By identifying variability in the quantity and quality of artefacts placed with the dead, the society of the living might be reconstructed (e.g. Arnold 1980; 1982; Shepherd 1979). These studies developed in parallel to legal and social interpretations of burial by Continental scholars (see Effros 2003; Härke 2000; James 1989). Very quickly, social approaches were augmented by further studies inspired by the structuralist and neo-Marxist critiques of the New Archaeology focusing upon the investigation of symbolism and ideology from mortuary remains. By the 1990s, it could be said that these approaches constituted a new 'orthodoxy' in the study of early medieval burials. Admittedly this orthodoxy is not strict and embraced many elements of both traditional and processual perspectives (see Scull 1993). Yet many of these 'post-processual' and 'contextual' approaches focus on five key inter-related strands of thinking.

First, many studies developed upon the quantitative methodologies and social approaches of the processual studies yet moved beyond seeing mortuary practices primarily in terms of status differentiation (e.g. Huggett 1996; Lucy 2002). Instead, research has addressed the multidimensional nature of grave-goods in revealing both vertical and horizontal social differentiation and social identities. The symbolic representation and social construction of age (Crawford 2000; Richards 1987) and gender categories (Brush 1988; Lucy 1998; Stoodley 1999) have become fashionable topics in recent research. Meanwhile other studies have re-appraised studies of early medieval households (Härke 1997a), communities (Lucy 1998) as well as regional and ethnic identities through burial analysis (Arnold 1980; Fischer 1988; 1995; Härke 1990; Lucy 2002). However, studies of status and rank (popular among processual approaches) continue to have a bearing on discussions of social structure and social change (Carver 2000; Härke 1997a; Stoodley 1999). The provision of artefacts with the dead is consequently recognised as influenced by complex social factors as well as by geographical and chronological variations (see Stoodley 1999).

Second, while some of these studies continue to attempt to 'read-off' social organisation or structure in a direct way from the burial record (with the proviso that it may not completely reflect the social organisation of the living community but an idealised community of the dead), others have recognised that the situation might not be that simple (Samson 1987). Instead of pursuing 'social organisation', it has been recognised that the burial record is a symbolic and ritualised medium in which social organisation is masked and mediated by a symbolic grammar based on contemporary ideologies (see Pader 1982; Härke 1997b and d; Richards 1987; 1992; 1995). Graves have therefore been regarded as symbolic texts that were intended to be 'read' by mourners (Halsall 1998; Pader 1982). This agenda promoted the view that an understanding of the complex symbolism of grave-goods requires both quantification and the careful focus upon the archaeological and social contexts of graves and cemeteries (Lucy 1998; 2002; Pader 1982).

Third, a related component of these studies is that early medieval mortuary practices were as much concerned with the ritual performances of the living than the deceased's identity. From this perspective, mortuary practices are contexts for social display functioning to legitimise political power and social identities. In other words, funerals were seen as displays of conspicuous consumption concerned with the society of the living rather than the fate of the deceased in which artefacts were buried with the dead by and for mourners and onlookers (e.g. Halsall 1998; Samson 1987).

Fourth, if material culture employed in mortuary practices is active, symbolic and used in ritualised contexts to display a materialised ideology, then it allows mortuary practices to be regarded as an important arena in which society reproduces itself. Some studies have gone further still in addressing the meanings of the symbolic statements made in mortuary practices and their broader socio-political and ideological significance. It has been argued that artefacts placed with the dead may symbolise and actively promote identities as well as broader conceptions of the world including origin myths and statements of political affiliation. In this sense, mortuary practices are concerned with constructing group identities rather than the display of the deceased's position in society. Death rituals are equally as much about connecting the past and present as with portraying an idealised social order (Carver 2000; Härke 1997b).

Finally, although many researches have complimented traditional enquiries into migration, cultural identity, kingdom formation and conversion, a central issue of many 'post-processual' and 'contextual' approaches has been the critical appraisal of earlier studies. In particular, the culture-historic paradigm that dominated traditional Anglo-Saxon archaeology has been a target of sustained criticism (Lucy 1998; Williams 2002). While not denying the historicity of population movements and ethnic groups in the past, recent accounts have been strongly critical of attempts to identify cultures and ethnic groups directly from the burial record. In many ways, this is a perspective that was inherited directly from the New Archaeology's focus on static systems theory and social evolution and its negative attitudes towards explaining culture-change in terms of migration and diffusion (see Arnold 1997). It also can be seen in relation to socio-political trends in Britain (Härke 1998).

Artefacts - Society, Symbolism and Ideology

One might cite numerous case studies to illustrate these five developments in recent early medieval mortuary archaeology but some of the more detailed and insightful studies may be mentioned by way of example. Heinrich Härke's study of the symbolism of weaponry in early Anglo-Saxon graves demonstrated the complex and shifting social and symbolic associations of weapons in relation to age, gender, status and ethnicity when placed in (predominantly) male burials of the fifth to seventh centuries AD (Härke 1990). Building upon Härke's work, Nick Stoodley (1999) has studied the costume of child and female burials using a similarly large sample of cemeteries. Equally, the seminal study by Julian Richards focused on the symbolism of pottery forms and decoration in early Anglo-Saxon cremation burials. This study provided an example of how quantitative methodologies can be employed in theorising the complex meanings of vessels for the cremated dead (Richards 1987). Meanwhile, Guy Halsall's discussion of ritual and social display in the Merovingian graves of the Metz region served to demonstrate the meaning of the deposition of grave-goods as well as the role of artefacts in helping to 'stage' the public performance of funerals (Halsall 1998). Both Halsall and Sam Lucy have used themes derived from social theory to critique traditional culture-historic interpretations of the furnished burial phenomenon (Lucy 1998; 2002). The symbolic significance of grave goods has been recently explored by Martin Carver in his discussions of the rich assemblage of artefacts buried in the late sixth and early seventh-century barrow cemetery of Sutton Hoo in Suffolk (Carver 2000). He argued that graves operated like poetry; through its theatrical composition and display it was intended to be seen and 'read' by mourners (see also Halsall 1998). Both burials and poetry in the early Middle Ages were public ritual performances, intentionally contacting layers of meaning and manifold allusions and associations within an elite ideology. Consequently, rich burial assemblages such as those interred within the mound 1 ship burial at Sutton Hoo contained many different, perhaps even contradictory, associations and meanings for those viewing or experiencing them. Like Halsall's textual analogy, Carver's poetic analogy helped him to support his argument that the artefacts buried at Sutton Hoo formed part of an ideological message promoting political affiliations. In combination these different studies provide us with a wealth of new perspectives with which to reappraise and appreciate the socio-political significance of early medieval furnished burial rites.

Early Anglo-Saxon Cremation Rites

So far we have seen how discussions of social structure, symbolism and ideology have been popular and fruitful approaches to the study of early medieval graves.

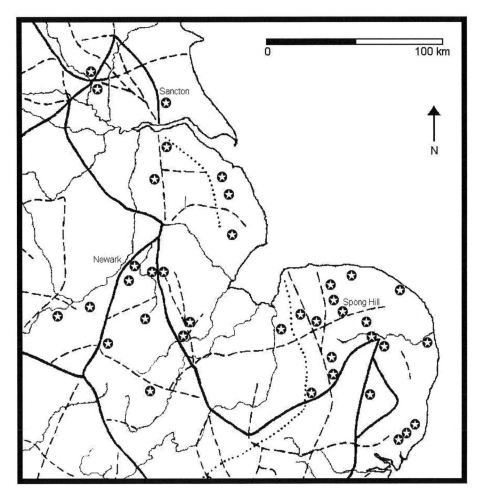

Figure 10.1: Distribution map of early Anglo-Saxon cemeteries in which cremation rites are the predominant method of disposal highlighting the sites of Newark, Sancton and Spong Hill where extensive excavations provide the richest data employed in this study.

Although the majority of these studies have focused upon the study of inhumation rites, this work has also inspired research into the early Anglo-Saxon cremation burials, including my own doctoral research (Williams 2000). The large urn-fields of hundreds and sometimes thousands of cremation burials dating to the fifth and sixth centuries AD form a discrete cluster in the 'Anglian' regions of Anglo-Saxon England, namely East Yorkshire, the East Midlands and East Anglia (Fig. 10.1). The cremation burial rites vary within and between cemeteries (see Richards 1987), although they usually consist of the shallow burial of a ceramic container bearing decoration often consisting of a range of inscribed, bossed and stamped motifs. Inside these urns were placed the cremated remains of one or sometimes two persons together with the burnt remains of sacrificed animals and a range of broken, burnt and distorted 'pyre goods'. Sometimes unburned artefacts, usually toilet implements or combs, were placed in the graves with the ashes. These 'grave goods' will be the central focus of this paper (Fig. 10.2).

The traditional approach to these burials has been to regard them as the clearest possible evidence of intrusive and immigrant Germanic groups settling in eastern England during the fifth century AD (e.g. Myres 1969). Recent studies by Catherine Hills have developed upon this work by showing the close parallels between the cremation rite and artefacts from the Spong Hill cemetery and cremation cemeteries from northern Germany and southern Scandinavia (Hills 1993). Meanwhile, social and symbolic approaches to early Anglo-Saxon cremation burials have been pioneered by the work of Julian Richards (1987) and Mads Ravn (1999) who employed quantitative and statistical analyses to identify patterns in the provision of urns and artefacts in relation to the identity of the deceased. This important work has been facilitated by invaluable osteological research, most recently those by Jackie McKinley and Julie Bond at Spong Hill and Sancton (McKinley 1994; Bond 1996; Timby 1993). The initial aim of my doctoral research was to build on these studies by providing a thorough study of mortuary variability in the early Anglo-Saxon cremation burial rite. The research also attempted to compliment the quantitative studies of the early Anglo-Saxon inhumation rites undertaken at the University of Reading by Heinrich Härke (1990) and Nick Stoodley (1999).

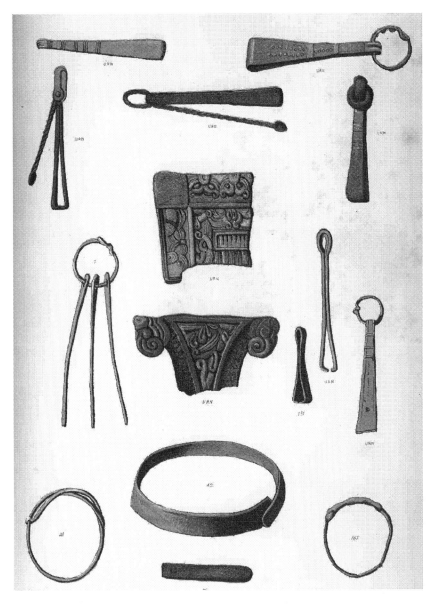

Figure 10.2: Toilet implements have been recognised in early Anglo-Saxon cremation and inhumation graves from antiquarian studies to the present day. This illustration is from R.C. Neville's 1852 publication Saxon Obsequies reporting finds from excavations at Little Wilbraham in Cambriddgeshire (after Nevill 1852).

osteological reports (e.g. Myres and Green 1973; see Hills 1980). Moreover, a number of the key sites that in future it is hoped will contribute numerous insights into early Anglo-Saxon cremation rites, were unavailable for study. Despite these problems, good data was obtained for the cemeteries of Newark (Kinsley 1989), Sancton (Myres and Southern 1973; Timby 1993) and Spong Hill (Hills 1977; Hills and Penn 1981; Hills *et al.* 1987; Hills *et al.* 1994).

As my analysis of the cemeteries developed, it was possible to identify patterns in the provision of artefacts and sacrificed animal remains in relation to the age and sex of the cremated human remains suggesting that the identity of the deceased had a bearing on the treatment that they received in death. For example, certain artefacts tended to be found with one gender. Tweezers for instance were more commonly found with males, and brooches with females. Equally, other items tended to occur with certain age categories as in the case of bone and antler combs where different types of comb were most commonly associated with distinctive age categories (Williams, forthcoming). At first it appeared that my study would concur with J.D. Richards (1987) and Mads Ravn (1999) that we can read a symbolic representation of social structure in the mortuary variability of the cremation graves.

Yet what was equally clear, as Richards (1987) has already noted, was that many of the aspects of mortuary variability found in the cremation rite were different from those recognised in contemporary furnished inhumation graves from eastern England (see Fischer 1988; 1995; Lucy 1998; 2002). For instance, the range and frequency of artefacts buried in cremation graves overlaps with, but is markedly different from, those interred in inhumation graves. For instance, whereas jewellery and weapons are common in inhumations, they are rare in cremation graves (Williams in prep). Meanwhile, toilet implements and combs are often discovered in cremation burials, but are only rare occurrences in inhumation graves (Williams, forthcoming). Moreover, while a series of correlations in the provision of both pyre- and grave-goods with the

My research entailed the compilation of a database of over five thousand cremation graves from across England (with the invaluable assistance of data already amassed electronically by Catherine Hills for the Spong Hill cemetery). Analysing this data was a methodological challenge. As well as my own limitations in handling large bodies of data using statistical methods there were also considerable problems with both the quality and quantity of the evidence. At an early stage I recognised that while publications had improved since the time of Julian Richards' study, many of the cemeteries available remained too poorly published to be of use in a quantitative social analysis. In particular, many of the older excavation reports lacked contextual data as well as deceased's social identity could be suggested, patterns were far less clear-cut in the cremation burials than in contemporaneous inhumation rites (e.g. Härke 1990; Stoodley 1999). For example, horses were most commonly sacrificed with young males at the Spong Hill cemetery, but horse sacrifice could accompany almost every age and gender category (Williams 2000). Social distinctions were clearly recognised in the treatment of the dead, but many of the rites appear ubiquitous rather than exclusive to particular identity groups.

Cremation as ritual technology

It was clear that, in addition to the methodological problems that the analysis faced, a theoretical problem had presented itself concerning the role of artefacts in the cremation rites of early Anglo-Saxon England. Why were patterns less clear and were manifest in the provision of different types of artefact in cremation burials than in contemporary inhumation graves?

There are two obvious responses to this problem. The first is rather naive and takes the evidence at face value and yet is often found in the academic literature. The argument goes that if it is difficult to reconstruct social identity, or the patterns are too complex to be identified, then perhaps the cremation burial context was not an important context for displaying social identities. In other words, those early medieval communities who cremated their dead did not emphasise identity in the same way as groups inhuming their dead. While archaeologists might often avoid studying cremation rites because of the seemingly richer opportunities for reconstructing social structure and symbolism from the inhumation graves (e.g. Crawford 2000), absence of evidence need not be evidence of absence (*contra* Brush 1988).

The second approach is more logical because it takes into account the ritual technology of cremation and its effects on human remains and artefacts. Rather than absence of evidence being evidence of absence, it might be argued that the cremation process could have destroyed many of the artefacts that were used to symbolise the dead. Consequently, we are unable to see the use of mortuary practices to symbolise and display social identities and social differentiation that had taken place prior to cremation. Patterns might equally be obscured by the fact that a minority of cremation burials contained multiple individuals. There is even the possibility that pyre-sites were re-used. Both processes might hinder the association of artefacts with discrete dead individuals and conceal potential patterns more easily perceived in the inhumation rite (Richards 1987).

This argument is linked to the assertion that, as McKinley (1994) correctly states, cremation in past societies would have involved many stages in a complex ritual sequence. These might include the preparation of the corpse, the building of the pyre, the procession to the cremation site,

sacrifice of animals, feasting and drinking rituals, and finally the 'composition' of artefacts and the body on the pyre. Following the cremation itself, rites might include the collection of the ashes, their transportation, burial and the subsequent building of a funerary monument to commemorate the dead. After the funerary sequence is completed, there may have existed further commemorative rituals focusing on the home, religious sites and the place of cremation and/or burial during seasonal ceremonies and anniversaries of the death. During these ritual practices, the deceased was transformed into an ancestor, or at least a member of the community of the dead (see Huntingdon and Metcalf 1991). Meanwhile, the entire ritual process may have been punctuated with a range of other social and religious exchanges, acts of sacrifice, songs, dance; in short, ritual performances serving to negotiate the changing relationships between the living and the dead. Hence, attempting to understand mortuary practices purely on the basis of the remains buried in the ground might be seen as a challenging and intractable task. From this perspective, issues of archaeological visibility are enough to explain the lack of clear patterns in the cremation data from fifth- and sixth-century England.

Going one stage further, it has been suggested by some archaeologists that the act of burying the cremated remains was of relatively limited importance in the funerary sequence. Instead it was the display of the dead with artefacts upon the pyre *before* the cremation that created an impressive public spectacle in which the wealth, status and identity of mourners and the deceased were promoted, negotiated and legitimised (see McKinley 1994). In particular, the laying out of the dead, clothed and surrounded by objects and sacrificed animals represents a comparable 'image in death' to that provided for onlookers surrounding an inhumation grave before back-filling (Bond 1996; McKinley 1994; see Carver 2000; Halsall 1998). Indeed, it seems evident from the osteological analysis of McKinley (1994: 83) for Spong Hill and Sancton that only token amounts of bone and artefacts were selected from the pyre for subsequent burial, giving us a distorted view of the range of artefacts and materials displayed with the dead.

Therefore social identity may have been important and it must be remembered that despite the distorting effect of the cremation there remain some clear patterns in the provision of pyre- and grave-goods in the cremation burials supporting this view. From this perspective it is simply the nature of the ritual technology of cremation that makes these patterns more difficult to identify in the archaeological record.

Artefacts and the Cremation Process

The first impression of this author's ongoing research was that the 'haziness' of the patterns did not reflect the reality of social identities in early medieval communities (explanation one) but instead concerned the complex nature of the ritual technology of cremation (explanation two). Yet for a number of reasons the choice of artefacts found in the post-cremation rite demanded further explanation. Certainly the ritual technology of cremation is the reason that patterns might not be as clear as in inhumation contexts, but this interpretation overlooks the social and ritual significance of cremation and post-cremation rites in past communities. Given the marked contrast in the experience and engagement between the living and the physical remains of the dead facilitated by cremation, it needs to be considered that inhumation and cremation created different ways of defining identities involving marked distinctions in the functions and symbolism of portable material culture.

This approach leads to an exploration of the possibility that our *expectation* of being able to see patterns in the provision of artefacts in graves as in inhumation graves may have been theoretically misplaced. This might be because our approach is based on the false premise that the artefacts – even those showing correlations with sex and age – were *primarily* present to communicate and display idealised elements of the deceased's identity. This is not to say that the deceased's identity was not important in the funeral (*contra* Brush 1988) nor is it claimed that identity was deliberately hidden by a masking ideology of equality created by the cremation rite (see Parker Pearson 1982). Instead, it is suggested that the artefacts were operating in a different way to current theoretical expectations.

Consequently, in order to understand artefact deposition in cremation graves, it becomes necessary to move beyond seeing the lack of clear patterns in artefact deposition as a problem of methodology, data quality, the irrelevance of the burial context in the funerary sequence or the effects of a masking ideology. Instead, having begun to investigate the implications of cremation as a ritual technology, it becomes important to theorise the roles of artefacts in this process. If cremation was simply about the social display of identity upon the pyre as McKinley suggests, then why were artefacts selected for burial at all? In fact, why were any of the ashes retrieved, handled, placed in a container, transported and burial in a communal cemetery? If the cremation was the element of social display of identity that mattered, then there seems little logic to these protracted rituals. In short, social display of an idealised identity for the deceased through material culture is a partial explanation at best when dealing with artefacts placed in cremation graves. Equally, if the outcome of early Anglo-Saxon cremation rites was a partial, distorted and fragmented assemblage of bones and artefacts, then this must surely have been an intended and often-repeated outcome of the ritual sequence. Post-cremation rites must therefore have held social significance within the society that experienced this rite. The decision to collect, transport and bury these fragmentary remains needs to considered to be a social and cultural option that requires our theoretical interest

rather than being dismissed as taphonomic and ritual 'noise' preventing our full recognition of early Anglo-Saxon social structure and ideology. This involves regarding cremation as not concerned with *representation* but instead with *transformation*. It also requires a move in focus from an emphasis on symbolism to social memory: strategies of remembering and forgetting.

Death and Social Memory

Death can be conceptualised and theorised in many ways, but more than any other it concerns the social, cosmological and ontological negotiation of relationships between the living and the dead. The key component linking mortuary practices to the identities of the living and the dead is the medium of social memory. Recent years have seen a burgeoning interest in anthropological and sociological studies of material culture and social memory (Hallam and Hockey 2001; Küchler 2002). These approaches have been adopted and adapted in a range of recent archaeological studies of death and memory in the prehistoric and historic past, providing a broad framework with which to apply these ideas to early medieval mortuary practices (e.g. Eckardt and Williams 2003; Fowler 2003; Jones 2001; 2003; Meskell 2003; Williams 2001). Social memory is what links death and identity, the ability to remember and forget elements of the deceased's life and social relationship and transform them into a manageable and coherent order. In many societies remembering involves the transformation of the deceased's memory from a dangerous ghost into that of a benign ancestor (Huntingdon and Metcalf 1991). In any particular society, different social categories of the dead can be provided with contrasting social memories. Social remembrance can involve the retrospective commemoration of how the dead were in life, or it can involve prospective memories of how the dead are perceived upon death or in an afterlife existence. Furthermore, social memory can be constructed and reproduced in many ways (see Küchler 2002). We often think about memory through commemorative practices of inscription (see Connerton 1989) such as obituaries, photographs and gravestones. Yet social memory can also operate through bodily practices of incorporation. Moreover, portable material culture and the human body can be central to the ways in which past societies remembered, particularly in pre-literate societies (but see Joyce 2003). The treatment and association of objects with the body can help to configure the way the dead are remembered and (equally) forgotten (see Hallam and Hockey 2001; Williams 2001).

In this light, cremation, a ritual technology focused on the transformation of the deceased's corporeality, can be understood as a technology of remembrance. Cremation breaks down the integrity and form of the body in a rapid display. The post-cremation rites of many societies are aimed at subsequently re-building a 'second body' for the

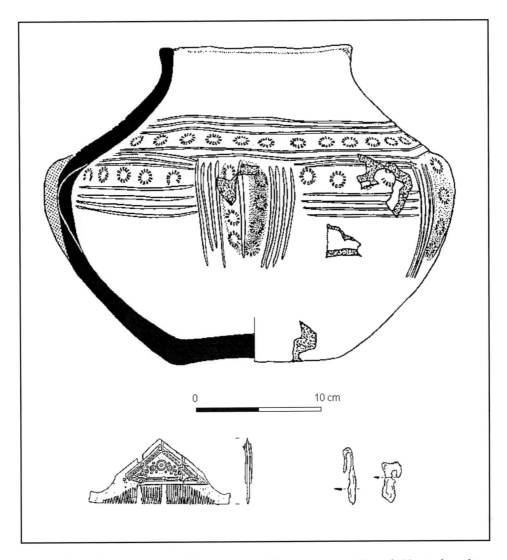

Figure 10.3: Cremation burial 204 from the Millgate cemetery, Newark, Nottinghamshire (redrawn after Kinsley 1989: 138). The urn contained the remains of an adult male, red deer antler, a composite triangular antler comb, iron shears, iron blade, as well as fragments of red glass and bronze (Kinsley 1989: 52).

deceased (Serematakis 1991). This process can serve in the selective remembering of the deceased and the network of relationships with the living through which the social person was constructed and maintained. This 'reconstitution' of the dead is a process of remembering aspects of the deceased as they were in life, but also one of forgetting by making the dead fit into archetypal and idealised identities appropriate for their new status as an ancestor or member of the community of the dead.

In this sense, portable artefacts were involved in the 'memory-work' of the funeral, a process in which the various material and physical elements of the deceased's personhood are reconfigured and arranged as a means of promoting, displacing and dispersing different social memories. Symbolism certainly played a part in this process and could be an effective means of remembering the dead. However, we also need to consider the role of objects as having mnemonic agency (their ability to both reflect and enact remembrance) through their presence, use and alteration in funerary contexts rather than simply

by referencing or signifying abstracted social attributes. In other words, remembrance might be achieved through symbolic representation in a direct way (*i.e.* by deploying artefacts to display or articulate aspects of social or ethnic identity), yet equally, objects might influence remembrance through their materiality and transformation. Artefacts might operate as symbols but also, as the anthropologist Alfred Gell has argued, objects might be seen as indexes (secondary agents) of social persons. In this sense, artefacts can be seen as extensions of the deceased's identity and having a social agency of their own (Gell 1998: 13-14; 96-154). In the early medieval funerary context, we might envisage this to mean that the artefact's deployment initiated the impact of its 'agency' (and indirectly the agency of the mourners) over the transformation of the dead body from living person to dead person. Moreover, the experience and engagement with both artefacts and the corpse during the funeral provided them with an agency to influence and direct the memories of funerary participants and mourners. Therefore, objects can be seen as symbolising identities but also as operating alongside mourners in strategies aimed at changing the body's social, cosmological and ontological state through selective remembrance. In addition, they can be considered to be indexes or extensions of the body and constituting elements of the deceased's personhood (Gell 1998; Hallam and Hockey 2001). Inspired by these theories, we can re-appraise artefacts in early Anglo-Saxon cremated graves as mnemonic devices serving in social remembrance through their close association with the dead body.

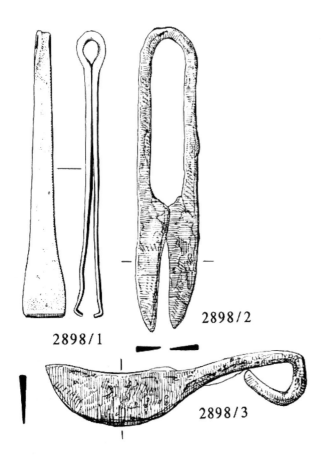

Figure 10.4: Toilet set consisting of bronze tweezers, miniature iron shears and miniature iron razor from cremation burial 2898 excavated at Spong Hill, Norfolk (after Hills, Penn and Rickett 1994: 211). Reproduced by kind permission of Ken Penn and Norfolk Museums and Archaeology Service.

Pots, Toilet Implements, Combs and the Body's Transformation

This argument is born out when we consider the nature of the artefacts associated with the cremated dead. Many items found in cinerary urns are clearly objects of costume that show the effects of heat and fire from the cremation. While many items would have been destroyed by the cremation, it appears that often items were

deliberately selected out of the pyre for inclusion with the post-cremation rites. Therefore, there was an intentionality in the process of collecting that is separate from the process of building the pyre and piling artefacts and materials onto it prior to cremation. Moreover, new objects were deliberately associated with the dead in the early Anglo-Saxon post-cremation rites. The most frequent unburned items found in cremation graves are the cinerary containers themselves. It remains unclear whether these richly and (sometimes) bizarrely decorated vessels were made especially for the funeral, or selected for their qualities from among pots used in the domestic setting, but it does appear that they differ from the normal range of domestic assemblages found in early Anglo-Saxon settlements (Richards 1992). Moreover, as Richards (1987) has argued, the identity of the deceased seems to have had a bearing on the form and decoration of the pot selected to contain the remains of the dead. Leaving aside the details of this variation (see Richards 1987), we need to ask what these objects were doing in the post-cremation rite after the spectacle of the burning pyre was long passed? Unlike cremation rituals in our societies, the early Anglo-Saxon cremation rite placed great emphasis upon the urn as container for all of the human and animal bone. In this sense, urns provided a new 'body' for of the deceased, and the decorated surface of the urn articulated a new 'skin' for the dead (see ManiBabu 1994).

A range of other items were selected and added to the assemblage in the post-cremation rites prior to burial. These are commonly classed as 'toilet implements' consisting of bronze and iron tweezers, razors and blades, shears and earscoops, some of them full-sized functional objects, other miniatures possibly serving as amulets among the living or specially made for the funerary ritual (Figs. 10.3-5). Another extremely common 'grave-good' were fragments of bone and antler combs (Williams, forthcoming). If the cremation was the important part of the public display social identity to the large assembled audience, why were these small, sometimes miniature, objects added to the ashes before burial? Certainly objects whose meanings are either deliberately ambiguous or consciously concealed from view can provide an alternative way of communicating identities, yet the post-cremation rite seems to contrast markedly with the pre-cremation display of the corpse. An explanation may lie in the possible role of artefacts in constructing a new 'body' for the dead in the post-cremation rites. Looking again at the combs and toilet implements as objects that had a role in a technology of transformation, it is both their functional and symbolic associations that gave them a role in refashioning rather than representing the deceased's body and hence his or her social identity in death. What is particularly interesting about these artefacts is that they are objects closely linked to the management of the body's surface during life. Combs in early medieval society were probably used to remove lice, prepare head and beard hair and may have formed parts of daily washing rituals.

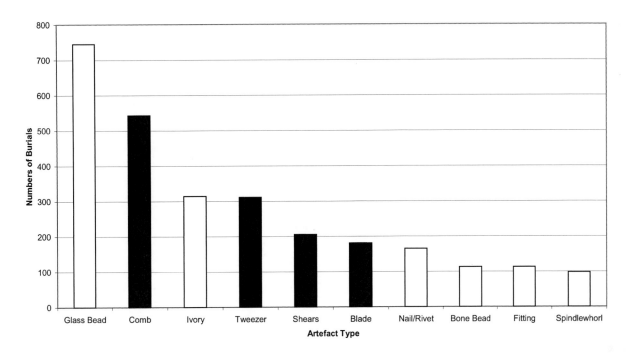

Figure 10.5: Top-ten most frequently occurring artefacts from early Anglo-Saxon cremation burials – objects usually placed on the pyre (pyre goods) in white, items that are selected especially for the grave (grave goods) in black.

These were personal activities, but they may have been performed by the individual or perhaps by slaves, servants or family members. Consequently these were not simply items of personal vanity, they were objects enmeshed in technologies of the self that connected social conventions of bodily appearance and adornment with intimate social practices, possibly involving the participation of others. Toilet implements can be understood in the same broad context. These were items that could have been used to pluck hair (tweezers), shave hair (razors) and cut hair and nails (shears). They are mainly found in adult cremation graves of both genders and may have been connected to the presentation of the deceased during physical and social maturity in early Anglo-Saxon society.

It is also worth noting that hair is often provided with magical associations in numerous societies including those from early medieval Europe (Williams, forthcoming). Not only is hair important in the presentation of the body and the constitution of identity, changes in regimes of hair management can be employed to articulate shifts from one identity to another during rites of passage (see Leach 1958). Toilet implements and combs may have even been used to prepare the hair of the body during the earlier stages of early medieval funerals. Therefore, these are items connected to the transformation of hair which in turn is frequently connected to the representation and transformation of identity. In this sense, combs and toilet implements could have held a special role in death rituals for both mourners and the deceased in reconfiguring memories and identities.

The significant point to make is that while similar items have been found in inhumation graves of the fifth and sixth centuries, antiquarians and archaeologists have long recognised that they are far more commonly found in cremation graves (Lethbridge 1951). While taphonomic factors might explain the greater survival of antler and bone combs in cremation graves where they are protected by a ceramic container from the erosion of the ground, this does not explain the high frequency of both bronze and iron toilet implements in cremation burials. Clearly, the management of the body's surface, and the treatment of hair held a particular significance in relation to the post-cremation rituals of early Anglo-Saxon England. At first this appears to represent a paradox: objects associated with hair placed in a cremation burial long after the hair had been destroyed by the funeral fire. Yet this very paradox may explain their meaning. Rather than seeing these as non-functional by either being miniature or impractical and by being placed with burnt ashes, they may have been items intended to articulate the construction of a new body's surface in the post-cremation rite. The very destruction of the body's surface during cremation both enabled and required the building of a new body, and the most effective way to articulate this may have been to place artefacts of hair-management in the grave.

Sustaining the argument is the notable absence of artefacts with other associations. The items most commonly seen as integral to the construction and display of personal and group identity – jewellery and weaponry are rarely found in early Anglo-Saxon cremation graves.

Practical explanations do not seem to explain their absence. It might be argued that the low frequency of brooches could be because these were objects that were most likely to be damaged beyond recognition by the cremation pyre since in inhumation graves they are often found attached to the costume on the torso region. Yet for other items there appears no similar explanation. It could be argued that swords were too large to be placed in an urn but this does not explain the absence of small spearheads, fragments of shield-boss, knives and the lower than expected frequency of buckles. On balance it appears that these artefacts were removed because of their significance in symbolising the deceased's social identity in life. They may have been frequently placed on the pyre only to be collected with the ashes and removed elsewhere. These items may have been too closely connected to the deceased's identity to emphasise the transformation that the cremation was intended to achieve (Williams, in prep.).

This argument suggests that a deliberate and intentional selectivity took place in the items and objects placed with the dead in the post-cremation rites. The objects interred were not merely the vestiges of an earlier impressive spectacle randomly shovelled into pots for rapid and secretive burial. Nor were they items that would have easily proved useful in impressive and elaborate social displays and in symbolising social identities to a wide audience. It is instead argued that the symbolism was concerned with transformation, and rather than solely with signifying aspects of identity. The concern was with objects acting as indexes or 'secondary agents' of the mourners serving to symbolise and enact the reconstitution of a social memory and identity of an ancestral identity that was distinct from the deceased's identity in life.

Discussion

As argued above, we have seen the rise of a new orthodoxy in the study of early medieval mortuary practices that has moved away from the identification of cultures, religious beliefs and social organisation to the discussion of death ritual in terms of social structure, symbolism and ideology. These theoretical approaches provide rich new possibilities for understanding the active and transforming effect of mortuary practices in shaping identities and socio-political structures against a background of rapid change. However, it is the contention of this paper that these perspectives can be themselves subject to critique. In particular this paper has highlighted some of the problems with focusing upon social display and attempts to read graves as symbolic texts. It might be suggested that, while valuable, these perspectives tend to place undue focus upon the socio-political strategies of the living rather than the close and intimate mnemonic engagements between the living and the dead during mortuary practices. It must be emphasised that this ongoing debate is a necessary and

healthy element of discussions of early medieval graves. Moreover, these arguments are aimed to compliment and augment rather than to dismiss earlier interpretations.

The sequence of pre-cremation activities, the cremation itself, and the post-cremation treatment of the cremated material can be interpreted in a new way. Inspired by, but contrasting somewhat with the views of scholars such as Pader (1982), Halsall (1998) and Carver (2000), cremation operated as a mnemonic technology rather than a symbolic text (see also Fowler 2003; Jones 2003). Indeed, the failure of recent studies of mortuary archaeology to understand cremation may lie in the expectations and assumptions derived from the study of inhumation burials concerning display and representation. As a theoretical approach, these ideas may have implications for understanding artefacts in early Anglo-Saxon cremation graves. Moreover, this may not simply be a viewpoint relevant to understanding the artefacts associated with cremation, since the inhumation rite might represent a comparable technology of transformation, but one that took a different trajectory. In both rites, artefacts could be used to symbolise social identities, but they were also operated as indexes (Gell 1998), objects with agency that articulated the shifting material form of the deceased's personhood through the funerary process through their close association with the corpse. In other words, both rites involved the careful staging of display, concealment and the translation and transformation of bodies and objects in acts of remembrance (see Williams 2001).

The specific implications of these arguments for our understanding of furnished burial in early medieval Britain require reiteration. If artefact placement in graves is not only (or primarily) about social display through the creation of a ritual tableau for mourners to see, then we need to think much more carefully about which artefacts are placed in graves and why. For cremation graves, it is argued that the artefacts such as combs and toilet implements have a mnemonic rather than a symbolic role. They serve to reconstitute a new body for the dead to encourage their selective remembrance and they are hence concerned with *transforming* memories rather with *representing* identities. The repeated burial of cremation urns in the same location over decades and even centuries allows us to understand the significance of placing relatively small and modest objects in graves. By creating new identities for the dead and fixing them in specific burial locations used by many different social groups, the histories and identities of these communities were closely linked to the place and the past. This was not achieved through raising permanent monumental tombs to the ancestors, but through the careful transformation of the deceased into a new ancestral form through the dissolution and reconstitution of their corpses and the deposition of mnemonic artefacts. From this perspective, cremation was repeatedly enacted using similar artefacts in order to construct of a community of ancestors who may have been believed to be closely and intimately connected to the living. Perhaps prior to the rise of the Christian cult of saints, the dead in early Anglo-Saxon England may have held powerful roles for the living as a focus for a cult of memory that linked the past and the present and served in the construction of identities through commemoration. Certainly it is argued that a more careful focus on the relationships between death, memory and material culture will be pivotal to any future studies of mortuary practices in Late Antique and early medieval societies.

Acknowledgements

I would like to thank the anonymous reviewer, the editors and Elizabeth Wilson for commenting on an earlier draft of this paper. Thanks also to those participating in the York conference for their constructive questions and comments, particularly Julian D. Richards. All errors remain my responsibility.

Bibliography

Arnold, C. J. 1980. Wealth and social structure: a matter of life and death, in P. Rahtz, T. Dickinson and L. Watts (eds.), *Anglo-Saxon Cemeteries 1979*: 81-142. Oxford: British Archaeological Reports British Series 82.

Arnold, C.J. 1997. *An Archaeology of the early Anglo-Saxon Kingdoms*. Routledge: London.

Bond, J. 1996. Burnt offerings: animal bone in Anglo-Saxon cremations. *World Archaeology* 28(1): 76-88.

Brush, K. 1988. Gender and mortuary analysis in pagan Anglo-Saxon archaeology. *Archaeological Review from Cambridge* 7: 76-89.

Carver, M. 2000. Burial as poetry: the case of Sutton Hoo, in E. Tyler (ed.), *Treasure in the Early Medieval West*: 25-48. Woodbridge: Boydell.

Connerton, P. 1989. *How Societies Remember*. Cambridge: Cambridge University Press.

Crawford, S. 2000. Children, Grave Goods and Social Status in Early Anglo-Saxon England, in J. Sofaer Derevenski (ed.), *Children and Material Culture*: 169-79. London: Routledge.

Eckardt, H. and Williams, H. 2003. Objects without a past? The use of Roman objects in early Anglo-Saxon graves, in H. Williams (ed.), *Archaeologies of Remembrance: death and memory in past societies*: 141-70. New York: Kluwer/Plenum.

Effros, B. 2003. *Merovingian Mortuary Archaeology and the Making of the Early Middle Ages*. Berkeley: University of California Press.

Fisher, G. 1988. Style and sociopolitical organisation: a preliminary study from early Anglo-Saxon England, in S.T. Driscoll and M.R. Nieke (eds.), *Power and Politics in Early Medieval Britain and Ireland*: 128-44. Edinburgh: Edinburgh University Press.

Fisher, G. 1995. Kingdom and community in early Anglo-Saxon eastern England, in L. Anderson Beck (ed.), *Regional Approaches to Mortuary Analysis*: 147-66. New York: Plenum.

Fowler, C. 2003. Rates of (Ex)change. Decay and growth, memory and the transformation of the dead in early Neolithic southern Britain, in H. Williams (ed.), *Archaeologies of Remembrance - death and memory in past societies*: 45-63. New York: Kluwer/Plenum.

Gell, A. 1998. *Art and Agency. An Anthropological Theory*. Oxford: Oxford University Press.

Hallam, E. and Hockey, J. 2001. *Death, Memory and Material Culture*. Oxford: Berg.

Halsall, G. 1998. Burial, Ritual and Merovingian Society, in J. Hill and M. Swan (eds.), *The Community, the Family and the Saint. Patterns of Power in Early Medieval Europe*: 325-38. Turnhout: Brepols.

Härke, H. 1990. Warrior Graves? The Background of the Anglo-Saxon Weapon Burial Rite. *Past and Present* 126: 22-43.

Härke, H. 1997a. Early Anglo-Saxon Social Structure, in J. Hines (ed.), *The Anglo-Saxons from the Migration Period to the Eighth Century: An Ethnographic Perspective*: 125-70. Woodbridge: Boydell.

Härke, H. 1997b. Material Culture as Myth: Weapon in Anglo-Saxon graves, in C. Kjeld Jensen and K. Høilund Nielsen (eds.), *Burial and Society*: 119-27. Aarhus: Aarhus University Press.

Härke, H. 1998. Archaeologists and Migrations: A Question of Attitude? *Current Anthropology* 39: 19-45.

Härke, H. 2000. Social Analysis of Mortuary Evidence in German Protohistoric Archaeology. *Journal of Anthropological Archaeology* 19: 369-84.

Hills, C. 1977. *The Anglo-Saxon Cemetery at Spong Hill, North Elmham Part I: Catalogue of Cremations*. Dereham.

Hills, C. 1980. Anglo-Saxon Cremation Cemeteries, with Particular Reference to Spong Hill, Norfolk, in. P. Rahtz, T. Dickinson and L. Watts (eds.), *Anglo-Saxon Cemeteries 1979*: 197-207. Oxford: British Archaeological Reports British Series 82.

Hills, C. 1993. Who were the East Anglians? in J. Gardiner (ed.), *Flatlands and Wetlands: Current Themes in East Anglian Archaeology*: 14-23. Dereham East Anglian Archaeology 50.

Hills, C. and Penn, K. 1981. *The Anglo-Saxon Cemetery at Spong Hill, North Elmham. Part II: Catalogue of Cremations*. Dereham.

Hills, C., Penn, K and Rickett, R. 1987. *The Anglo-Saxon Cemetery at Spong Hill, North Elmham Part IV: Catalogue of Cremations*. Dereham.

Hills, C. Penn, K. and Rickett, R. 1994. *The Anglo-Saxon Cemetery at Spong Hill, North Elmham. Part V: Catalogue of Cremations*. Dereham.

Huggett, J. 1996. Social analysis of early Anglo-Saxon

inhumation burials: archaeological methodologies. *Journal of European Archaeology* 4: 337-65.

Huntingdon, R. and Metcalf, P. 1991. *Celebrations of Death*, 2nd edition. Cambridge: Cambridge University Press.

James, E. 1989. Burial and Status in the Early Medieval West. *Transactions of the Royal Historical Society* 5th series, 39: 23-40.

Joyce, R.A. 2003. Concrete Memories: Fragments of the Past in the Classic Maya Present (500-1000 AD), in R.M. Van Dyke and S.E. Alcock (eds.), *Archaeologies of Memory*: 104-26. Oxford: Blackwell.

Jones, A. 2001. Drawn from memory: the archaeology of aesthetics and the aesthetics of archaeology in Earlier Bronze Age Britain and the present. *World Archaeology* 33(2): 334-356.

Jones, A. 2003. Technologies of Remembrance. Memory, materiality and identity in Early Bronze Age Scotland, in H. Williams (ed.), *Archaeologies of Remembrance - death and memory in past societies*: 65-88. New York: Kluwer/Plenum.

Kinsley, A. 1989. *The Anglo-Saxon Cemetery at Millgate, Newark-on-Trent, Nottinghamshire.* Nottingham: University of Nottingham.

Küchler, S. 2002. *Malanggan. Art, Memory and Sacrifice.* Oxford: Berg.

Leach, E. 1958. Magical Hair. *Journal of the Royal Anthropological Institute* 88(2): 149-164.

Lethbridge, T. C. 1951. *A Cemetery at Lackford, Suffolk.* Cambridge: Cambridge Antiquarian Society. Quarto Publication. New Series. No. VI.

Lucy, S. 1998. *The Early Anglo-Saxon Cemeteries of East Yorkshire: An Analysis and Reinterpretation.* Oxford: British Archaeological Reports British Series 272.

Lucy, S. 2002. Burial practice in early medieval eastern England: constructing local identities, deconstructing ethnicity, in S. Lucy and A. Reynolds (eds.), *Burial in Early Medieval England and Wales*: 72-87. Leeds: Maney.

ManiBabu, M. 1994. Post-Cremation-Urn-Burial of the Phayengs (Manipur). A Study on Mortuary Behaviour. *The Eastern Anthropologist* 47: 157-71.

McKinley, J. 1994. *The Anglo-Saxon Cemetery at Spong Hill, North Elmham. Part VII: The Cremations.* Dereham: East Anglian Archaeology 69.

Meskell, L. 2003. Memory's Materiality: Ancestral Presence, Commemorative Practice and Disjunctive Locales, in R.M. Van Dyke and S.E. Alcock (eds.), *Archaeologies of Memory*: 34-55. Oxford: Blackwell.

Myres, J.N.L. 1969. *Anglo-Saxon Pottery and the Settlement of England.* Oxford: Clarendon.

Myres, J.N.L. and Green, B. 1973. *The Anglo-Saxon Cemeteries of Caistor-by-Norwich and Markshall* London: Society of Antiquaries.

Myres, J.N.L. and Southern, W.H. 1973. *The Anglo-Saxon Cremation Cemetery at Sancton, East Yorkshire.* Hull.

Neville, R.C. 1852. *Saxon Obsequies.* London: Murray.

Pader, E. J. 1982. *Symbolism, Social Relations and the Interpretation of Mortuary Remains.* Oxford: British Archaeological Reports International Series 82.

Parker Pearson, M. 1982. Mortuary practices, society and ideology: an ethnoarchaeological study, in I. Hodder (ed.), *Symbolic and Structural Archaeology*: 99-114. Cambridge: Cambridge University Press.

Ravn, M. 1999. Theoretical and methodological approaches to Migration Period burials, in M. Rundkvist (ed.), *Grave Matters: Eight studies of First Millennium AD burials in Crimea, England and southern Scandinavia*: 41-56. Oxford: British Archaeological Reports International Series 78.

Richards, J. 1987. *The Significance of Form and Decoration of Anglo-Saxon Cremation Urns.* Oxford: British Archaeological Reports British Series 166.

Richards, J. 1992. Anglo-Saxon Symbolism, in M. Carver (ed.), *The Age of Sutton Hoo*: 131-149. Woodbridge: Boydell.

Richards, J. 1995. An Archaeology of Anglo-Saxon England, in G. Ausenda (ed.), *After Empire. Towards an Ethnology of Europe's Barbarians*: 51-66. Woodbridge: Boydell.

Samson, R. 1987. Social structures from Reihengräber: mirror or mirage? *Scottish Archaeological Review* 4: 116-26.

Scull, C. 1993. Archaeology, Early Anglo-Saxon Society and the Origins of the Anglo-Saxon Kingdoms, in W. Filmer-Sankey and D. Griffiths (eds.), *Anglo-Saxon Studies in Archaeology and History* 6: 65-82. Oxford: Oxford Committee for Archaeology.

Serematakis, N. 1991. *The Last Word. Women, Death and Divination in Inner Mani.* Chicago: University of Chicago Press.

Shepherd, J. 1979. The social identity of the individual in isolated barrows and barrow cemeteries in Anglo-Saxon England, in B.C. Burnham and J. Kingsbury (eds.), *Space, Hierarchy and Society*: 47-79. Oxford: British Archaeological Reports International Series 59.

Stoodley, N. 1999. *The Spindle and the Spear.* Oxford: British Archaeological Reports British Series 288.

Timby, J. 1993. Sancton I Anglo-Saxon Cemetery. Excavations Carried Out Between 1976 and 1980. *Archaeological Journal* 150: 243-365.

Ucko, P. 1969. Ethnography and the archaeological interpretation of funerary remains. *World Archaeology* 1: 262-80.

Williams, H. 2000. *"Burnt German of the Age of Iron" Early Anglo-Saxon Mortuary Practices and the*

Study of Cremation in Past Societies. Unpublished Doctoral Thesis, University of Reading.

Williams, H. 2001. Death, Memory and Time: A Consideration of the Mortuary Practices at Sutton Hoo, in C. Humphrey and W.M. Ormrod (eds.), *Time in the Medieval World*: 35-71. Woodbridge: Boydell.

Williams, H. 2002. Remains of Pagan Saxondom? - the study of Anglo-Saxon cremation rites, in S. Lucy and A. Reynolds (eds.), *Burial in Early Medieval England and Wales*: 47-71. Leeds: Maney.

Williams, H. forthcoming. Material Culture as Memory - combs and cremation in early medieval Britain. *Early Medieval Europe.*

Williams, H. in prep. Keeping Remembrance at Arms Length – weaponry, cremation and social memory in early Anglo-Saxon England.

11: Living amongst the dead: From Roman cemetery to post-Roman monastic settlement at Poundbury

Christopher Sparey-Green

York was an apposite location for a paper on this topic since it is here that, significantly, the only real parallel for the cemetery at Poundbury, Dorchester, Dorset can be found. The city of Constantine's elevation and the starting place of the imperial conversion is the only other urban centre in Britain to have produced a large, ordered cemetery containing the use of gypsum plaster burials. Poundbury, however, has not only produced more such burials but contains mausolea, some richly decorated. The cemetery was also succeeded by a complex settlement and it is the transition from cemetery to settlement during the earliest post-Roman centuries which will be examined here.

The publishing of separate volumes on the cemetery and settlements at Poundbury, Dorset, although necessary because of the complexity of the site, had the effect of divorcing the late Roman cemetery from its contemporary and later settlements (Sparey Green 1987; Farwell and Molleson 1993). Woodward discussed aspects of the cemetery in the Wessex Trust publication of the cemetery and the speaker has followed up various aspects of the burial rite as well as re-interpreting the sub-Roman settlement (Woodward 1993; Sparey-Green 1993 and 1997). Since then new information concerning the wider context of this site has accumulated; the cemetery is now the subject of various research projects and the author is collating new information on the parallels to the cemetery, the mausolea and the special burials.

At Poundbury the sequence within the Roman period from suburban settlement to cemetery is fairly clearly understood although the extent and nature of the settlement remains uncertain. Cemeteries 1 and 2 (using the writer's preferred terminology: Sparey-Green 1993) were small- scale and closely associated with the early occupation area. The larger Cemetery 3 also started within the settlement but, in contrast, expanded into enclosures occupying the hillside below the Roman aqueduct and Poundbury Camp itself. The cemetery's expansion was marked by the interment of various special and focal burials, the construction of mausolea or chapels and then the burial of rows of simple interments in a well regulated layout. The organisation of the burial ground (contra Philpott 1991: 226-227) is not the result of late Roman bureaucracy controlling burial places but a reflection of the customs established within the community using the site (Sparey-Green 2002: 98-99). The form of burial would be most appropriate to a strictly Christian community although overt symbolism and unambiguous iconography for the belief of those using the site was largely absent.

The extensive cemetery itself became the focus for a new phase of settlement early in the post-Roman period, this being very different in character and the subject of a major re-organisation prior to a sudden abandonment and destruction. Through the Saxon and medieval periods the site was unoccupied and probably used as agricultural land, although settlement may have continued at the nearby West Mills (Sparey Green 1987: 93-94). The walled area of Dorchester remained a focus of settlement during that time, but by the middle Saxon period a new foundation existed across the valley at Charminster, a name with an obvious significance (Hall 2000; Fig. 11.1).

The location of the main Late Roman cemetery 3 may have depended simply on the availability of existing fields on the hillside above the suburban settlement. The site looked east to the Roman town and the Frome valley beyond but was set some 500m from the town defences and 300m from the nearest road to Ilchester. The ground immediately eastward is not known to have contained any major cemetery although a smaller but closely similar graveyard did exist nearer the town, adjoining the road to Exeter and other road-side cemeteries (Biek et al. 1981). The question thus arises whether the site was deliberately located distant from the urban population and separate from the other dead, those visiting the site enjoying a fine view of the town and the eastern skyline, the burial place not intended to be admired by passing travellers.

The main cemetery (Cemetery 3) originated within the courtyard of a group of simple work buildings (R12-14) on the western side of the occupied area (Sparey-Green 1987: 66). This burial area (3B) was composed of oriented coffined burials often of juveniles or infants accompanied by a few gravegoods including coins of the late third century. At the centre lay an adult burial, Focal burial F1, described below, the grave set beside a stone base covered in brick concrete and served by a small drain. The adjacent Buildings R13-14 had been used for iron-working and could have served as an undertaker's workshop before they were abandoned in the late third and early fourth century, at approximately the time that a major coin hoard of Carausian date was deposited between the two buildings (Frere 1987: 345; King 2004).

Burial extended early in the fourth century into the first of the more formal burial area (Cemetery 3A), occupying the nearest of the enclosures uphill. The cemetery appears to have expanded into a second enclosure (Cemetery 3C) during the later fourth century, the burial rite altering over time, the burial zones marked by several significant interments, the foci of particular groups. Environmental evidence suggests that at least Cemetery

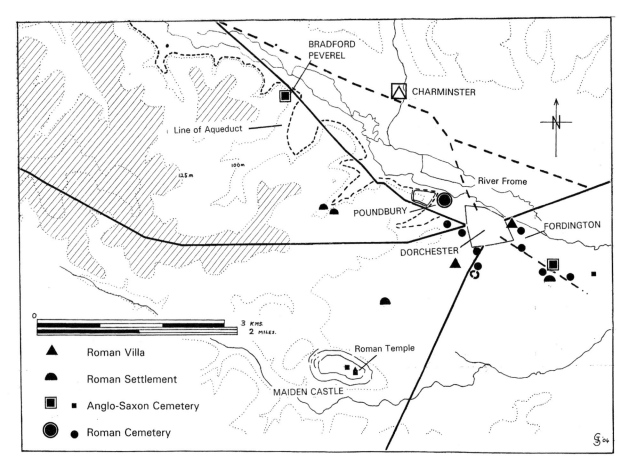

Figure 11.1: Poundbury in the context of Roman and Anglo-Saxon sites in the area,
including the minster at Charminster.

3A had been under close-cropped grassland immediately prior to interments (Sparey Green 1987: 65). Although the new use for burial might seem to mark the end of farming, there is no reason why the maintenance of sheep flocks here should not have continued. Indeed there would be practical and even symbolic reasons for maintaining them, rather in the manner that pagan temples had their sacred animals, as at Uley. In the medieval period in the southwest of Britain, there is at least one case of a church keeping flocks in the churchyard, and on a small scale nowadays country churchyards use sheep as lawnmowers. The as yet unpublished finds from the enclosure ditches and grave fills in this area include glass and pottery dating to the end of the Roman period.

Several mausolea were erected over special groups in stone or lead-lined coffins, two of these notable for their painted interiors and worn internal floor surfaces, suggesting their particular veneration or regular use, perhaps as cemetery chapels. The scale of burial indicates that this served a large population, undoubtedly urban. A third and little studied area to the south west of the main burial zone (Cemetery 3D) contains further interments and may have formed the latest stage of the site, beyond the limits of the post-Roman settlement and potentially contemporary with it.

Only some aspects of the cemetery will be described, particularly the special graves and mausolea which were important features within the succeeding post-Roman settlement. Amongst the rows of ordinary graves there are three main groups of burial that appear unusual and, in some cases, to be the earliest features in the horizontal stratigraphy of the layout of the grave rows. These could be characterised as Focal burials, Special Burial Groups and the Mausolea burials. Focal Burials (F1-3) are a rare feature of the developed cemetery which deserves highlighting, such burials being unusual both in their form and in their relationship to surrounding interments. Three such graves can be tentatively identified, the first (F1) at the centre of the initial area, Cemetery 3B, described above. This burial was a plaster-packed lead-lined coffin (376) containing an adult male which had been succeeded by an infant grave (386) into the top of which had been inserted a New Forest ware jug of early or mid fourth century type, a unique sequence on the site. The most significant of this type is 243 A-C (F2). This consisted of a male aged 50 buried with two infants set either side of him in the same grave pit, his hands on their skulls. They had been buried beneath a partially charred wooden door, the grave not marked in any obvious way but set centrally within the area of cemetery 3A and 3C at a point which should have been occupied by another mausoleum. The grave was surrounded by a cluster of ordinary graves set on a common alignment with this burial suggesting it was of some significance and remembered. Another unusual grave (F3) (1339) was of a male aged 40 set within an open area to the north of mausoleum R8, this spot approached by an apparent path leading uphill from the settlement. An iron plaque, possibly in a shape of an Ankh symbol, appeared to have been some decorative fitting, possibly on the underside of the coffin lid above the head. There was no clustering of burial here save for some infants and a series of un-coffined adult graves, which may belong late in the series.

Focal Burial 2 (F2) remains the most puzzling, the unusual combination of a man with children, and the symbolism of the hands on skulls recalling Christ's blessing of children (*Mark* 10: 13-16) and also alludes to baptismal rites where the celebrant would place his hands upon the head of the intitiate (Picard 1986: 8). Furthermore, this burial might also indicate the status of the adult since, if indeed an allusion to baptism, then under normal circumstances this would have been a bishop or at least someone with delegated authority (Tertullian, *De Baptismo,* 17). Equally interesting and more numerous are the Special Burials, the gypsum plaster packed coffins of various types that occur at regular intervals across the site. These burials could be contained in stone, lead-lined wooden or massive wooden coffins clustered in at least nineteen Special Burial Groups (SBG1-19) without surviving monuments and another eleven groups within buildings (Mausolea R1-3 and 7-11). The total number of such graves was at least sixty-six and possibly more, those in wooden coffins not having been identified in all cases. Without detailing the location of the Special Groups, seven occur in Cemetery 3A, set at regular intervals throughout the enclosure with a particularly large group in the centre where nine lead-lined coffins and one Portland stone coffin occurred within a dense cluster of graves. Patches of open ground around this group suggest the location of bases for the support of a columnated structure, one of the bases perhaps having survived, reused in a post-Roman feature nearby. Two mausolea, R9 and R10, occurred in the southwest corner, the first surrounding two lead-lined, the second two lead-lined and a stone coffin. Another seven groups were identified within the exposed area of 3C besides five mausolea, the special burials here commonly in massive wooden or stone coffins. Lastly, two isolated special burials in stone coffins occurred in 3D, the least investigated area to the south, this area also producing two ditched grave enclosures R4-6. No tombstones have been identified other than one possible plain stone marker.

The mausolea at Poundbury probably form the largest group of funerary structures found on a single site in Roman Britain and may be representative of a type that has often lain unrecorded, this simple form of above-ground, roofed structure leaving only limited remains. Here I will only discuss aspects of their use, the traces of activity within them and then their influence on the post–cemetery land-use. Eight built mausolea were found within the exposed part of the cemetery, at least one other lying in an unexcavated area. All the buildings appear to be of a simple rectangular plan, approximately 4.7m by 6.5m although there remains some doubt about the incompletely excavated R1-3; Mausoleum R2 was probably wider than the others and R3 appears to have been at least 7.3m long. All were aligned E-W with evidence for entrances on the western uphill side in at least two cases. These simple roofed buildings overlay groups of interments although the relationship of graves to buildings is complex, the funerary use multi-phase, in some cases commencing before the erection of the building, sometimes possibly post-dating construction. There is also evidence in at least one case of interment extending into the period of dereliction as well as two cases of the robbing of special burials, discussed below. Several mausolea produced signs of activity, both domestic and craft-related, within their interior. R1 contained a scatter of Ham stone chips and dust on its worn internal floor, debris presumably from finishing a coffin that must remain *in situ*. R2 contained similar traces of a worn floor. Other graves nearby and in R7 and R10 produced similar debris from the finishing of sarcophagi on site.

The most significant mausolea were R8 and R9, marked out by their internal decoration, the reconstructed sections of painted plaster from the former described in Davey and Ling, the decorative scheme of walls and ceiling thereafter outlined by the writer but now the subject of re-interpretation in the light of new comparative material (Davey and Ling 1982: 106-110; Sparey-Green 1993b). Very little plaster was recovered from R9 but in R8 the decoration consisted of ranges of figures along the south wall in purple, green and white robes or tunics, some figures carrying rods, one figure at least with a white head-dress. A central lost figure appears to have had a small Chi-Rho set above it on the blue background. The east wall had at least one nude figure, the legs surrounded by sweeps of blue and white, possibly water, while of another clothed figure only the cuff of a garment and the hand could be discerned. Part of the west wall, close to the presumed entrance, had been re-plastered and a new scene painted of a city in semi-aerial perspective, including possibly a gateway and the front of a courtyard building with doorway. On the barrel-vaulted ceiling figures in white may have formed another register above those at ground level, part of the design also including floral borders around polygonal or circular panels. It is tempting here to see a suite of paintings familiar from better preserved tombs. The lower row of figures might be portraits of the living, those above, the dead relatives. The scene on the east wall was perhaps a depiction of a baptism or of Adam and Eve. The opposite western end bore part of a cityscape which may now be compared with not only a scene of the Holy City from the third century tomb of the Aurelii in the Catacombs in Rome but also the recently discovered 'painted city' mural from a Flavian building beneath Trajan's Baths (Borda 1958: 316; La Rocca 2001). At a later date depictions of cities also occur in the background of paintings illustrating scenes from *Genesis* and, most notably, in the early Byzantine map of Jerusalem in the Madaba pavement (Ferrua 1990: 82-83; Donner 1992: 87-94). Such subject matter may also relate to the stylized depiction of cities in maps like the Peutinger Table. The surviving painted surface was so fragmentary as to militate against so grand an interpretation but the scale and quality of the surviving sections is such as to indicate an unusually highly decorated funerary structure, way beyond that normally identified in Roman Britain. This then questions whether this was merely a mausoleum and not a small church in a funerary context decorated with a series of inter-related figured scenes which, although not certainly identified could be of a biblical nature.

The date of construction and the period of use of the building can be estimated on the evidence of unpublished finds. The construction trench contained Black Burnished Ware (BB1) of a distinctive late form while, within the building, an occupation layer and trampled surfaces associated with a stone base in the south-west corner produced more pottery of this type and fragments of late glass ware. Some of the latter were from vessels similar to those found at Burgh Castle and could have come from either drinking vessels or even glass lamps. A pierced coin with prominent Chi-Rho from the eastern interior floor could suggest the deliberate deposition or dedication of an object of Christian significance, such as a *bulla* worn by a child until the age of majority, as is visible on a small bronze from Trier (Green 1970: 138).

These finds would suggest construction late in the fourth century and a period of use continuing into the fifth century. Pottery from the robber trenches of R3 and R8 suggest the final robbing did not take place until the late medieval or early post-medieval period, a time when a significant quantity of pottery was introduced to the topsoil across the site, probably as a result of the manuring of the site during a renewed phase of arable use. There is, then, every possibility that at least these mausolea stood as ruins if not as structures still in use, throughout the post-Roman period. Their presence may thus have been visible and the site remembered in some way when the Abbey of Bindon held land at West Mills nearby.

One casual find deserving mention is the small bronze bowl and miniature axehead found in 1943. The former object is akin to a miniature hanging bowls of the early post-Roman period but is closer in size to a censer or lamp, akin to the vessel found in Glastonbury, although that was of a more exotic origin (Rahtz 1993: 99). The axehead is an example of a miniature tool which, while not associated with a particular cult, certainly was associated with pagan shrines such as that at Woodeaton (Green 1976: 177-178). The findspot remains uncertain

but should lie in the upper, western part of the cemetery, in cemetery 3C.

Continued activity in Poundbury Camp itself is suggested by the refacing of the western rampart and the placing of a late Roman coin hoard within the rampart front (Sparey Green 1987: 69). A square parch mark within the interior also suggests a structure near the centre of the camp but is undated and may be a seventeenth century plague house. On the eastern side, above the cemetery, the presence of aquatic snails and fourth century pottery in the base of the aqueduct channel suggests this still contained water in the 4th century (Sparey Green 1987: 51). Earthworks of side channels below the northwestern corner of the hillfort and to its west suggest it may have fed water-mills at the base of the hillside close to the river. The virtual absence of hand-querns from the Roman and post-Roman settlements would suggest other facilities for the production of flour had existed.

The published chronology of the cemeteries' development depends on dateable gravegoods but, as noted above, other finds of glass and pottery from graves, boundary ditches and mausolea may allow refinement and extension of the present chronology. Apart from mausoleum R8 significant groups come from the southern and western boundaries of cemetery 3A, the latter levelled when the core area expanded into the larger uphill area 3C (Sparey-Green 1987: 65). The latter ditch was superseded by a row of burials which cut a fill containing both pottery groups and debris from the finishing of stone coffins, sealed by the bank material. This could potentially give a date for both cemetery expansion and the introduction of the use of Hamstone for coffins.

A significant group within the cemetery were those adult burials either in shallow, uncoffined or stone cist graves, this series often overlapping the neat rows of coffined inhumations (Fig. 11.2). This series could have co-existed with the pattern of post-Roman activity, most of these graves lying in the open ground, clustered in groups near R9 and 10 and around R8 and the apsidal structure PR4 erected beside this mausoleum (Sparey-Green 1997: 129). Three lay close to the focal burial F2 of the man and two children. Other groups adjoined F3, the focal burial with the monogrammed coffin. This group of graves need more exact definition and study but they superficially appear to include an unusually high number of females and particularly elderly females (Farwell and Molleson 1993: 162). The possible significance of this will be discussed below. The type of grave is exemplified locally at Ulwell and has been discussed by Rahtz in connection with the cemetery at Cannington, these cemeteries falling in the fifth to seventh century (Cox 1988; Rahtz *et al.* 2000: 422-423).

Attention should also be drawn to the three graves in Cemetery 3D which lay within trenched or ditched

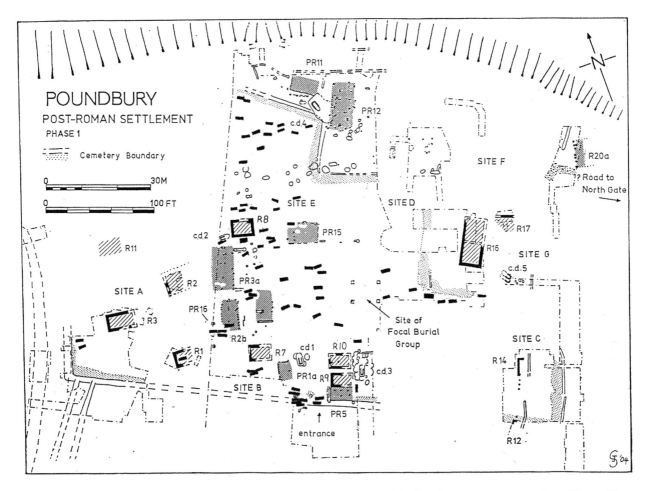

Figure 11.2: Plan of the Phase 1 post-Roman settlement on the site of the late Roman cemetery at Poundbury. The black rectangles indicate the latest adult inhumations, the areas of close hatching indicate the major buildings.

enclosures. These enclosures respected the south boundary of Cemetery 3C and lay beyond the limits of the sub-Roman settlement so could have co-existed with either. In their rite of burial, including the use of nailed wooden coffins, they did not fall within the definition of the late burials. The enclosures can be found locally on Cranborne Chase in Iron Age contexts but also occur in the Roman period, as in the larger bank and ditch enclosures surrounding small groups of inhumations on the Roden Downs, Berkshire (White 1970; Hood and Walton 1948). The rite recurs in early post-Roman Christian contexts, as at Tandderwen, Denbigh, Clwyd (Brassil *et al.* 1991).

There are also some rare cases, not previously recognised, of graves dug into mausolea after their partial demolition or dereliction, one unexcavated burial (Grave 3) having been cut into mausoleum R1, its upper fill sealed by redeposited walling blocks. Finally, there are at least three burials cut into post-Roman features which would belong to a yet later phase but these were of a distinct type, the dead crouched or even trussed and inserted into the fill of features (Farwell and Molleson 1993: 83). Although numerically insignificant these

categories of burial serve to show a more complex history for the use of the site, burial continuing even after the disuse of both the mausolea and the post-Roman settlement.

The post-Roman settlement sequence has already been re-defined and here only some wider discussion of the site and its possible interpretation will be attempted, developing from the most recent discussion (Sparey-Green 1997: 127-135). An overlap between the use of the site for burial and its occupation has been suggested while the two mausolea with internal decoration, R8 and R9, also appear to have been retained as important features of the new layout (Sparey-Green 1987: 83-85). Throughout cemetery 3 disturbance of graves was generally rare and this was also the case with the succeeding settlement. Where graves had been cut into by pits from the occupation this is presumed to have been accidental but there are some notable cases where special graves have been heavily disturbed. The most significant disturbance is that within mausolea R3 and R7 where grave pits had been re-excavated and the coffins partly broken up and removed, the backfilled debris containing fragments of coffin, plaster and human bone. The observed, very damaged remains of R11 may also suggest that this had been similarly disturbed. The excavated pits appear to fall early in the post-Roman sequence and to have been dug neither in the course of domestic activity nor for the robbing of stone since, as noted above, the mausolea walls were possibly standing until the medieval period. In this respect the first coffin found in 1855, to the south in cemetery 3D, is notable since this not only appears somewhat weathered but is now minus its lid. Nothing is known of its contents but the possibility remains that this burial, set within what is postulated as the latest extension of the cemetery, was a reused coffin base taken from R3 or R7 in the sub-Roman period. Such reuse of Roman coffins is, of course, recorded in the case of the burial of Queen Aetheldreda (Bede, *Eccl. Hist.*, IV, 19). The presence of broken coffin fragments in the pits could be evidence that it was the contents that were sought, either valuable gravegoods or even the bones themselves. Disturbed human bones occurred in some post-Roman features and deserve further study as to their nature and location, the most significant being the fragment of calvarium built into the drystone wall inserted into a sub-Roman pit beside building PR1a; this had to be a deliberate placing within the wall, perhaps a placatory gesture to the disturbed dead. Until this and other disturbed cemetery material have been examined the question must remain open as to whether there could be evidence for relic hunting.

The first phase of the post-Roman settlement is generally aligned with that of mausolea and cemetery boundaries, the new structures set amongst the existing buildings and appended to them. In the case of PR 1-5 these were located to fill the gaps between mausolea R7-10, the most significant or largest scale buildings lying in a range between R7 and R8, with others set downhill between R7 and R9 and R10. There may also have been another structure downhill of R8 creating almost a 'villa' type layout of main range with two wings, the whole facing east and downhill to the position of the largest Special Burial Group (Sparey-Green 1997: 131; Special Burial Group 5 appears as 'Site of Focal Burial Group' on Fig. 11.2). Phases 2 and 3 of the settlement represented a reorientation and a re-planning, with new structures and outer enclosures set at angle across this plan with the axis now more exactly east-west and ignoring the Roman land divisions.

The number of agricultural structures was originally seen as evidence for the purely domestic and agricultural nature of the occupation, the possibility that this may have been a lost monastic site being dismissed by the writer as unproven and unprovable (Sparey-Green 1997: 150-151). Early monastic texts, however, contain many references to farming activities and to innovations in this field; such communities have been seen as pioneers (Morris 1973: 432-434). The provision of water supplies and mills were important innovations on such sites and allusion has already been made to the evidence for these on the present site. Corn drying ovens are described in

Saints Lives from Wales and Ireland and the remains of a drying or malting oven has, for instance, been identified in the early monastic site at Hoddom, SouthWest Scotland (Lowe 1993). The presence of several at Poundbury would be entirely compatible with this being a monastic settlement.

The apsidal structure PR4, adjacent to mausoleum R8, was one of the most distinctive features of phases 2 and 3, its plan apparently not of some utilitarian structure but built to receive massive timbers and with a paved doorway on its north side. It may have been a free-standing structure but it was set downhill of and aligned with mausoleum R2, and could have been set at the eastern end of a surface-built extension of that, the least known but widest of the mausolea. The apsidal structure was oriented with a group of burials beneath it, enclosing four of them and, as already noted, adjoined a number of shallow cist and uncoffined graves. One notable find from the structure was a column capital reused as a basin, an object of potential liturgical use (Green 1987: 108, Fig. 76, 28).

Sunken floored huts are now well known from late Roman and early Anglo-Saxon settlements but here they form an important element of the later phases, contemporary with PR4 and occupying the hillside below it. Five of these can be recognised (PR6-10) besides at least four other small surface huts, R19, R20b, PR1b and PR13 all bounded by small enclosures, as if they formed individual cells. A cluster of such buildings within Burgh Castle are associated with the monastic settlement of Fursey although there they are not set in an enclosure system.

The poverty of material culture has recently been remarked on as an indication of how difficult such sites would be to identify, the lack of distinctive pottery making it and comparable sites almost invisible (Esmonde Cleary 2001: 93-95). At the mundane level this seems typical of the region during the post-Roman period and at Poundbury contrasted with the large quantities of basic domestic refuse, particularly the animal bones. All containers must have been of organic substances or metal which had then be conserved and re-used. Although late Roman or sub-Roman exotic amphora sherds were identified these derived from the latest Roman settlement levels. Amongst the rudimentary iron tools the plain knives were remarkably sophisticated in their technology, other elements of the tool kit comprising whetstones and stone rubbers. Combs were the most common artefact and like the spindle whorls were presumably part of weaving equipment. The bone pins seem too small and delicate for dress use and may have been tools for delicate craftwork.

Cereals in use were of new varieties developed in the late or early post-Roman period and, as suggested above, the absence of quern stones, other than rare fragments of lava quern, might indicate the continued existence of a mill operated off the aqueduct or the river below. A mill existed later on the river 200m to the east at West Mills, this probably one of the Domesday mills and held by Bindon Abbey in the early medieval period.

The occupation of a cemetery as a permanent settlement site is unusual if not unique in late Roman Britain and is even more noteworthy in view of the potential overlap of the earliest phase of post-Roman settlement with the latest burials. As noted above, these burials comprised a disproportionate number of women, raising questions as to the nature of the community interred here and perhaps occupying the site. A similar bias in the make-up of a population at this time can be recognised at the Lamyatt Beacon temple where a small rectangular building was adjoined by a group of at least sixteen unaccompanied and oriented inhumations (Leech 1986: 268-274). Ten of the thirteen adults were female, the whole group notably above average height for the period. Radiocarbon dating placed two skeletons in the sixth to ninth centuries AD. As Leech pointed out, other temples in the south-west have produced small buildings and post-Roman cemeteries, the former similar to known early Christian oratories, the latter comprising burials that conform with a Christian style of interment. Comparison can also be made between the simple rectangular buildings and the albeit slightly larger mausolea at Poundbury but, whereas the majority of these sites marked the Christianisation of a pagan religious site, at Poundbury it is the transformation and development of a cemetery of a Christian character which included foci for veneration. In the early post-Roman period these venerated structures were incorporated into a living place for the faithful, gathered at a spot made holy by those interred there.

The structure of the population through each phase of the cemetery, as defined here, deserves re-examination but the existence of female believers at this date as a group, or at least an important element, within a Christian community, recalls the writings of Egeria, a female pilgrim to the Holy Land in the late fourth century who addressed her writings to fellow female believers ('Dominae venerabilis sorores', Peregrinatio, 20.5; translated by Wilkinson 1981: 118). It is also noteworthy that a late Roman burial from Sycamore Terrace, York contained an open-work bone plaque with the text 'Soror ave vivas in Deo' (Royal Commission on Historical Monuments 1962: 73, Fig. 58 and 135, no. 150). The presence of jewellery and glass vessel grave goods need not contradict interpretation of the text as Christian and, although the use of the word soror could simply refer to a familial relationship, its use as part of such an invocation may be significant.

The number of females interred at Poundbury at a date in the late fourth or early fifth century could then imply that the first inhabitants of the burial place were just such a community, a 'form of late fourth century Christian sisterhood' (Thomas 1981: 52-53). To suggest the existence of female monasticism at this early date in

Britain is speculative but this may only reflect our lack of evidence or inability to recognize the transient or ambiguous remains of such sites. Within two centuries religious houses of this type are recorded locally, at for instance, Wimborne and Shaftesbury, and these were perhaps re-foundations of earlier British foundations. The references to pilgrimage from the western provinces in the fourth century also puts the city-scape in mausoleum R8 in a new light for, if a scene of the Holy City, this possibly commemorated the return of just such a traveller in the late fourth or fifth century. And this pilgrim was remembered in the first post-Roman phase, the mausoleum-church becoming an important element in the new layout of structures which also incorporated R9, the other mausoleum-church with painted interior. Still at the centre of the complex was the largest group of special burials, marked by some monument now lost or simply a site remembered. This early phase was also a working farm marked by the number of drying ovens for cereals and perhaps one barn like structure (PR12). The later phases of post-Roman settlement might also have been occupied by some form of monastic community but differently organised. Now, there were small huts separated by boundaries which served as the cells of individual monks, the apsidal structure, whether or not part of a larger building, a small church or oratory. A group of believers may have deliberately chosen this spot to dwell on in as simple a manner, making use of whatever resources they could to set up on a holy site close to Dorchester. The mausolea–churches continued to be venerated as the most obvious foci even if the burial places of the most revered individuals, including the central special burial group, were lost by that stage. At some point attempts were made to hunt for relics amongst the ruins leading to the disturbance of some special burials. Throughout the life of the settlement the very simplicity of the structures and the rarity of artefacts could be more than a reflection of the economic collapse from the high point of material culture in the late fourth century and might be a deliberate asceticism.

If the origin of the settlement overlapped the late use of the burial ground the end of the site is more easily defined. The major structures of the final phase were rapidly abandoned with evidence for the burning and levelling of drystone structures and the burial of animal carcasses in features, suggestive of rapid clearance if not a violent end to the site. The few radiocarbon samples from the drying ovens place their use in the fifth to sixth century, in the earlier phase of the settlement, allowing the later stages of the settlement to overlap with the coming of the Anglo-Saxons. The creation of Wessex is a shadowy event in this area, with few historical references to the settlement of this area in the mid seventh century, but the name 'Durn saete' might refer to the new settlers or dwellers in and around Durnovaria, the Roman name of Dorchester. Archaeological evidence for Anglo-Saxon burials and settlement is now known south east of Dorchester and another cemetery has been identified at Bradford Peverel, only 2 km to the northwest of Poundbury, close to the Roman road to Ilchester that passes the south edge of the present site (Green 1984; Davies *et al.* 2002: 171-179, 199; Hinton 1998: 40-41)

The foundation of a new Anglo-Saxon ecclesiastical system in Dorset included the creation of minster churches, the nearest at Charminster on the opposite side of the Frome Valley, 1.5 km to the north (Hall 2000: 25 and 93). There is little information on its origin but the form of the name, *Cernminstre*, incorporating the Celtic river name Cerne, and its location on Royal lands, suggests a foundation in the early eighth century. The early date and proximity to Poundbury raise the interesting possibility that this was in some way a successor to the postulated British monastic foundation. Recent research on the origins and development of minsters in Dorset and neighbouring counties suggests that elsewhere such a process took place, the new Anglo-Saxon foundations eclipsing and then replacing their British predecessors (I am grateful to Teresa Hall for information on this and for access to forthcoming papers on this topic).

The evidence for Charminster should be contrasted with that for the other early Anglo-Saxon settlement close to Dorchester. Woodward promoted Fordington, on the other side of the town from Poundbury, as an example of continuity from a Roman cemetery to an early church (Woodward 1993). The character, however, of the late Roman burials in the vicinity was more variable and much more typical of normal provincial inhumation cemeteries while the earliest structures beneath St George's Church were the foundations of its late Anglo-Saxon predecessor, with no sign of intervening cemetery or ecclesiastical use. Instead, Poundbury provides better evidence for a cemetery of a special and Christian character, the site then the focus for an early monastic community supplanted in the early eighth century by an Anglo-Saxon foundation at Charminster, the minster on the Cerne.

Acknowledgements

I am most grateful to James Gerrard for alerting me to the significance of the Lamyatt Beacon cemetery and Enid Allison for reminding me of the York inscription. I am also particularly indebted to Teresa Hall for information on her recent research on Dorset Minsters and for access to forthcoming papers on this topic.

Bibliography

Biek, L., Paterson, M. and Green, C.J.S. 1981. A Roman Coffin Burial from the Crown Buildings Site, Dorchester, with particular reference to the head of well preserved hair. *Proceedings of the Dorset Natural History and Archaeological Society* 103: 67-100.

Borda, M. 1958. *La Pittura Romana*. Milan.

Brassil, O. and Britnell, W.J. 1991. Prehistoric and early medieval cemeteries at Tandderwen, Denbigh, Clwyd. *Archaeological Journal* 148: 46-97.

Cox, P.W. 1988. A Seventh-century Inhumation Cemetery at Shepherd's Farm, Ulwell, near Swanage, Dorset. *Proceedings of the Dorset Natural History and Archaeological Society* 110: 37-48.

Davey, N. and Ling, R. 1982. *Wall-Painting in Roman Britain*. London: Britannia Monograph 3.

Davies, S.M., Bellamy, P.S., Heaton, M.J. and Woodward, P.J., 2002. *Excavations at Alington Avenue, Fordington, Dorchester, Dorset, 1984-87*. Dorchester: Dorset Natural History and Archaeological Society Monograph 15.

Donner, H. 1992. *The Mosaic Map of Madaba, an Introductory Guide*. Kampen.

Esmonde Cleary, S. 2001. The Roman to medieval transition, in S. James and M. Millett (eds.), *Britons and Romans: advancing an archaeological agenda*: 90-97. London: Council for British Archaeology Research Report 125.

Farwell, D.E. and Molleson, T.L., 1993. *Excavations at Poundbury 1966-80, Vol. II, The Cemeteries*. Dorchester: Dorset Natural History and Archaeological Society Monograph 11.

Ferrua, A. 1990. *The Unknown Catacomb, A Unique Discovery of Early Christian Art*. New Lanark.

Frere, S. 1987. Roman Britain in 1986. *Britannia* 18: 302-59.

Green, C.J.S. 1970. Interim Report on Excavations in the Roman Cemetery, Poundbury, Dorchester, 1970. *Proceedings of the Dorset Natural History and Archaeological Society* 92: 138-40.

Green, C. Sparey, 1984. Early Anglo-Saxon Burials at the 'Trumpet Major' Public House, Alington Avenue, Dorchester. *Proceedings of the Dorset Natural History and Archaeological Society* 106: 149-52.

Green, M.J. 1976. *The Religions of Civilian Roman Britain*. Oxford: British Archaeological Reports British Series 24.

Hall, T.A. 2000. *Minster Churches in the Dorset Landscape*. Oxford: British Archaeological Reports British Series 304.

Hinton. D.A. 1998. *Discover Dorset:Saxons and Vikings*. Wimborne.

Hood, S and Walton H. 1948. A Romano-British Cremating Place and Burial Ground on Roden Downs, Compton, Berkshire. *Transactions of the Newbury District Field Club* 9(1): 10-62.

King, C.E., 2004. The Poundbury Hoard of Third-Century. *Antoniniani. Proceedings of the Dorset Natural History and Archaeological Society* 126.

La Rocca, E., 2001. The Newly Discovered City Fresco from Trajan's Baths, Rome. *Imago Mundi, The International Journal for the History of Cartography* 53: 121-24.

Leech, R. 1986. The Excavation of a Romano-Celtic Temple and a Later Cemetery on Lamyatt Beacon, Somerset. *Britannia* 17: 259-328.

Lowe, C. 1993. Hoddom. *Current Archaeology* 135: 88-92.

Morris, J. 1973. *The Age of Arthur, A History of the British Isles from 350 to 650.* London: Weidenfeld.

Philpott, R. 1991. *Burial Practices in Roman Britain, a Survey of Grave Treatment and Furnishing AD 43-410.* Oxford: British Archaeological Reports British Series 219.

Picard, J. 1986. Ce que les textes nous apprenant sur les equipements et le mobilier liturgique necessaires pour le bapteme. *Pretirage des Rapports de la Region Rhone-Alpes, XI Congres Internationale D'Archeologie Chretienne.* Lyon.

Rahtz, P.A. 1993. *Glastonbury.* London: English Heritage.

Rahtz, P.A., Hirst, S. and Wright, S.M. 2000. *Cannington Cemetery.* London: Britannia Monograph Series 17.

Robertson, A.S. 1952. The Poundbury Hoard of Roman Fourth Century Copies and Their Prototypes. *Numismatic Chronicle 6th Series* 11: 87-95.

RCHM(E). 1962. *An Inventory of the Historical Monuments in the City of York, Volume 1, Eburacum, Roman York.* London: Royal Commission on Historic Monuments of England.

Sparey-Green, C. 1987. *Excavations at Poundbury Volume I: The Settlements.* Dorchester: Dorset Natural History and Archaeological Society Monograph 7.

Sparey-Green, C. 1993a. The Rite of Plaster Burial in the Context of the Romano-British Cemetery at Poundbury, Dorset, England, in M. Struck (ed.), *Romerzeitliche Graber als Quellen zu Religion, Bevolkerungsstruktur und Sozialgeschichte*: 421-432. Mainz.

Sparey-Green, C. 1993b. The Painted Plaster, in D. Farwell and T. Molleson, *Excavations at Poundbury 1966-80, Vol II, The Cemeteries*: 135-40. Dorchester: Dorset Natural History and Archaeological Society Monograph 11.

Sparey-Green, C. 1997. Poundbury, Dorset: settlement and economy in late and post-Roman Dorchester, in K. Dark (ed.), *External Contacts and the Economy of Late Roman and Post-Roman Britain*: 121-152. Woodbridge: Boydell.

Sparey-Green, C. 2002. Where are the Christians? Late Roman Cemeteries in Britain, in M. Carver (ed.), *The Cross goes North, Processes of Conversion in Northern Europe, AD300-1300*: 93-107. Woodbridge: Boydell.

Thomas, C. 1981. *Christianity in Roman Britain to AD 500.* London.

White, D.A. 1970. The Excavation of an Iron Age Round Barrow near Handley, Dorset 1969. *Antiquaries Journal* 50: 26-36.

Wilkinson, J. (ed. and trans.) 1981. *Egeria's Travels to the Holy Land.* Jerusalem and Warminster.

Woodward, A. 1993. Discussion, in D. Farwell and T. Molleson, *Excavations at Poundbury 1966-80, Vol. II, The Cemeteries*: 215-239. Dorchester: Dorset Natural History and Archaeological Society Monograph 11.

12: Religious Heresy and Political Dissent in Late Antiquity: A comparison between Syria and Britain

Daniel Hull

Heresy, politics and monasticism; this paper concerns the political role of heresy in Late Antiquity, and the role which monasticism played in articulating the link between the two. It is not immediately clear how a complex question such as this can be answered by the relatively sparse evidence base for fourth to sixth century Christianity in Britain. Yet elsewhere in the Late Antique world, debates of this nature have been raging for some time. Not only is the archaeological evidence so much more available, but the interplay between that evidence and the broader political trends of the period have been addressed more fully. What follows therefore is an attempt to relate arguments about Late Antique heresy to Britain, by using frameworks of thought formed on the basis of the archaeology of the Eastern Mediterranean. Is it simply that our evidence for Christianity in Late Roman Britain is so sparse that our questions have been less ambitious, or was it that the social and political situation here was genuinely different? Can we use models created elsewhere to reform our understanding here in Britain? In short, has the political role of Late Antique heresy not been addressed because of our approach, or the nature of the material itself?

To begin with, this paper will concern itself with a set of monastic sites of the fifth and sixth centuries in a region known as the Limestone Massif between Aleppo and Antioch in northern Syria. On another level, this set will serve as a case study to explore the broader question of whether heretical Christian sects should be viewed as primarily religious movements, or as political catalysts which drove populations across the late Roman world into processes of secession. This debate will then be related to Britain in order to ask whether such processes were at work here.

This dilemma will be addressed in four ways. To begin with, the origins and development of the debate concerning the role of Late Antique heresy will be introduced. Secondly, I will present my own hypothesis, which is that consideration of the 'political' aspects of heresy have tended to be too restrictive, deriving from problems of definition, and that the broader implications of the way in which monasticism was established are at risk of being missed. Thirdly, I will attempt to illustrate this through an exploration of a data set from northern Syria, using both documentary and archaeological evidence. Finally, I will return to the broader issue at stake, by attempting to address the implications for our knowledge of Late Antique Britain.

Early monasticism in northern Syria

Popular depictions of early Christianity in Western Asia are characterised by Stylites and cave dwellers, wandering through the rural landscape of northern Syria and south-east Anatolia. Hovering on the margins of society in the fourth and early fifth centuries, these roaming ascetics inspired, advised, troubled and agitated the rural population (there are many accounts available which illustrate this, but see, for example, Price 1985). Yet by the later fifth and early sixth century, this colourful, ephemeral movement had begun to be institutionalised through a very large building programme, carried out within the context of an established Church hierarchy. Quite what a monastery

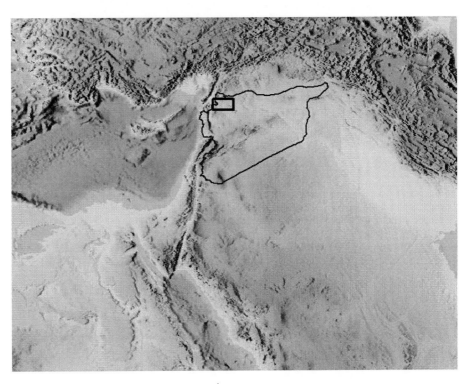

Figure 12.1: Relief map of western Asia showing the position of Syria, with the case study shown to the north-west.

Figure 12.2: An institutional monastery of the late fifth century. Qal'at Sim'an in northwest Syria.

may be in the fourth and fifth century is a matter for debate. However, for reasons of the brevity of this paper, it can be summarised as a locus with multiple elements for the purposes of dedicated, residential Christian worship, involving at least an attempt at subsistence. Although monasticism was a varied phenomenon during its early development, we can be sure that institutions such as Qal'at Sim'an, Dayr Turmanin and Dayr Dehes matched up to this definition. This is corroborated by the documentary evidence of a series of letters sent to Constantinople by a number of institutions in this region (Tchalenko 1958: 66-83). Furthermore many of the settlements which stand close to these sites bear place-names with the word *dayr*, of Syriac origin and continuation into Arabic, which means monastery. Using this evidence, there are at least 49 possible monastic institutions within the northern Limestone Massif (Jebel al-A'la, Jebel Barisha, Jebel Halaqa and Jebel Sim'an) alone, an area encompassing just over 2000km².

Arguably, the catalyst for the institutionalisation of monasticism in northern Syria, was a particular kind of Christian heresy know as Monophysitism. This heresy, which sees Christ as having one nature - both God and man at the same time - rather than the Orthodox view that he has two natures in one, began a long, drawn-out process of schism in the Christian world from the time of Apollinarius in the AD 360s (Frend 1972; Daniel-Rops 2001: 140-149). The denouement was reached at the Council of Chalcedon in AD 451, when Monophysitism was declared officially heretical. Adherents to the Monophysite position are today broadly referred to as the Eastern Churches, and more specifically of the Syrian

Orthodox (or Jacobite) Church, the Armenian Orthodox Church and the Coptic Churches of Egypt and of Ethiopia.

Woodward and the 'national' debate

This situation prompts a great many questions. What was the impact of this outlawing of a version of the Christian faith which had many adherents? Were such moves symptomatic or causal of broader socio-political processes? The origin of this debate regarding the relationship between heresy and nationalism springs from Woodward who proposed as early as 1916 that Christian heresies of the fourth and fifth centuries fuelled nationalist political movements, and that, furthermore, it was these movements which brought down the Roman state. He wrote (Woodward 1916: 102):

> ...had there been no theological disagreements other battle cries would have been found. But the religious differences in themselves, apart from the local patriotism and jealousies with which they were connected, are sufficient to arouse the fiercest passions; and it is probable that the strife might have been less bitter had the instruments been less dangerous; though, again, it must be remembered that the fusion of religion and politics was, in what we have called a Christian age, almost unavoidable.'

Woodward employed a series of case studies from the Late Antique world - from Egypt and Syria, from Armenia, from the Gothic regions, also from Spain,

114

Burgundy and elsewhere - to illustrate his point. For Syria, for example, he justifies the link between religious and political dissent on the following grounds. Northern Syria had a number of prominent theological schools, which produced literature in Syriac, the indigenous language of the region. This native tongue was used in the liturgy of the Monophysite service, just as Coptic was used in Egypt. Furthermore the Syrian church had a large number of its own churches, some of which are architecturally distinct in various ways from structures of the Orthodox rite. Finally, the Orthodox, Byzantine government appeared to at least recognise the danger of this link between heresy and political dissent, as persecution of the Monophysite faith was carried out systematically during the reign of Justin I (518-27), and intermittently by Justinian (527-565).

On reflection, Woodward's argument is made in crude terms, and derives from a tradition of nineteenth century scholarship - ultimately begun by Gibbon's *Decline and Fall of the Roman Empire* - which held that the 'intolerant zeal of the Christians' was responsible for the destruction of the Roman Republic (Gibbon 1788, cited in Low 1960: 143-44). Wayward religious beliefs were seen as linking automatically with wayward anti-Imperial sentiments. Such an argument did not seem to require a careful definition of what 'nationalism', as Woodward called it, *meant* for Late Antique society, nor indeed how political motivation related to theological motivation.

More recently, there has been a certain degree of scepticism about use of the term 'nation' in an archaeological context. It is worth considering this term for a moment in order to be clear about whether it is appropriate to use it within the context of late Roman political disintegration. Although the word is used abundantly in discussions by Banks (1996), Díaz-Andreu (1996 and 2004), Silbermann (for example, 1988) and others, this is often with reference to how archaeology is used to contribute to our sense of nationhood in the present, rather than its application to groups in the past. The most active in deconstructing the term 'nation' within the latter context have been Marxist historians and archaeologists. Harman, for example, points out the difficulty of defining a 'nation' since this term does not equate neatly with characteristics such as language, culture or those who inhabit a particular geographical entity, and there are modern nations in existence which present exceptions to each of these categories (Harman 1992). He proposes the argument, following Hobsbawm, Anderson and others, that nations are 'imaginary' entities (Hobsbawm 1990; Anderson 1991). Furthermore, they are an invention of sixteenth century Europe, especially of Holland and England, and are essentially a product of, and a means by which to facilitate, capitalism. Harman argues that the first nations were constructed within the context of states, and that stateless nations came later, created by those wishing to emulate (and react against) the nation states who ruled them. Discussion of nations without states being formed in reaction to existing power

structures has been very active recently with reference to indigenous political identity in Australia (Purvis 1996) and North America (Guibernau 1999), but less so within Europe and Western Asia. However, the political theorist Ignatieff has given some substance to the discussion (1999). He adapts Sigmund Freud's work in accounting for how political identities are constructed (1977; 1985a; 1985b). Political identities are only formed where the threat of competing identities is present. Such competition occurs when two or more social groups are in close contact with one another, and when they share large numbers of common attributes. According to Ignatieff, it is closeness and similarity, not distance and difference, which force the construction of political identities. In other words, homogenising ideologies, like Hellenized Christian orthodoxy, create simultaneous drives towards heterogeneity. While Hellenism, it has been argued, was a long-term concept which somehow transcended community differences, Hellenization was a more aggressive form of 'cultural domination' (Bowersock 1990: *xi*). It was against this domination that Monophysite Christianity, whether by consequence or by design, reacted. But it is difficult to come up with an appropriate definition of this reaction, since identity operates on so many different levels. If the term 'nation' is not appropriate for the late Roman period, then how should we describe those groups who, with varying degrees of theological difference from Imperial Orthodoxy, sought secession in the fourth to sixth centuries?

There has been much use of the term 'ethnic group' in the last fifteen years or so. In some cases, nation is akin to ethnicity, and indeed there is often a perceivable overlap between the two. Ethnicity is the way people think of themselves collectively, which transcends the immediacy of gender, status, family and trade. Those collective thoughts can be based on a variety of concepts, and are often bound together by descent, belief and purpose. It is the collective sense of those thoughts which 'guide everything from the ways in which people speak to each other and arrange their buildings and other social spaces to the artefacts they make, how they use them and what they come to symbolize' (James 1999: 69; Jones 1997). Within the context of Western Asia, ethnicity is necessarily more fluid than nation, with boundaries (both conceptual and territorial) which are more difficult to define. It is historically contingent, changing by emphasis, degree and method through time, according to circumstances. Politics, and the adjective political, can be described in this context as the ways in which social groupings interact with the state or other power which governs them. It is about the mediation of identity on a local level with the power which seeks to control resources and ideology on a broader scale. What we are concerned with here, therefore, is not so much the relationship between heresy and nation, or indeed heresy and ethnicity, but heresy and political identity. It is that special link between theological dissent and organised secession which concerns us here.

There has been much discussion in the last decade and a half about the extent to which communities in Late Roman Western Asia may be described by terms such as national or ethnic group, and the role which religious heresy may have played in the formation of such groups. I will not embark here on a full review of these arguments, since they are beyond the scope of this paper. However, summarising the major ones may help with the complexity of the debate.

One of the most direct challenges to Woodward's 'nation' hypothesis came in 1959 from A.H.M. Jones, who completely dismissed any notion of a link between heresy and nationalism (Jones 1959). For Jones, 'there is no hint of any anti-imperial movement, much less any rebellion, during the period of close on two centuries that elapsed between the Council of Chalcedon and the Arab conquest' (Jones 1959: 288). His problem with this association lies within the specific circumstances of each situation. For example, we cannot say, as Frend has, that the Donatists of North Africa were properly a 'national' movement, because their political ambitions were driven only by a small number of the elite for their own gain (Jones 1959: 283, *contra* Frend 1985).

But it is difficult to be clear what Jones expected of a 'national' movement, as he never actually states explicitly what it is that he is disqualifying exactly. The closest we come to an explication is the following extraordinary statement:

> Did the average Copt say to himself, 'I am an Egyptian and proud of it. I hate the Roman oppressor, and will at the earliest opportunity cast off the alien yoke. Meanwhile I insist on speaking my native Coptic instead of Greek, the language of the foreign government, and I refuse to belong to its church. I do not know or care whether Christ has one or two natures, but as the Romans insist on the latter view, I hold the former'? [Jones 1959: 280]

Jones' analysis is in fact a skin-deep hunt for the stark, clear borders which were an integral part of the early and mid-twentieth century *zeitgeist* of European nationhood in which Jones was working. And if 'nation' is inappropriate, he does not suggest an alternative term.

Millar approached the problem rather differently, by first defining what he regards as a religious group with a discernible political agenda (Millar 1987). For him, *Jewish* identity had all of the necessary mechanisms for us to regard it as a politically coherent group: a religious text which carried political messages, a 'national' language, a system of law, recognised interpreters of that law (in this case, rabbis), social institutions and a communal leader. But Millar is cautious about assigning other groups a specifically political label. More recently, he has argued of the Syriac speaking Monophysites of northern Syria that they certainly do not represent a nation, nor indeed an *ethnos*, during the late Roman

period, on the grounds that that language was not the primary public language of worship until somewhat later (Millar 1998).

Sebastian Brock has concentrated more on the issue of written language. For him, it is significant that certain social groups had a literary tradition in a language other than Greek or Latin. In Northern Syria, for example, Syriac was being used in a literary sense by the third century, and by the mid-fourth had an established literary tradition, with its own subject matter and various theological writers. However, Brock too is cautious about assigning a *political* status to those using this language. For him, this literature, and all of its associations with the Monophysite church, do not add up to nationalist aspirations. In common with Jones, he asserts that the fact that many writers using such languages *also* wrote in Latin and Greek disqualifies them from being regarded as truly nationalist (Brock 1999: 157; Jones 1959).

So, it appears there is some consensus that in the case of the Syriac speaking Monophysite Christians of northern Syria, they were united by the region they inhabited, perhaps in the language they spoke, in their literary tradition, in belief and liturgy and in the public architecture they produced. At the same time, however, there has been an almost unanimous consensus that such factors do not constitute a national group, nor indeed a coherent *ethnos*. However, this does not necessarily disqualify them form having a collective political intent.

The archaeological evidence

We have already summarised some of the factors which, on the basis of documentary evidence, suggest a social coherence of, and perhaps a political organisation to, the Syriac speakers of northern Syria. And if this region saw the formation of a coherent community, promoting its identity through language and religious heterodoxy, how, when and why did this happen? Progress on this issue might be made by studying material culture, the 'silent witness' of identity and political agenda as expressed in monuments. So what of the archaeological evidence?

This is the problem on which I am currently engaged through a programme of PhD. study, and I offer two interim statements – on the economy and on the form of ecclesiastical sites.

The region had, since the second century, prospered on the olive oil trade (Tchalenko 1953; Callot 1984; Kennedy and Liebeschuetz 1988). Olive oil presses survive well in both domestic and industrial settings, and there are many examples extant. On closer examination, many of the larger presses are in fact part of, or very close to, monastic complexes, implying monastic involvement, and quite possibly control, of the trade from the time of the construction of monastic institutions in the late fifth/early sixth centuries. This trade, and indeed the economy in general appear to subside during the upheavals of the mid-sixth century, a period marked by plague, warfare with Persia and earthquakes. However, in spite of this decline, churches and monastic buildings in the region continue to be constructed until the early seventh century, over fifty years after the widespread construction of other monumental architecture ceases (Kennedy and Liebeschuetz 1988: 69). Furthermore, it is precisely during this period that Seleucia, the main Mediterranean port for this part of Syria, begins to decline. This decline had resulted in extensive depopulation *by the time of* the Arab conquest of AD 637 (Kennedy and Liebeschuetz 1988: 70). This could imply that the economy of the region was becoming less and less linked to that of

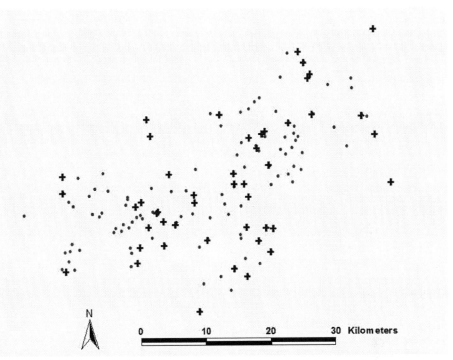

Figure 12.3: Distribution plot showing position of monasteries (marked as crosses) and settlement, showing the partial correlation between the two.

the Mediterranean, as it had been during the Roman period. This internalising may have been a long term process, as Paul Reynolds has noted that the ceramic types used in the interior of northern Syria during the Late Roman period are self contained, and have almost nothing to do with the ceramics used on the coast (Paul Reynolds pers. comm.).

It would be an attractive conclusion to draw from this that northern Syria becomes a coherent, self-contained region from at least the late fifth century, with its own religious ideology, its own language, its literary tradition marrying these two factors together and its own self-contained economic processes. They do this, it could be argued, in reaction to the homogenising ideology of the Byzantine state. Understanding quite how religious thought connects with political protest is a complex issue. However, though speculative at this stage, it would be equally attractive to conclude that Monophysite monasticism was organising this process of secession. It acted as an intermediary between theological disagreement and public action. Peter Brown has proposed that the early precursor of the monastery, that network of Holy Men who so agitated the Syrian countryside in the fourth and fifth centuries, began this process. They did this through their 'constant symbiosis with the life of the surrounding villages', hovering on the margins of rural units, acting as arbitrators in times of dispute, negotiating with the urban landlords, and in a spiritual role, an allayer of anxiety' (Brown 1971: 82). In short, he (or she, and there were plenty of Holy Women) were the new authority, the 'professional in a world of amateurs' (Brown 1971: 97). By the late fifth and sixth

centuries, when monasteries became truly monumental institutions, this role had solidified, and their position as arbitrators and controllers from the margins of settlement is there for us to read archaeologically in the landscape. Although research is ongoing, it seems that monastic complexes are placed carefully on the margins of the settlement pattern, closely connected with communications networks, as well as the water and agricultural resources. This is in marked contrast to the pagan ritual landscape of the third century, based on remote hilltop temples, removed from the centres of social and economic activity.

So while it may now no longer be appropriate to go along with Woodward's hypothesis that such identities were in fact 'national' in nature during the late Roman period, there may be some currency in seeing them as nevertheless politically driven, since they often involved some form of mediation between the ways in which locally constructed group identities were formed, and how those identities were then used to interact with Imperial power. It seems that emergent monasticism may have mediated in this way in the fifth and sixth centuries.

Having first discussed the debate regarding heresy and nationalism in Late Antiquity, then explored a case study from northern Syria, where does this leave us with regard to Europe, and more specifically Britain? Of course, each situation is different, and broad generalisations across vast tracts of the Old World are unlikely to be profitable. However, are we in a situation where we can at the very least compare the historical processes at work? Having examined a comparatively rich evidence base, is it worthwhile applying such hypotheses to a region where the data – both in terms of documents and archaeological material – is more scarce?

The case for Britain

There have been various useful assessments of Christianity in fourth and fifth century Britain by, for example, Frend (2003), Petts (2003), Mawer (1995) and Watts (1991). Frend concludes that although it was sufficiently present and organised in episcopal terms to take part in the theological debates of Late Antiquity, like the Council of Arles in AD 314, the evidence for Christianity in the private sphere, is 'scanty' (Frend 2003: 81). Petts is more optimistic, regarding that evidence as sufficient 'to allow important things to be said about the nature of late Roman religion and society' (2003: 7).

Archaeologically, we have, of course, evidence for the churches themselves at places like Silchester, Richborough, Icklingham, Colchester House in London, Lincoln and others, although the dating of these structures has at times been ambiguous, and there is 'little consistency in their layout or architectural features' (Lane 2001: 151). Rodwell claims of Roman London that it was a fully Christian city under Constantine, and that it had at least 13 churches (1993: 91-93). High status artefacts, such as the small disc with a chi-rho from Rookery Farm near Newmarket, the chi-rho amulet from Shepton Mallett and the silver spoons in the Mildenhall treasure, have suggested use of an established set of Christian symbols. Graffiti, such as the chi-rho symbols on amphora sherds at Congresbury Cadbury, provides further support for this (Rahtz *et al.* 1992: 244). The Durobrivae hoard suggests a 'sophisticated liturgy' (Frend 2003: 83), though how widespread this was we do not know. There are various examples too of baptismal vessels of various kinds, especially lead tanks (Watts 1991). Christian mortuary practice is suggested in the form of incised gravestones, such as the chi-rho stone from Maryport (Petts 2003). Christian burial is also implied, though not necessarily in a decisive sense, of the evidence from Poundbury, Ilchester, Lankhills, Northover, Bradley Hill, Cannington and others (Rahtz *et al.* 2000). Mosaic evidence, particularly those from Hinton St. Mary, Frampton and Fifehead Neville, has been discussed, particularly with regard to the interpretation of the Christian and non-Christian symbolism represented.

Within this evidence for Christianity, there is some evidence for heterodoxy. For example, Perring suggests of the aforementioned mosaic pavements, that they represent Gnostic practice among the villa-owning elite of the South West in the fourth century, on the basis of the allegorical scenes depicted (Perring 2003). He has argued that mosaics depicting similar scenes occur as early as the first half of the second century, as at Fishbourne (Cunliffe 1971). Although it is not yet clear

whether this is unambiguously Gnostic practice, or whether simply Gnostic-inspired, there is at least enough evidence to suggest diversion from the norm within the symbolism used.

There is, of course, a broader discussion to be had about whether *heterodoxy* can properly be called *heresy* in Britain at this time. In Western Asia, and to an extent in Continental Europe too, heresy is clearly more evident. This is especially the case after Christianity was made formal by the Council of Nicaea in AD 325, as heresy stands in greater contrast against the backdrop of the Orthodox views of the establishment. Later in the fourth century, for example, Priscillian's semi-Manichaean views in the mountains of Spain, provoked violent repercussions from central government (Green 1998: 33). By the AD 380s, under Theodosius, anti-heretical edicts were becoming more and more common. Figures such as Augustine of Hippo, that 'champion of Catholic Orthodoxy', provided the Christian world with an established theological background against which heretical views could be defined (Green 1998: 39). A problem exists therefore if heresy is only defined as such by those who oppose it. Like the word 'cult', it 'is something strange that other people do, and its strangeness is owed mainly to observations by strangers' (Carver 1993: *v*). This reminds us of Johnson and Olsen's (1992: 420) summary that identity is defined as much by the others around it than by itself. So if the evidence for the orthodox position is not yet sufficiently well defined for Britain, defining the opposition is a still harder task. And if the Orthodox establishment had no knowledge of, and thus did not react against, a particular theological stance, then it is difficult to distinguish heresy from the diverse substructure of practices and micro-beliefs which may have characterised Christianity in Late Roman Britain.

Pelagianism in Britain

The formal process of excommunication may be one method, if the evidence is available to us, by which a heresy may be distinguished from heterodoxy. For the British Isles during the period in question, however, we are limited to just one clear cut example of excommunicated heresy. This is the case with the views of Pelagius, since he was officially excommunicated by the Vatican in ad 418. Pelagian theology essentially concerned itself with the nature of free will. His notion, as evidenced by a diverse corpus of documentation by both Pelagius and his followers, was that man was responsible for his own deeds, whether good or evil, and could therefore save himself by his own actions, rather than necessarily with the intervention of divine grace. This position clashed markedly with the views of Augustine which were much more assertive of the doctrine of predestination. We know that Pelagius' views were sufficiently well known for Augustine to attack them directly in *De Remissione* and *Sermons* 293 and

294. We also know that the Gaulish bishop Germanus visited Britain at least once in order to tackle followers of Pelagius (Petts 2003: 46-7). Quite how Pelagius' views relate to, first of all, religion 'as lived' in an ordinary sense, and as evidenced therefore by material culture, and specifically to practice in Britain, is a more complex task to disentangle. The first point to make here is that we have, in fact, almost no evidence for the role which Pelagianism may have played in Britain. It is almost certain that Pelagius was British born, but it is equally certain that he spent much of his adult life outside Britain, and that he died in Palestine. Furthermore, there is nothing in his theological views which we can be sure bears a specifically 'British' character, whatever that may mean. Indeed, the protagonists in the Pelagian movement, according to Bonner's recent review of the evidence, were figures such as Rufinus the Syrian and Julian of Eclanum (Bonner 2002: 145; Cróinín 2001; Morris 1965; Rees 1988 and 1991). There were others who have been associated with Pelagianism and also had some form of link, whether by origin or by other means, with Britain, such as Faustus of Riez. Conclusions regarding their activities and influence within Britain itself are, alas, nothing more than speculation (Bonner 2002: 146). So although it is true that we have a substantial quantity of historical documentation for Pelagian theology, it provides very little information about Britain, and still less about the substructure of religious practice carried out by the population.

The second point to make here is that the archaeological recognition of Pelagian views is made rather complex by our ignorance of any of the symbols which may have been used to differentiate such views from the Orthodox establishment. In the case of the Limestone Massif of northern Syria discussed above, we have distinctive architectural plans which relate to the nature of the liturgy (for example, Baccache 1980; Castellana 1992; Donceel-Voûte 1988; Loosley 1999; Tchalenko 1958) and a corpus of incised motifs (Naccache 1992). Although neither plan nor motif can be related specifically to Monophysite theology, they are common in areas where Monophysite Christianity is know to have been predominant from the first half of the fifth century onwards. In Britain, the imagery on the Frampton mosaics allows lengthy discussions, such as that by Perring, to take place on whether they were Gnostic or not. We have no equivalent portfolio of specifically 'Pelagian' images to draw that heresy into similar discussions.

Thus, having questioned two sources of speculation for our interpretation of Pelagianism, this brings us to a third issue, of whether there is a relationship between Pelagian discourse and political revolt in late Roman Britain. Does Woodward's statement, mentioned at the beginning of this paper, that 'the fusion of religion and politics was...almost unavoidable' ring true for Pelagianism (Woodward 1916: 102)? Myres has suggested that British Pelagianism 'must have provided precisely the emotional and spiritual stimulus necessary to make the repudiation of the old corrupt regime possible and the path to independence a reality' (Myres 1960: 31). His argument rests on the interpretation of the word *gratia*, which Pelagius' followers are often described as campaigning against. Myres translates the word as 'favouritism' or 'corrupt', and extrapolates this to argue that 'Pelagians were revolted at a social and political regime which permitted and encouraged such injustice' (Myres 1960: 27). Indeed it would be hasty to conclude that Britain was necessarily separated from anti-establishment movements with a theological content (whether in origin or by consequence) taking place in Contintental Europe. However, Myers' evidence is limited, and there currently exists no direct evidence that the views of any other prominent heretics, such as Priscillian, ever found purchase with communities in Britain.

Such movements, where they existed, appear to have been reacting against the increasingly ardent position of the establishment throughout the course of the fourth and early fifth centuries. Yet the establishment's own position was far from clear in a doctrinal sense, as the successive church councils of the following century and a half suggest. Within Britain, Frend has argued that the church was in decline from the end of the fourth century onwards because it lacked the strength of Episcopal infrastructure present in, for example, Late Roman Gaul (Frend 2003). Quite how local variations were played out amid the socio-political complexity on the ground is therefore more difficult to ascertain. With regard to the mosaic pavements of possibly Gnostic origin, Perring (following Williams 1999) argues that they were not necessarily vehicles for dissent, but could have been *conformist* in their intention. This is argued on the grounds that '(t)he retrospective, eclectic, syncretic, and Hellenistic form of Orphic-Gnostic-Christianity suggested by the evidence indicates that the ideas were not being developed as part of any challenge to the existing status quo but instead *conformed to* the existing beliefs and prejudices of a Romano-British élite society' (Perring 2003: 121; my italics).

This statement returns us to a problem raised earlier in this paper. How is it that religious thought connects with political protest? Which acts as the vehicle for which, and how do they move around and find support within new communities? I have argued above that monasticism may have acted as both a catalyst and a directive force for Monophysite thought in fifth and sixth century northern Syria, by providing leading figures, an organisational infrastructure repeated in village after village, and landscape forms which enabled communities to feel bound both to themselves and to the central space of the monastery. Assessing the role of *monasticism* within the politics of heresy, as I have argued is at least tentatively possible for northern Syria (and elsewhere), is more difficult to assess in Britain. This is largely because of the ambiguity of what actually constitutes a monastic institution. This ambiguity has been furthered by the temptation to project the later 'monastic' nature of sites towards earlier roots. It has been argued that *possible* sites exist, such as, for example, Glastonbury Tor, Cadbury Congresbury (Rahtz 1992) and Brean Down for the south-west, Llandough and Llancarfen for south Wales, or Lullingstone for the south-east (Dunn 2000: 139). More recently still, Christopher Sparey-Green presents in this volume a possible monastic site at Poundbury, argued on the basis of multiple mausolea, a managed and predominantly female cemetery, an apsidal structure and the presence of agricultural structures. However, assigning such complexes the monastic label with any certainty is risky, given the problems of defining what monasticism is in Late Roman Britain, compounded by the ambiguity of dating such sites. Indeed, as an example of this ambiguity, for Charles Thomas, the very dividing line between sub- and post-Roman Britain is marked by the appearance of *'full'* monasteries for the *first time* in the late fifth century (Thomas 1981: 348). Without a 'background' of firmly identified sites to clearly demonstrate the signature-type and use of monasteries at this time, it is difficult to be certain about the identification of new evidence coming through. Even if we can identify a monastic tradition, investigating the possibility of a link with heresy is more difficult where those heresies are secretive and potentially piece-meal in their distribution. The secrecy and free will often emphasised by Gnosticism, for example, has traditionally been incompatible with institutional monasticism.

This brings us to a final point of comparison between the heresies of western Asia and those of northern Europe in the fourth and fifth centuries. Whilst the debates which characterise the theological terrain of the Councils of Ephesus (AD 431) and Nicaea (AD 451) concerned the nature of Christ, the great debates of northern Europe were more about the nature of humankind. Those who raged against what they saw as the 'established' view that the fate of an individual in the afterlife is essentially predestined, focussed instead on free will, by asserting that such matters are dictated by actions in life. At the risk of simplifying this difference, an emphasis on free will is perhaps less likely to find expression in collective institutions such as monasteries, than in the private houses of everyday life. If indeed we do have a significant Pelagian presence in late Roman Britain, then that presence is perhaps less likely to be found in a monastic setting. Bonner's view is that instead, 'Pelagius and his disciples did not go out into the desert and build monasteries, but sought to live as monks and nuns within society as a whole' (Bonner 2002: 148).

Conclusion

It seems then, at the end of this journey from east to west, that the issue of whether heretical Christian sects could be viewed as political catalysts remains unresolved. Although some of the evidence for Western Asia suggests that an argument along these lines can be made, this is crucially different from the British material in that it derives from a widely practiced, well documented sect.

By comparison, it seems that too many questions remain unanswered in Late Antique Britain by an evidence base which seems, as yet, insufficient in providing good definition of the heresies practiced. Is it in fact the case that the binary opposition of 'heresy' versus 'orthodoxy' is not appropriate for what was a more heterogeneous religious situation in Britain? Furthermore, deciding on the issue of whether monasticism played a role in turning heresy to political advantage is hampered by the difficulties of what constitutes a monastery.

Acknowledgements

Many thanks are due to Prof. Martin Carver and Reverend Prof. William Frend for reading and commenting on earlier drafts of this paper. Steve Roskams and Dominic Perring also made some valuable recommendations. The PhD. from which this paper derives is funded by the Arts and Humanities Research Board, and hosted by the Department of Archaeology, University of York.

Bibliography

Anderson, B. 1991. *Imagined Communities: Reflections on the Origin and Spread of Nationalism*. London: Verso.

Baccache, E. 1979. *Églises de Village de la Syrie du Nord. Volume 2; planches*. Paris: Librairie Orientaliste Paul Geuthner.

Banks, I. 1996. Archaeology, nationalism and ethnicity, in I.Banks, J.O'Sullivan, and J.A.Atkinson (ed.), *Nationalism and Archaeology*: 1-11. Glasgow: Cruithne Press.

Bonner, G. 2002. The Pelagian Controversy in Britain and Ireland. *Peritia*, 16: 144-155.

Bowersock, G. 1990. *Hellenism in Late Antiquity*. Cambridge: Cambridge University Press.

Brock, S. 1999. Greek and Syriac in Late Antique Syria, in S. Brock (ed.), *From Ephrem to Romanos. Interactions between Syriac and Greek in Late Antiquity*: 149-160. London: Variorum.

Brown, P. 1971. The rise and function of the Holy Man in Late Antiquity. *Journal of Roman Studies*, 61: 80-101.

Callot, O. 1984. *Huilleries Antiques de Syrie du Nord*. Paris: Librairie Orientaliste Paul Geuthner.

Carver, M. 1993. *In Search of Cult: Archaeological Investigations in Honour of Philip Rahtz*. Woodbridge: Boydell Press.

Castellana, P. 1992. Note sul bema della Siria settentrionale. *Note sul bema della Siria settentrionale*, 25: 90-100.

Cróinín, D.Ó. 2001. Who was Palladius, 'First bishop of the Irish'? *Peritia*, 15: 205-237.

Cunliffe, B.W. 1971. *Fishbourne: a Roman Palace and its Garden*. London: Thames and Hudson.

Daniel-Rops, H. 2001. *The Church in the Dark Ages*. London: Phoenix Press.

Díaz-Andreu, M. and Champion, T. 1996. *Nationalism and Archaeology in Europe*. London: UCL Press.

Díaz-Andreu, M. forthcoming. Britain and the Other: the archaeology of imperialism, in H. Brocklehurst and R. Phillips (ed.), *History, Nationhood and the Question of Britain*. New York: Palgrave.

Donceel-Voûte, P. 1988. *Les Pavements des Églises Byzantines de Syrie et du Liban. Décor, Archéologie et Liturgie*. Louvain-La Neuve: Département d'Archéologie et d'Histoire de l'Art.

Dunn, M. 2000. *The Emergence of Monasticism: from the Desert Fathers to the Early Middle Ages*. Oxford: Blackwell.

Frend, W.H.C. 1972. *The Rise of the Monophysite Movement*. Cambridge: Cambridge University Press.

Frend, W.H.C. 1985. *The Donatist Church: A Movement of Protest in Roman North Africa*. Oxford: Clarendon Press.

Frend, W.H.C. 2003. Roman Britain, a failed promise, in M.O.H Carver (ed.), *The Cross Goes North*: 79-91. York: York Medieval Press.

Freud, S. 1977. The taboo of virginity. *On Sexuality*. Pelican Freud Library, vol. xii. Harmondsworth: Penguin.

Freud, S. 1985a. Group psychology and the analysis of the ego. *Civilisation, Society and Religion*. Pelican Freud Library, vol. xii. Harmondsworth: Penguin.

Freud, S. 1985b. Civilisation and its discontents. *Civilisation, Society and Religion*. Pelican Freud Library, vol. xii. Harmondsworth: Penguin.

Green, V.H.H. 1998. *A New History of Christianity*. Stroud: Sutton Publishing.

Guibernau, M. 1999. *Nations without States. Political Communities in a Global Age*. Cambridge, Oxford and Malden: Polity Press.

Harman, C. 1992. The return of the national question. *International Socialism*, Autumn 1992: 3-61.

Hobsbawm, E.J. 1990. *Nations and Nationalism since 1780. Programme, Myth, Reality*. Cambridge: Cambridge University Press.

Ignatieff, M. 1999. Nationalism and toleration, in S. Mendus (ed.), *The Politics of Toleration*: 77-106. Edinburgh: Edinburgh University Press.

James, S. 1999. *The Atlantic Celts*. London: British Museum Press.

Jones, A.H.M. 1959. Were ancient heresies national or social movements in disguise? *Journal of Theological Studies* 10 (2): 280-298.

Jones, S. 1997. *The Archaeology of Ethnicity. Constructing Identities in the Past and Present*. London and New York: Routledge.

Johnson, H. and Olsen, B.J. 1992. Hermeneutics and archaeology. *American Antiquity* 57 (3): 419-436.

Kennedy, H. and Liebeschuetz, J.H.W.G. 1988. Antioch and the villages of Northern Syria in the Fifth and Sixth AD: trends and problems. *Nottingham Medieval Studies* 32: 65-90.

Lane, P. 2001. The archaeology of Christianity in global perspective, in T. Insoll (ed.), *Archaeology and World Religion*: 148-181. London and New York: Routledge.

Loosley, E. 1999. The early Syriac liturgical drama and its architectural setting, in T. Insoll (ed.), *Case Studies in Archaeology and World Religion*. Oxford: British Archaeological Reports Supplementary Series 755.

Low, D. 1960. *The Decline and Fall of the Roman Empire by Edward Gibbon*. London: Chatto and Windus.

Mawer, F. 1995. *Evidence for Christianity in Roman Britain: The Small Finds*. Oxford: Tempus Reparatum.

Millar, F. 1987. Empire, community and culture in the Roman Near East: Greeks, Syrians, Jews and Arabs. *Journal of Jewish Studies* 38: 143-164.

Millar, F. 1998. Ethnic identity in the Roman Near East, 325-450: language, religion, and culture, in G. Clarke and D. Harrison (ed.), *Identities in the Eastern Mediterranean in Antiquity. Proceedings of a conference held at the Humanities Research Centre, Canberra*: 158-176. Mediterranean Archaeology 11.

Morris, J. 1965. Pelagian literature. *Journal of Theological Studies* 16: 26-60.

Myres, J.N.L. 1960. Pelagius and the end of Roman rule in Britain. *Journal of Roman Studies* 50: 21-36.

Naccache, A. 1992. *Le Décor des Églises de Villages d'Antiochene du IVe au Viie Siècle. Tome I: Texte*. Paris: Librairie Orientaliste Paul Geuthner.

Perring, D. 2003. Gnostic readings in fourth century Britain: the Frampton pavements reconsidered. *Britannia* 34: 97-127.

Petts, D. 2003. *Christianity in Roman Britain*. Stroud: Tempus Publishing.

Price, R.M. (trans.) 1985. *A History of the Monks of Syria, by Theodoret of Cyrrhus*. Kalamazoo: Cistercian Publications.

Purvis, T. 1996. Aboriginal peoples and the idea of the nation, in L. Smith and A. Clarke (ed.): *Issues in Management Archaeology*: 51-57. St.Lucia: University of Queensland.

Rahtz, P., Woodward, A., Burrow, I., Everton, A., Watts, L., Leach, P., Hirst, S., Fowler, P. and Gardner, K. 1992. *Cadbury Congresbury 1968-73. A Late/Post-Roman Hilltop Settlement in Somerset*. Oxford: British Archaeological Reports British Series 223.

Rahtz, P., Hirst, S. and Wright, S. 2000. *Cannington Cemetery: Excavations 1962-3 of Prehistoric, Roman, post-Roman, and Later Features at Cannington Park Quarry, Near Bridgwater,*

Somerset. London: Society for the Promotion of Roman Studies.

Rees, B.R. 1988. *Pelagius: a Reluctant Heretic*. Woodbridge: Boydell Press.

Rees, B.R. 1991. *The Letters of Pelagius and his Followers*. Woodbridge: Boydell Press.

Rodwell, W. 1993. The role of the church in the development of Roman and early Anglo-Saxon London, in M.O.H. Carver (ed.), *In Search of Cult. Archaeological Investigations in Honour of Philip Rahtz*: 91-99. Woodbridge: Boydell Press.

Silberman, N. 1988. *Between the Past and the Present: Archaeology, Ideology, and Nationalism in the Modern Near East*. New York: Holt, Reinhart and Winston.

Tchalenko, G. 1953-1958. *Villages Antiques de la Syrie du Nord*. Paris: Librairie Orientaliste Paul Geuthner.

Thomas, C. 1981. *Christinaity in Roman Britain*. London: Batsford.

Watts, D. 1991. *Christians and pagans in Roman Britain*. London: Routledge.

Williams, M.A. 1999. *Rethinking Gnosticism*. Princeton: Princeton University Press.

Woodward, E.L. 1916. *Christianity and Nationalism in the Later Roman Empire*. London: Longmans.

13: Before 'the End':
Hadrian's Wall in the 4th Century and After

Robert Collins

The study of the transition from late Roman to Early Medieval Britain is highly problematic across the entire British Isles. In the past decade, more attention has been given to sub-Roman sites along Hadrian's Wall (e.g. Casey 1993; Dark and Dark 1996; Wilmott 2000). These sites were part of a unified frontier system during the Roman period. Therefore, while the sites cannot be seen as anything more than individual locations, it is possible to understand the wider context within which this transition occurred by more carefully considering the late Roman frontier zone. This, however, identifies two problems that must be addressed.

1. Hadrian's Wall is generally conceived of as a large monument connecting a number of sites, and these sites on the Wall are examined in isolation, divorced from the rest of the Wall. While the sites are compared and contrasted, there is little integration of the Wall as a whole and the interrelationships of the sites along it.

2. There is no suitable explanation of "the end" of Hadrian's Wall when the Roman frontier "collapsed". The "end" is often believed to be related to troop withdrawals for continental campaigns, or it is left ambiguous, often with the implicit assumption that without pay the soldiers would disperse (Breeze and Dobson 2000: 246).

The first problem is solved by considering data from a case study area that incorporates a number of sites in relatively close proximity and by analyzing them in an integrated landscape study. Ideally, the information provided from a number of sites should also indicate the nature of the final phases of Hadrian's Wall in the case study area that can then be compared to other case studies (Collins, in prep.). This case study approach is made easier by focusing upon two fundamental elements of the northern frontier: the need to supply a standing garrison and the primary function of Hadrian's Wall as a monument of traffic control. For the purposes of this paper, by considering the evidence for food provisioning and gate blocking, we can then provide a greater context by which to understand any transition from a late Roman frontier.

The Case Study: Birdoswald

Desktop research was conducted that focused on a case study in the western-central sector of Hadrian's Wall, centered on the site of Birdoswald in modern Cumbria and encompassing the area within 10 km from the fort (see Figures 13.1 and 13.2). The site itself has provided excellent archaeological evidence for the transition from the late Roman to the Early Medieval periods (Wilmott *et al.* 1997). The case study area is quite suitable for a

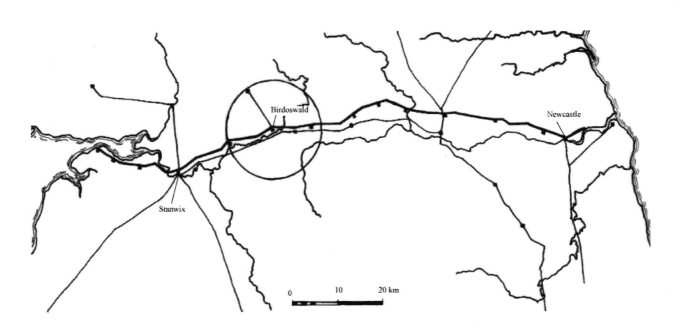

Figure 13.1: Hadrian's Wall and the Birdoswald case study area (adapted from Wilmott 1997).

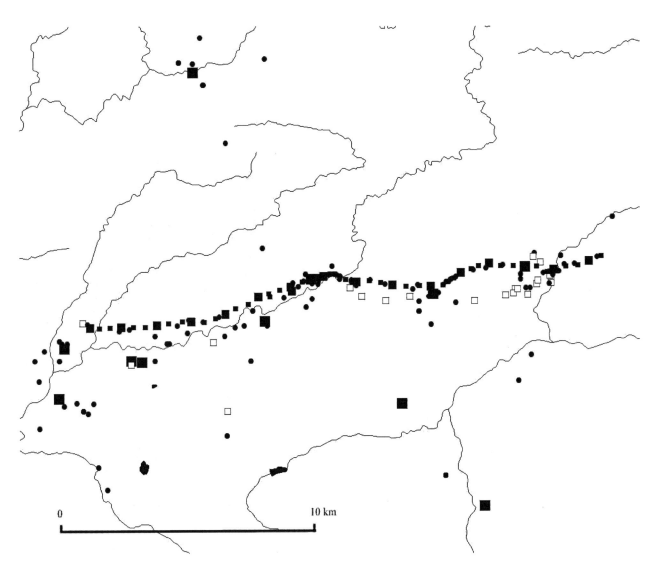

Figure 13.2: The Birdoswald case study area, indicating the location of all Roman period sites and findspots.

landscape consideration of this transition, as the Wall in this sector is well studied archaeologically. While most of the excavations took place over fifty years ago, and the primary research emphasis was generally to establish a chronology for construction of Hadrian's Wall, an overview of activity at these sites can be established. It is also worth noting that there is a diversity of sites available for consideration, including a bridge, aqueducts, a water mill, and "native" farmsteads in addition to the typical forts, milecastles, and turrets. The area also has the benefit of contributing environmental evidence. To be sure, not all the sites are contemporary, but an integrated approach will help flesh out an understanding of the landscape of the locale beyond that of a number of frontier postings for a soldier.

Provisioning

The evidence for provisioning is found in three forms. First, there are the pollen studies; second, there are the local farmsteads; and finally, there is the archaeological evidence from the fort at Birdoswald (see Figure 13.3).

Palynological Evidence

The palynological evidence for the case study is provided by three pollen sites: Midgeholme Moss, Fellend Moss, and Walton Moss. All three sites present regional pictures of the vegetation history, so can be used for the case study area as a whole rather than providing specific information for local proximity. Unfortunately, there are no pollen sites that present a localized picture for the relevant period of this case study in the Birdoswald area (e.g. Fyfe and Rippon, this volume).

Midgeholme Moss is the closest site in proximity to Birdoswald, north of the fort by less than a kilometer. Two studies have examined cores from the mire basin site: Innes (1988) and Lewis (1993). During the Roman period, the landscape was predominantly cleared, but it was hardly treeless, as arboreal pollen accounts for approximately 30% of the pollen (Wiltshire 1997: 37). The maximum clearance, however, was achieved during the Roman period. The area remained largely cleared, as there was no increase in woodland indicator taxa, though there was a spread of *Salix* (willow) across the site (not

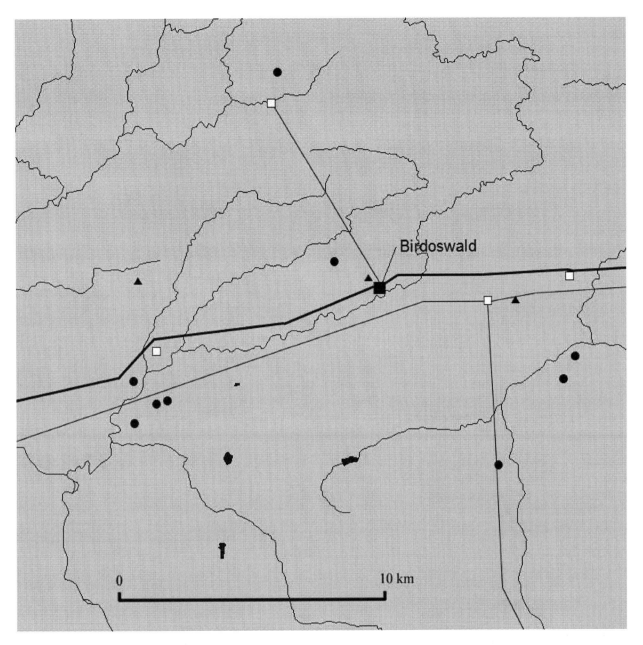

Figure 13.3: The location of sites providing evidence for provisioning in the case study area. Forts are indicated by squares, farmsteads by circles, and pollen sites by triangles.

the region) during the period between cal. AD 440-780 (Wiltshire 1997:35).

At Fellend Moss, east of Birdoswald by only a few kilometers, maximum levels of clearance established in the Roman period are continued and maintained up to *c.* 620, determined through numerous calibrated radiocarbon dates (Davies and Turner 1979). Maximum forest clearance was achieved under the Romans. Anthropogenic indicators for the 4th to 7th centuries included some evidence of cereal cultivation, but most agricultural indicators suggested pastoral activity. After *c.* 620, there is an increase in woodland coverage (*contra* Dark 1996:28, who argues that woodland regeneration occurs before the radioncarbon-dated level).

Clearance activity leveled out at Walton Moss by the 4th century and those levels of clearance were maintained, until a further increase in clearance occurred in "monastic times" (Dumayne and Barber 1994). Furthermore, studies at Walton Moss have revealed wet shifts extrapolated from calibrated radiocarbon dating and sediment accumulation rates. These wet shifts occurred at *c.* AD 200, 490, and 650 (Hughes *et al.* 2000).

The overall pattern emerging from the regional pollen studies suggests roughly continued levels of clearance from the Roman period until at least the early 7th century, if not later. The only evidence for cereal cultivation comes from Fellend Moss, but we must remember Huntley's (2000: 68) warning that "cereal pollen is notorious at being under-represented at traditional pollen sites" such as those studied in northern Britain. So the pollen sites cannot answer questions about local practices effectively, but the demonstration that there is not rapid forest regeneration at a regional scale in the sub-Roman period is at least suggestive of maintained levels of agricultural practice. It is possible that the agricultural regimes may have changed, but the regimes being practiced required or made use of similar levels of land clearance.

"Native" Farmsteads

The "native" farmsteads available in the case study are important, as the surplus from these sites would have been helpful, if not essential to support the garrison based at Birdoswald. All the farmsteads are situated in river valleys. But only the farmstead at Watch Hill is within 5 km of Birdoswald, to its northwest. The only river valley in the vicinity of Birdoswald is the Irthing, and the course of the river south of Hadrian's Wall falls between the wall and the Stanegate. This area may have been restricted by the Roman authorities, keeping people from establishing farmsteads there. Perhaps the land was included in a fort's immediate *territoria*, providing land for grazing of the garrison's livestock or other purposes. Another problem arises, though, upon considering the spatial relationship between these farmsteads and Birdoswald. With the exception of the farmstead to the northwest of Birdoswald, all the other farmsteads are closer to other forts, as the crow flies and in terms of distance by road. Therefore, these farmsteads may not have been provisioning Birdoswald in the late Roman period, but the forts they were closest to.

There are two more interesting sites to consider, though. At some point after the late 3rd century, the walls of Turret 52a were used as shelter and foundation for a structure, probably of agricultural or domestic function (Bruce and Daniels 1978: 221), and a hut was built in the ruins of Turret 51b, with a *terminus post quem* in the late 4th century (Woodfield 1965). The evidence from these two turrets might suggest a changing use for Milecastle 52. Unfortunately, other than information from the gates, no further archaeological evidence can be gleaned as the construction of a post-medieval farmhouse has destroyed any evidence for internal structures (Simpson and Richmond 1935). The low number of "native" farmsteads does not necessarily mean that the land was not worked, however. Geophysical survey has revealed the extent of *vicus* buildings to the east and west of Birdoswald (Biggins and Taylor 1999), and the *vicus* could have housed the labor forces connected to the fort garrison that worked the land (James 2001: 80).

Faunal and Macrobotanical Evidence

The excavations at Birdoswald have provided faunal and macrobotanical evidence that must also be considered.

The faunal evidence at the fort fits King's (1984) model of a Roman military diet dominated by cattle (Izard 1997: 363-70). The later Roman period remains from the *horreum* demonstrate 14% had butchery marks, and there was a lower ratio of caprine metapodials to humerus and tibia. This may indicate the removal of bones in the skinning process. However, there was no discernible pattern of selective disposal of specific parts of animals, though there seemed to be few larger cattle bones, which may have been disposed of elsewhere.

The relative proportion of bones of identified age has led to the interpretation that mature/older cattle were brought to the site and slaughtered. There is also evidence that the cattle were a local breed due to the high incidence of a reduced talonid on the third molar at a 25% frequency, compared to the normal 10-20% frequency of most Roman assemblages (Izard 1997: 369). This suggests either a restricted or a local supply of the fort, with the military possibly lacking the authority to choose mature animals carrying the optimum quantity of meat (compare this to the evidence from Carlisle: Stallibrass 2000). However, it may be that the contribution of prime cattle to local dairy production was more important to the military than the consumption of cattle at the optimum age for butchering. Furthermore, the low proportion of bones from pigs and chicken, high-status food in the imperial core, may reflect their consumption by higher-status individuals at the fort – the officers – who would have been fewer in number relative to enlisted soldiers (Izard 1997: 369).

The plant macrofossil evidence comes primarily from the sub-floor fillings of the *horrea*. The deposits from 197 seem to be more secure and indicative of the plant diet and use of the *horreum* in Period 5, from approximately AD 350-400 (Huntley 1997: 142-144). Most of the charred seeds were from cereal and associated weeds. Wheat was the most frequently recovered cereal from the site as a whole, making up 34.4% of cereal grains. Identifiable bread wheat only consisted of 3.9% while hexaploid wheat consisted of 27.4% and a further 68.7% was unidentifiable. The source of this wheat is unknown, however. It seems rather unlikely that it was grown in the immediate area given the altitude and high rainfall of the area. It is probable that wheat is being brought in from further afield, *via* a supply fort like South Shields.

After wheat, barley was the next most common cereal at 29.1%. Barley would be more suitable for local growth given the climatic conditions it favors. The presence of large amounts of barley chaff reinforces a notion of local production, though it could simply mean it was being processed in the fort rather than grown locally. This last point is significant, though. If the barley is being processed at the fort, then it means the army must use its own labor to process the crop rather than demand it in a processed form. One might argue from this that the military could not or did not exercise authority on its suppliers. However, this could also be interpreted by the fact that barley might be used in different forms, such as food for draft animals, so a processed crop would not be desired. It may also have been easier to transport unprocessed barley, perhaps with a reduced risk of spoilage. Furthermore, there is the possibility that forts along Hadrian's Wall had access to mills built by the army. East of Great Chesters fort at Haltwhistle Burn Head, pieces of large millstones were found that would have necessitated a power mill to grind (Anon. 1910: 167). Close to Birdoswald, there is the possibility that a mill was built near Willowford Bridge, which carried the Wall across the River Irthing (Bidwell and Holbrook 1989: 94). Army control of local mills could have provided a further means of economic exploitation/domination in the frontier zone.

The only other seeds at Birdoswald worth noting are the grassland species, which may indicate the cutting of hay for animals at the fort. As the evidence comes from a late Roman context, the amounts indicated by the samples could potentially reflect changing amounts or arrangements for the provisioning of the fort. Unfortunately, there are no samples from earlier periods in the fort to compare with.

When we consider the discoveries provided through the different forms of evidence, we reach some interesting conclusions. The pollen cores indicate that levels of clearance are maintained. So in crude measurements, the amount of land being exploited for agriculture is basically the same through the late Roman and post-Roman period. There do not seem to be many farmsteads in the case study area, however. Given the extensive aerial photographic record of Cumbria, this is not likely to be due to a bias in coverage. It is possible that the ancient farmsteads have been replaced by modern ones, but this seems unlikely. Given the lack of evidence for rural settlement, it seems likely that much of the grain provisions are coming in from outside the range of ten kilometers. However, perhaps most of the exploitation of the land around Birdoswald was through labor forces associated with the garrison at Birdoswald and based in the *vicus*. The evidence from the fort supports the notion of local provision, based on the pathology from cattle

teeth and from barley remains. That would mean, then, that wheat would have to be imported to the fort. As long as the Roman state exercised authority in Britain, this would not be a problem, but in the early 5th century this may have changed.

Gate Blocking

Breeze and Dobson (2000: 40) identified that the primary function of Hadrian's Wall was to control the movement of people and goods. Two important features in the landscape would have dictated this movement. The Wall curtain would have limited movement to certain points – milecastles and forts. By directing people to these points, the military could exercise considerable authority over people and the goods they traveled with. The second feature was the road system. In the case study area, the Stanegate provided an east-west communications route, while the Maiden Way fulfilled the same role north-south on the western side of the Pennines. These roads were the basis of troop movements for the army and connected the locale to places outside of the vicinity on major Roman roads. These roads would also be available for civilian use and would have facilitated the transportation of bulk goods. This would be important in the later Roman period when tax-in-kind was more common (Hopkins 1980). Exclusive to the control of the army was the Military Way, which ran behind the Wall in some places, or on the north bank of the Vallum in others. It seems likely that there was also a network of local trackways, though identifying these can be problematic.

Perhaps the best indicator of the control of traffic through the Wall is the changes that were made to the gates of forts and milecastles (see Tables 13.1, 13.2, and 13.3). The gates probably acted in the same way as many of the gates into Roman and other cities of the empire – as customs points (Palmer 1980). Evidence suggestive of this can be seen in the structures built to either side of the Maiden Way leading north out of the fort of Birdoswald (Biggins *et al.* 1999: 160). Of the five forts in the case study, only two have any evidence for changes to the gates: Birdoswald and Great Chesters (see Figure 13.4).

Table 13.1: Gate alteration at forts in the case study area, in terms of the geographic position of the gates.

	North gate	South gate	East gate	West gate
Birdoswald	?	T	P, possible collapse resulting in T	P
Great Chesters	?	P	?	T
Castlesteads	?	?	?	?

Table 13.2: Gate alteration at forts in the case study area, in terms of the forts' layout

	Porta praetoria	*Porta principalis sinistra*	*Porta principalis dextra*	*Porta decumana*
Birdoswald	?	P	P, possible collapse resulting in T	T
Great Chesters	?	?	P	T
Castlesteads	?	?	?	?

Table 13.3: Gate alteration at milecastles in the case study area

	Gate type	North gate	South gate
Milecastle 44, Allolee		?	?
Milecastle 45, Walltown		?	?
Milecastle 46, Carvoran		?	?
Milecastle 47, Chapel House	II or III	?	?
Milecastle 48, Poltross Burn	III	N	N
Milecastle 49, Harrow's Scar	III	?	N
Milecastle 50, High House	III	N	N
Milecastle 51, Wall Bowers	III	?	--
Milecastle 52, Bankshead	III	N, then T	N, then restored?
Milecastle 53, Banks Burn	III	?	?
Milecastle 54, Randylands	III	?	N
Milecastle 55		?	?
Milecastle 56, Walton		?	?

N = narrowed gate   P = portal of double gate blocked   T = total blockage of gate
? = unknown or evidence destroyed   -- = left to original size

At Birdoswald, Wilmott (1997: 191-193) has attempted to integrate the findings of the earlier excavations with his own periodization of the site. The *portae principalis dextra* and *sinistra* (east and west gates, respectively) each had one of two portals blocked in the early 3rd century. The *porta decumana* (south gate) also had one portal blocked, probably contemporary with the *portae principales*. At some point in the 4th century, the remaining portal of the *porta decumana* was blocked and the ditch was re-cut in front of it, eliminating access to the gate. It is important to note that there is no mention of the blocking of the remaining portal of the *porta principalis dextra*, though there is a note that the arch may have collapsed into the gate passage, effectively blocking the gate (Wilmott *et al.* 1997: 192-193). However, the date at which this happened is unknown. Unfortunately, we have no knowledge of the north gate, the *porta praetoria*, as it lies under the modern road.

Like Birdoswald, there is evidence for the blocking of the *porta decumana* at Great Chesters in the 4th century (Gibson 1903: 31). There is also an indication from probable walling stones that the west portal of the *porta principalis dextra*, or the south gate, was blocked in the late 2nd/early 3rd century (Haverfield 1894: 197). Unfortunately, the north and east gates of the fort have not been investigated.

It is unfortunate that we do not have any information from the northern gates of either fort, as these gates permitted traffic through the Wall. At Birdoswald it seems likely that one portal of the north gate was blocked in the early 3rd century, based on the evidence from the other gates. This may also be true for the north and east gates at Great Chesters, if we use the south and west gates as an indicator. It seems plausible to suggest that at some point in the late 4th or early 5th century, the north

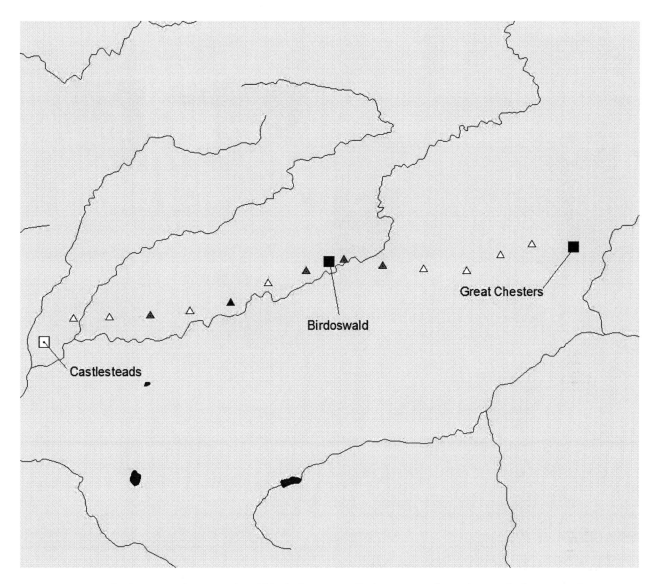

Figure 13.4: The location of narrowed and blocked gates. Filled squares indicate forts with changes to the gates. Hollow squares indicate no evidence for gate changes. Filled triangles indicate gate blocking at milecastles, while shaded triangles indicate gate narrowing. Hollow triangles indicate no data available for gate alterations at milecastles.

gate at one or both forts could have been blocked completely if there was a further need for redirection of trans-Wall traffic. Complete blockage of the north gate at Birdoswald is less likely, however, as the Maiden Way passed through the fort.

The evidence from milecastles seems to be fairly consistent (see Appendix 1 for references). Six of the thirteen milecastles in the case study demonstrate a narrowing of at least one of their gates (see Figure 13.4). This has the effect of reducing passage to pedestrian traffic only. So anyone with a large cart or wagon would have to travel to a fort to move their goods through the Wall, unless they wanted to unload their goods and reload them on another wagon on the other side of the Wall. This narrowing seems to occur in the late 2nd or early 3rd century. The narrowing can take two forms (see Figure 13.5). It can narrow from both sides of the gate, leaving a

centered passageway, as at Milecastle 49, or a reducing wall can be built out from one side of the gate, forcing traffic to approach the left hand side of the gate externally. This is seen at Milecastle 48, Poltross Burn. In the case of Milecastle 52, Bankshead, the north gate was narrowed and then blocked up completely in the 4th century.

By the early 3rd century, the number of through-points along Hadrian's Wall had been reduced. Prior to this, access through the Wall would have been possible every mile, in theory. But by the later period, we only know of 14 crossing points through the Vallum to the forts in the later period (Breeze and Dobson 2000: 40, 59). Nor has there been enough research to demonstrate how frequent access across the ditch north of the Wall was. Furthermore, we must consider the topography. Milecastles were placed regularly, sometimes sited on a

A

B

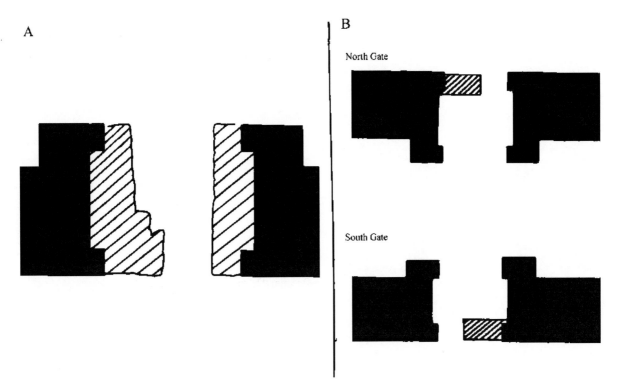

Figure 13.5: Gate narrowing. A. Milecastle 49, demonstrating narrowing from both sides, leaving a central passageway (adapted from Richmond 1956). B. Milecastle 48, narrowing is achieved through the construction of wall across one portal (adapted from Gibson and Simpson 1911).

steep slope instead of in the dip between slopes to control access. In other cases, the north gate would open up to a cliff face. So the actual number of gates at milecastles approachable by civilians would be fewer than it initially seems.

In terms of this case study, Milecastle 45 would be inaccessible from the north, and the approach to Milecastle 49 from the north would be limited by the Irthing and the steep slopes to either side of the river. From Milecastle 49 to Milecastle 53, approaches from the south would be limited by the steep slopes behind the Wall cut by the Irthing. At Birdoswald, entering or leaving the fort from the north is easy enough, topographically speaking. But south of the Wall, the topography would make it easier to approach from the east or west.

Traffic along the Wall would have been directed to certain points depending upon the needs of the party crossing through. In theory, pedestrian traffic could cross at most milecastles. However, pedestrian traffic may have had to walk along the Military Way until a Vallum crossing could be reached. Those traveling with goods in a wagon or cart would need to pass through a fort. Presumably anyone moving large herds of animals through the Wall would also have to use a fort. So we may have to remember the influence that the Wall would have on the practice of transhumance.

In general, then, consolidation of access through the Wall begins in the late 2nd/early 3rd century. Total blocking of gates in some instances in the 4th century further reduced the number of crossing points. There are two possible reasons for this gate blocking. There may have been reduced traffic along and through Hadrian's Wall from the late 2nd century, allowing valuable space within fort and milecastle gates to be used differently, or the army wanted to more effectively direct traffic through the Wall. There is little evidence to support the first possibility, but the second reason, keeping in mind the use of the Wall as an architectural feature of control, is highly likely. Furthermore, the gates that provide north-south access through the Wall probably acted in the same way as many of the gates into Rome and other cities of the empire – as customs points (Palmer 1980). Thus, Hadrian's Wall actually acts as a barrier more effectively in the late Roman period rather than its earlier inception by reducing the number of access points and thereby directing traffic.

Conclusions

The evidence suggests that forts were reliant on the locale for the supply of some goods, but it may have been necessary to supplement local provisions with imported quantities of grain. In terms of controlling movement across the line of the Wall, the forts and milecastles, with the assistance of the local topography and the Vallum seemed to have directed the flow of traffic well to preferred access points.

The case study area flags up an interesting contradiction. The perception of Hadrian's Wall in the past was of a modern type of border, but research has shown that the Wall actually acted as a line of access between two different zones. Yet over the course of centuries, gates were blocked and narrowed, forcing movement through more tightly defined points. So that in the late Roman period, Hadrian's Wall becomes more of a barrier against movement than it was before. Thus, more restricted and localized access created nodes of control for power groups. It is perhaps through this mechanism of control of movement that we can see the rise of a late and sub-Roman military elite.

One final question must be asked. How does this inform our view of the Late Antique transformation on Hadrian's Wall? It is possible the garrisons would be reliant upon imported grain. If this was so, then it seems likely a garrison would dissolve quickly after the loss of state sponsorship. On the other hand, if local surplus production was high enough to meet the demands of the smaller garrisons of the late Roman period (Coello 1996; James 1984), then it is feasible, in terms of provisioning needs that a garrison could survive past AD 410.

Furthermore, if Roman officers had truly become integrated in their posting communities (Whittaker 1994: 243-278), then the officers would possess the authority to maintain their soldiers, and thus, their power. I would like to suggest, therefore, without taking further time to expound upon late Roman social dynamics, that we must consider provisioning as the key physical (as opposed to social) component of continuity of settlement between the late Roman and sub-Roman periods on Hadrian's Wall. This has to be studied in a landscape context, building upon site-by-site analysis and environmental evidence. This is likely to result in a greater understanding of Late Antique frontiers and subsequent transformation.

Appendix 1: Site Specific Citations for Gate Blocking at Milecastles

Milecastle		
Milecastle 47, Chapel House	Simpson *et al.* 1936	
Milecastle 48, Poltross Burn	Gibson and Simpson 1911	
Milecastle 49, Harrow's Scar	Richmond 1956	
Milecastle 50, High House	Simpson 1913	
Milecastle 51, Wall Bowers	Simpson and Richmond 1935a	
Milecastle 52, Bankshead	Simpson and Richmond 1935a	
Milecastle 53, Banks Burn	Simpson and Richmond 1933	
Milecastle 54, Randylands	Simpson and Richmond 1935b	

Acknowledgements

I would like to extend my thanks to Steve Roskams (University of York), Dom Perring (University of York), and James Gerrard (University of York) for comments on drafts of this paper. Bette Hopkins and Elizabeth Williams at the Cumbria and Northumberland SMRs, respectively, also provided assistance and information. This paper contains maps based on copyright digital map data owned and supplied by Harper Collins Cartographic and is used with permission.

Bibliography

Anon. 1910. Discoveries *Per Lineam Valli. Proceedings of the Society of Antiquaries of Newcastle-upon-Tyne* 4: 167.

Bidwell, P. T. and Holbrook, N. 1989. *Hadrian's Wall Bridges*. London: English Heritage.

Biggins, J. A., Robinson, J. and Taylor, D. 1999. Geophisical Survey, in P. Bidwell (ed.), *Hadrian's Wall 1989-1999*: 157-160. Knedal: Titus Wilson and Son.

Breeze, D. and Dobson, B. 2000. *Hadrian's Wall*, 4th edition. London: Penguin.

Bruce, J. C., and Daniels, C. 1978. *Handbook to the Roman Wall with the Cumbrian Coast and Outpost Forts*, 13th edition. Newcastle: Hill and Son.

Casey, P. J. 1993. The end of Fort Garrisons on Hadrian's Wall: A hypothetical Model, in Vallet and Kazanski (eds.), *L'armée romaine et les barbares du IIIe au VIIe siécle*: x-x. Rouen: Musée des Antiquités Nationales.

Collins, R. in prep. *Social and Economic Transformations on Hadrian's Wall from the 4th to the 7th centuries*, PhD. thesis, Department of Archaeology, University of York

Coello, T. 1996. *Unit Sizes in the Late Roman Army*. Oxford: British Archaeological Reports International Series 645.

Dark, K. and Dark, P. 1996. New Archaeological and Palynological Evidence for a Sub-Roman Reoccupation of Hadrian's Wall. *Archaeologia Aeliana* series 5, 24: 57-72.

Dark, P. 1996. Palaeoecological evidence for landscape continuity and change in Britain *ca* A.D. 400-800, in K. Dark (ed.), *External Contacts and the Economy of Late and Post Roman Britain*: 23-51. Oxford: Boydell Press.

Davies, G. and Turner, J. 1979. Pollen diagrams from Northumberland. *New Phytologist* 82: 783-804.

Dumayne, L. and Barber, K. 1994. The impact of the Romans on the environment of northern England: pollen data from three sites close to Hadrian's Wall. *The Holocene* 4: 165-73.

Gibson, J. P. 1903. On Excavations at Great Chesters (*Aesica*) in 1894, 1895, and 1897. *Archaeologia Aeliana* series 2, 24: 19-62.

Gibson, J. P. and Simpson, F. G. 1911. The Milecastle on the Wall of Hadrian at the Poltross Burn. *Transactions of the Cumberland and Westmorland Antiquarian and Archaeological Society* 11: 390-461.

Haverfield, F. 1894. Notes on Excavations at Aesica in 1894. *Archaeologia* 55:195-98.

Hopkins, K. 1980. Taxes and Trade in the Roman Empire (200 B.C.—A.D. 400). *Journal of Roman Studies* 70:101-125.

Hughes, P. D. M., Mauquoy, D., Barber, K. E., and Langdon, P. G. 2000. Mire-development pathways and palaeoclimatic records from a full Holocene peat archive at Walton Moss, Cumbria, England. *The Holocene* 10: 465-479.

Huntley, J. P. 1997. Macrobotanical evidence from the *horrea*, in T. Wilmott *et al.*, *Birdoswald, Excavations of a Roman fort on Hadrian's Wall and its successor settlements: 1987-92*: 141-44. London: English Heritage.

Huntley, J. P. 2000. Late Roman Transition in the North: the Palynological Evidence, in T. Wilmott and P. Wilson (eds.), *The Late Roman Transition in the North*: 67-71. Oxford: British Archaeological Reports British Series 299.

Innes, J. B. 1988. *Report on pollen analysis, from Midgeholme Moss, Birdoswald, Cumbria*, unpublished. Institute of Prehistoric Science and Archaeology, University of Liverpool.

Izard, K. 1997. The animal bones, in T. Wilmott *et al.*, *Birdoswald, Excavations of a Roman fort on Hadrian's Wall and its successor settlements: 1987-92*: 363-70. London: English Heritage.

James, S. 1984. Britain and the late Roman army, in Blagg, T. and King, A. (eds.), *Military and Civilian in Roman Britain*: 161-186. Oxford: British Archaeology Reports British Series 136.

James, S. 2001. Soldiers and civilians: identity and interaction in Roman Britain, in S. James and M. Millett (eds.), *Britons and Romans: advancing an archaeological agenda*, x-x. York: Council for British Archaeology.

King, A. 1984. Animal bones and the dietary identity of military and civilian groups in Roman Britain, German, and Gaul, in T. Blagg and A. King (eds.), *Military and Civilian in Roman Britain: cultural relationships in a frontier province*: 187-217. Oxford: British Archaeological Reports British Series 136.

Lewis, M., 1993. *A palynological investigation of deposits from Midgeholme Moss, a valley mire adjacent to Birdoswald Roman Fort, Hadrian's Wall, Cumbria*, unpublished dissertation. King's College, University of London.

Palmer, R. E. A. 1980. Customs on Market Goods Imported into the City of Rome, in J. H. D'Arms and E. C. Kopff (eds.), *The Seaborne Commerce of Ancient Rome: Studies in Archaeology and History*: 217-33. American Academy in Rome.

Richmond, I. 1956. Excavations at Milecastle 49 (Harrow's Scar), 1953. *Transactions of the Cumberland and Westmorland Antiquarian and Archaeological Society* 56: 18-27.

Simpson, F. G. 1913. Excavations on the line of the Roman Wall in Cumberland during the years 1909-12. *Transactions of the Cumberland and Westmorland Antiquarian and Archaeological Society* 13: 297-397.

Simpson, F. G. and Richmond, I. A. 1933. Banks Burn to Randylands. *Transactions of the Cumberland and Westmorland Antiquarian and Archaeological Society* 33: 262-70.

Simpson, F. G. and Richmond, I. A. 1935a. Bankshead Milecastle, 52. *Transactions of the Cumberland and Westmorland Antiquarian and Archaeological Society* 35: 247-56.

Simpson, F. G. and Richmond, I. A. 1935b. Randylands Milecastle, 54. *Transactions of the Cumberland and Westmorland Antiquarian and Archaeological Society* 35: 236-44.

Simpson, F. G. *et al.* 1936. Milecastles on Hadrian's Wall Explored in 1935-6. *Archaeologia Aeliana*, series 4, 13: 258-73.

Stallibrass, S. 2000. Cattle, culture, status and soldiers in northern England, in G. Fincham *et al.* (eds.), *TRAC 99: Proceedings of the Ninth Annual Theoretical Roman Archaeology Conference, Durham 1999*: 64-73. Oxford: Oxbow

Whittaker, C. 1994. *Frontiers of the Roman Empire: A Social and Economic Study*. London: Johns Hopkins University Press.

Wilmott, T. *et al.* 1997. *Birdoswald, Excavations of a Roman fort on Hadrian's Wall and its successor settlements: 1987-92*. London: English Heritage.

Wilmott, T. 2000. The late Roman transition at Birdoswald and on Hadrian's Wall, in T. Wilmott and P. Wilson (eds.), *The Late Roman Transition in the North*: 13-23. Oxford: British Archaeological Reports British Series 299.

Wiltshire, P. E. J. 1997. The pre-Roman environment, in T. Wilmott *et al.*, *Birdoswald: Excavations on a Roman Fort on Hadrian's Wall and its successor settlements, 1987-92*: 25-40. London: English Heritage Archaeological Reports.

Woodfield, C. 1965. Six Turrets on Hadrian's Wall. *Archaeologia Aeliana*, series 4, 43: 87-200.